Praise for *Four Seasons*

"There's something different about a Four Seasons hotel. It's like gravity doesn't have the same effect there ... I've often wondered how they do it. Now I know. It's an inspiring story."—Morgan Freeman

"Fascinating."—*National Post*

"A terrific read by one of the smartest men in any business."—Larry King

"An appealing memoir and instructive attempt to sum up [Sharp's] business philosophy."—*The Wall Street Journal*

"The heartfelt autobiography of a compassionate family man and the dazzling success story of a legendary entrepreneur ... Remarkable."—*Toro Magazine*

"Sharp is one of Canada's great business success stories ... He's the living example of what a business leader can and should be."—Rick Waugh, president and CEO, Scotiabank

"Four Seasons truly sets the gold standard for excellence. Isadore Sharp is an amazing guy!"—Donald Trump

"The breezily told story of the man who transformed the hotel business, hospitality, and, in many ways, business itself."—Don Tapscott, bestselling author of *Wikinomics*

"No one—in our generation—has established a global brand name so totally identified with unquestioned quality as Issy Sharp."—Peter Munk, founder and chairman, Barrick Gold Corporation

"A brilliant example of true success, this is the story of a great business leader and his iconic company—as well as a chronicle of perseverance and self-confidence in adversity."—Dr. Sherry Cooper, executive vice-president, BMO Financial Group

"Sharp has animated and applied the Golden Rule as business principle ... How uplifting it is to see how a philosophy built on so much common sense so directly leads to such uncommon success!"—Danny Meyer, CEO of Union Square Hospitality Group and author of *Setting the Table*

"Sharp shares the story of his astonishing rise out of the Toronto ghettos to founder, chairman and CEO of ... the largest group of five-star hotels in the world … His story is impressive and inspiring—the company was named one of Fortune's 100 Best Companies to Work For in America, and weathered 9/11 and the SARS outbreak with aplomb—a good rags-to-riches story." —*Publishers Weekly*

"An entertaining and educational peek inside the wonderful world Issy Sharp has created at Four Seasons … A must read for anyone who aspires to excellence and meaning in their life."—Roger Martin, dean, Rotman School of Management, University of Toronto

"A compelling story of an entrepreneur and his success."—*Booklist*

"Regardless of your business, regardless of your price point, Four Seasons offers invaluable lessons to us all."—Tom Peters, author of *In Search of Excellence*

"Brilliant, incisive, and honest. A story of engagement, imagination, ambition and charm."—Michael Silverstein, author of *Trading Up*

"Sharp dared to take on the biggest by being the best. Today, his legacy is clearly not just a global chain of fine hotels … but a pioneering approach to business that always puts people first."—Gordon M. Nixon, president and CEO, RBC

"This isn't just another rags-to-riches story but a story about a leader who embodies three essential qualities of exemplary leadership—trust, integrity, and optimism—how he leveraged those values to create quality at Four Seasons, and how just about every business that cares about excellence can do the same." —Warren Bennis, Distinguished Professor of Business, University of Southern California; author of *Judgment*

"For my money, Isadore Sharp is one of the smartest entrepreneurs Canada's produced."—Seymour Schulich, author of *Get Smarter*

"A consummate hotelier, Isadore Sharp is in the pantheon of entrepreneurs who reinvented innkeeping, with Cesar Ritz, Conrad Hilton and Kemmons Wilson. *Four Seasons* reveals how Sharp re-conceived the hotel as a discreet oasis of small-scale serenity and assiduous service to guests."—David Olive, author of *No Guts, No Glory*

"I'm always proud to point out that Four Seasons … was founded and developed by Canadian Issy Sharp. It's a great credit to Canada."—Jim Pattison, chairman and CEO, The Jim Pattison Group

PENGUIN CANADA

FOUR SEASONS

ISADORE SHARP is the founder, chairman, and CEO of Four Seasons Hotels, Inc. He opened the first Four Seasons in Toronto in 1961, and the company now operates eight-two luxury hotels and resorts around the world, with more than forty additional properties under development. He and his wife, Rosalie, are prominent philanthropists. They divide their time between Toronto and Palm Springs, California.

FOUR SEASONS

The Story of a
BUSINESS PHILOSOPHY

ISADORE SHARP

WITH ALAN PHILLIPS

PENGUIN
CANADA

PENGUIN CANADA

Published by the Penguin Group

Penguin Group (Canada), 90 Eglinton Avenue East, Suite 700, Toronto, Ontario, Canada M4P 2Y3
(a division of Pearson Canada Inc.)

Penguin Group (USA) Inc., 375 Hudson Street, New York, New York 10014, U.S.A.
Penguin Books Ltd, 80 Strand, London WC2R 0RL, England
Penguin Ireland, 25 St Stephen's Green, Dublin 2, Ireland (a division of Penguin Books Ltd)
Penguin Group (Australia), 250 Camberwell Road, Camberwell, Victoria 3124, Australia
(a division of Pearson Australia Group Pty Ltd)
Penguin Books India Pvt Ltd, 11 Community Centre, Panchsheel Park, New Delhi – 110 017, India
Penguin Group (NZ), 67 Apollo Drive, Rosedale, North Shore 0745, Auckland, New Zealand
(a division of Pearson New Zealand Ltd)
Penguin Books (South Africa) (Pty) Ltd, 24 Sturdee Avenue, Rosebank, Johannesburg 2196, South Africa

Penguin Books Ltd, Registered Offices: 80 Strand, London WC2R 0RL, England

First published in Viking Canada hardcover by Penguin Group (Canada), a division of Pearson Canada Inc., 2009
Simultaneously published in the United States by Portfolio, a member of Penguin Group (USA) Inc.

Published in this edition, 2010

2 3 4 5 6 7 8 9 10 (WEB)

Copyright © Four Seasons Hotels, 2009

Manufactured in Canada.

LIBRARY AND ARCHIVES CANADA CATALOGUING IN PUBLICATION

Sharp, Isadore
Four Seasons : the story of a business philosophy / Isadore Sharp with Alan Phillips.

ISBN 978-0-14-317088-4

1. Sharp, Isadore. 2. Four Seasons Hotels & Resorts.
3. Hotelkeepers—Canada—Biography. 4. Hotel management.
I. Phillips, Alan II. Title.

TX910.5.S53A3 2010   647.94092   C2009-906852-4

American Library of Congress Cataloging in Publication data available

Visit the Penguin Group (Canada) website at **www.penguin.ca**

Special and corporate bulk purchase rates available; please see
www.penguin.ca/corporatesales or call 1-800-810-3104, ext. 2477 or 2474

TO ALL OUR PEOPLE—
PAST, PRESENT, AND FUTURE—
WHO HAVE CREATED AND WILL CONTINUE TO MAINTAIN
THE SUCCESS OF FOUR SEASONS

CONTENTS

ABOVE: *The entrepreneur has nothing to hide.*

CENTER LEFT: *Canoe trip, Algonquin Park, Ontario.*

CENTER RIGHT: *Isadore at his bar mitzvah.*

BELOW LEFT: *West Prep Junior High, Toronto.*

BELOW RIGHT: *Catalina Island, California.*

FOREWORD

Isadore has always been a dreamer. In the classroom, he spent more time gazing out the window than studying the blackboard. Issy longed for the freedom to be outdoors playing football or hockey or whatever sport was in season. With all the illusions of an eight-year-old, one of his first resolves was to be a champion pole vaulter. His patient sister Beatrice would hold out a broom handle for an hour while Issy repeatedly ran across the lawn with his pole (a rake handle), gathering the speed to leap over the broom. He saw no reason why this goal should not be within his reach. The aims of his ambitions, of course, changed with the years.

"Well, if not a pole vaulter, perhaps I should join the Marines," he said. We were at war with Germany, and boys just a little older were joining up to serve a cause that seemed to Issy higher and more important than any career. When people ask him who served as his mentors and role models, he answers, "Those men who volunteered for the army in wartime. They put their lives on the line for their principles."

But since he was denied the chance to be a war hero, Isadore drifted into the business world, still carrying the illusions of the dreamer—which he has never lost: he refused to settle for the pragmatic dicta of maturity. Issy also skipped skepticism and "Let's be sensible." People said he was naïve, with a kind of glandular optimism. Perhaps. But as it turned out naïveté served him well. Issy trusted everyone. He still does.

And trust and integrity have been the foundation of Four Seasons. Issy was a leader with no notion of the prescribed tenets of how to run a company and no MBA. He made a lot of brash decisions—against the trends and the pundits' advice—stubbornly trusting in intuition, an intuition born of long experience. And Issy has an almost zealous code of social commandments and believes that ethics is the religion that unites and motivates his people. "The only thing you can control," Isadore says, "is your attitude." He has a strong belief in his decisions, which to him are just common sense. Bucking the naysayers can be a lonely responsibility, but his parents taught him to welcome responsibility.

Over the years, I've had the pleasure of watching his mind work. In bed, before first light, I sometimes find him with arms crossed behind his head, gazing up at the ceiling and weighing possibilities. I know he'll come up with the right answer. Business books credit Isadore with "a talent for innovation" and the mind of an "integrative thinker." Roger Martin applauds Issy's capacity for "holding two opposing ideas" while simultaneously producing "a synthesis that is superior to either . . . idea."

I DERIVE MUCH *naches* (joy) from watching Issy the evangelist in action speaking at each hotel on his travels. These talks have become the stuff of legend. He is half-sitting on a high stool, one leg bent resting on a rung, his slim build loosely framed by a fine suit, and you can count on the color of the cufflinks matching the tie—maybe lavender or topaz. He speaks with the charisma of a late-night TV host. Isadore exudes a psychic energy and intellectual vigor that is contagious and constant, even though he might visit fifteen hotels in seventeen days. The whole staff typically arrives in the ballroom at four P.M., and he brings everyone into his confidence, reporting the news of the company just as he would if he were addressing his board of directors. I like how Barbara Talbott put it: "Issy's speeches reflect the hallmarks of his personality, namely, his humility, appreciation, inclusiveness, and understatement."

What sets Issy apart is his innate humanity. He honestly believes that every person has potential, and it's opportunity that makes the difference.

And watch him structure a business deal—Issy could write the book on negotiating. As he says, "You have to address the needs of the other guy." He has a facility for coming up with just that right point, and on cue. "When I lose this timing," he says, "I'll quit." And he'll never respond in anger, and therefore has no need for remorse. Nothing gets his dander up. He's imperturbable.

As I said in my memoir: "Throughout the years, I've watched in disbelief as Issy's aspirations have come to fruition. Early on he made some audacious statements that sounded like pipe dreams. He told me once that his aim was to make the name Four Seasons a worldwide brand, synonymous with luxury, like Rolls-Royce. 'Sure,' I thought, 'with only about ten hotels—hardly likely,' but I didn't let on. My most valuable contribution to his success has been my silence."

After fifty-five years, my husband, Isadore, continues to be very kind and very wise—an unbeatable combination. And as long as there is a Four Seasons, Isadore Sharp will be remembered as the man who made the company.

ROSALIE WISE SHARP
August 24, 2008

Finally, in 1972, in my first office with a window.

INTRODUCTION

So much of long-term success is based on intangibles.
Beliefs and ideas. Invisible concepts.
—ISADORE SHARP

People often ask me about my original vision for Four Seasons. Well, the truth is that there was no vision or grand scheme. In 1961, when I built my first hotel, I knew nothing about the hotel business. My only professional experience was in building apartments and houses. I was just a builder, and the hotel was just another real estate deal. I never thought this was going to be a career, nor did I ever imagine I would one day find myself building and managing the largest and most prestigious group of five-star hotels in the world.

I approached the business of innkeeping from a customer's perspective. I was the host, and the customers were my houseguests. I decided what to build and how to operate by asking myself: What would the customers consider important? What will the customers recognize as value? Because if we give them good value, they will unhesitatingly pay what they think it's worth. That was the first strategy, and it continues to this day.

The company evolved slowly at first, and I'll admit I made a few mistakes along the way. But I never made the mistake of putting profit ahead of people, and I believe part of Four Seasons' worldwide acclaim is built primarily on the strong relationships I've built over the years with owners, partners, and board members who shared my standards, and with the thousands of employees, managers, and executives who helped make the company such a success.

Looking back over the last forty years, I've identified the four key strategic decisions that formed the rock-solid foundation of Four Seasons. These are now known as the four pillars of our business model. They are quality, service, culture, and brand.

Curiously, the last of these four key objectives was set way back in 1986. Sometimes people ask, "Does that mean you haven't thought of anything new since then?" I tell them that we make new initiatives every year, but nothing so far that has been as fundamentally important. Our main focus is to continue refining and reinforcing those original four pillars.

It's not as though lightning struck and I said, "I've got an idea," and we put it all together in a day. These decisions evolved over twenty-five years, each decision supporting the one before. Over the years, we've initiated many new ideas that have been copied and are now the norm in the industry. But the one idea that our customers value the most cannot be copied: the consistent quality of our exceptional service. That service is based on a corporate culture, and a culture cannot be mandated as a policy. It must grow from within, based on the actions of the company's people over a long period of time.

Four Seasons is the sum of its people—many, many good people.

PART I

THE IMMIGRANT'S SON

Ah, to build, to build! That is the noblest of all arts.

—LONGFELLOW

ABOVE: *Max Sharp in Israel, 1924. He made the canoe from a piece of sheet metal.*

CENTER: *Max Sharp*, chalutz *(pioneer), on the first kibbutz in Israel, 1924. He is in front with hand on hip.*

BELOW LEFT: *Mom's brother Max Godfrey, whose daring I inherited.*

BELOW MIDDLE: *My mother, Lil Gotfrid, 1925.*

BELOW RIGHT: *Max Sharp marries Lil Gotfrid, 1926.*

CHAPTER 1

Lil and Max

It was my parents who unintentionally determined my career. They grew up in Poland, Lil in Ostrowiec, Max in Oswiecim (now tragically famous as Auschwitz), where my grandfather, a pious Jew, was considered "the village wise man." He had seven boys and five girls, but the family was forcibly separated by World War I and increasing pogroms: squads of thugs breaking into Jewish homes, seizing their furniture, beating them up, often burning down their houses.

Max's father and older brother Louie enlisted in the army, and Max, age thirteen, went to Kraków to live with his grandparents. At seventeen, with a visa obtained in Vienna, he went to Palestine, then known only as an ancient Asian region on the Mediterranean coast, a part of the Ottoman Empire taken over after World War I by Britain.

Settlers in what would later become the State of Israel were struggling to make the desert livable, and for Max and his young companions, it was not an easy life. By day, he helped plant eucalyptus trees to dry up the swamps and marshes to make productive fields, and by night he fought off marauding bandits. He became a builder and was later one of the founders of Deganya, Israel's first kibbutz, now a sizable city. We have an early picture of him and his comrades looking very young and stern. And you can see from their faces and bearing that these young men, boys really, were different from others, in that they were possessed by an uncommon purpose: to build a country from scratch.

In the meantime, my mother's oldest brother, Max Godfrey, had emigrated, one of the early Polish Jews to reach Canada, paying his way by working on ships and ending up by chance in Toronto.

My uncle Max soon threw off his immigrant ways along with his Yiddish accent. He was a jaunty and debonair salesman, confident and charismatic. Coming into a room, he made an immediate impression.

I admired Uncle Max and believed we were alike in many ways. And though I was much less brash, the Godfrey genes have served me well. Max was resolute, and gradually, as he prospered, he brought over most of his family, one by one. That included my father's brother, Louie Sharp, who had married Max's sister.

Louie kept in touch with his youngest brother and talked him up to Godfrey, who was looking for a suitable husband for his young sister, Lil. That was the reason Godfrey gave Louie the money that brought my father from Israel to Toronto.

Louie was in the plastering business, and since Dad had learned plastering in Israel, they became partners. Max Godfrey, having seen that Dad was a hard worker, now considered him a suitable catch for his sister. "Lil's a nice young girl," he told my father. "You'll like her. We should bring her over here so you can get married." Arranged marriages were then common among Jewish families, so when Dad agreed, Godfrey brought his sister over.

My mother at sixteen was tall and attractive, uneducated but discerning and decisive. She wasn't about to marry just anyone she was told to. Max, who idolized her from the moment they met, had several rivals, one of them wealthy. But Lil was drawn to Max's vitality and his gentle ways, and on June 12, 1927, they were married. I'm told that for their honeymoon, Max stayed home from work until nine A.M.

Dad and Louie did not remain partners for long. Mother thought Louie took advantage of Dad and, forceful as always in her opinions, minced no words about it. I would come home and hear them arguing vehemently. But always it would end the same way: my mother saying, "OK, OK, Louie! Come to dinner Friday, and bring Rose and the kids." Regardless of differences, family always came first.

Louie went into building apartments and eventually became wealthy. Dad continued, alone, as a plasterer, earning ten dollars a week; he had as yet insufficient English or technical know-how to imitate Louie. But he was learning, watching how all the other tradesmen—bricklayers, carpen-

Max and Lil Sharp with daughters Beatrice and Edith, six months before I came along.

My three sisters, Edie, Bea, and Nancy, with me, 1934.

The four Sharps sixty years later, Max and Lil looking on.

6 •   THE IMMIGRANT'S SON

ters, electricians, plumbers—did their jobs. He improved his English by studying the daily newspaper and listening to people talk.

Mom and Dad first lived in downtown Toronto in what was known then as the Ward, moving from 81 Brunswick Avenue, where I was born, to Euclid, Crawford, Clinton, and Major streets. While living in the Ward, my mother gave birth to four children: Edith in 1927, Beatrice in 1929, me in 1931, and Nancy in 1933.

Toronto today is Canada's largest city, its major commercial center, but in the twenties, thirties, and forties it was only one fifth as big. Religion ruled, and on Sundays all commerce, including movies, plays, and concerts, was shut down. Peddlers bought and sold old clothes and hawked fruits and vegetables. Bread, milk, and ice were delivered by horse and wagon, and children ran behind the iceman's cart for free slivers of ice. Behind the iceman came the street-cleaner picking up the steaming refuse from the horses, which drank from dark-green cast-iron water troughs ornamenting the main thoroughfares.

The Ward was the heart of Toronto's Jewish ghetto. There were six churches there, and 72 percent of residents were Protestants, who looked askance at Jews.

At the back of the houses on our street and the street opposite ours was a lane heaped with cinders dumped from all the coal-burning furnaces on both streets. The lane was a playground for me and other Jewish kids, and playtime often meant throwing back cinders at non-Jewish kids who'd attack us. It was some time before I realized that this wasn't just normal play but a childish gang war with children brought up to hate Jews. Anti-Semitism was so rampant that some Jewish kids anglicized their names. I occasionally thought about it but decided it wasn't for me.

Once, when we were playing, I was hit on the forehead with a stone-hard cinder. I rushed into the house, crying, blood running down my cheek (I still have a slight scar). My mother gave me a quick look and slapped me across the face—she had seen at once that I wasn't badly hurt. "Look what you did to your shirt!" she said. Then she cleaned my face, covered my cut with a Band-Aid, and ordered me to "go back out and play."

THAT WAS THE KIND OF LADY my mother was: strict but kind, understanding and practical, always acting with common sense, always knowing the right thing to do, what people now call tough love. Whatever she asked us to do was always for family, never herself. She had a surprising lack of vanity. She eventually became overweight but never lost her gracefulness. As Rosalie says, she didn't walk; she glided, like the prow of a sailing ship breasting a wave.

Our mother was the undisputed head of our family, and in business, social, and family affairs, her word was law. At home, we children did unquestioningly whatever she told us. But outside the house, at an early age, we were independent. I remember walking alone to kindergarten, trying to figure out how to get there. My parents never thought of taking me or picking me up. Not only had they too little time; they expected us to be as self-sufficient as they were as youngsters.

As a boy in a household of girls, I received no special treatment. My mother, I believe, considered women more capable than men, because in Ostrowiec her mother had run the family coal business while her father studied the Torah. She herself was outstandingly efficient, a take-charge person following a matriarchal tradition.

Neither she nor Dad had books from which to read us bedtime stories, and they couldn't have read them if they had. Our early childhood learning was from our parents' actions and from the street, not untypical of immigrants bringing up youngsters here at that time.

In 1937 my parents left the Ward for the newer, nicer north end of the city to buy cheap land and build a house for us. But Dad came into business at the worst possible period: the deepest depression in North American business history. Often he took jobs anywhere he could get them. Once, when he was excavating a basement with horse and plough, he broke his shoulder. But he shrugged it off and uncomplainingly kept on working, something I never forgot.

Before long, he decided he'd learned enough to become a plastering contractor. But his English was still problematic at best. On his first job, he misread the plans. He didn't realize that the plans showed only half the building, because the other half, as the plans explained, was identical;

this was a common practice then. As a result, his quote—readily accepted, of course—was 50 percent too low.

He didn't comprehend this until he was well into the job. He could have picked up his tools and walked away, leaving someone else to finish it. But he had made a commitment and felt honor-bound to keep it. So he finished the house without lowering quality and worked for the next several years paying off his resulting debt. I was only told of this later, but it became for me an invaluable lesson in business ethics that I have remembered throughout my career.

When we moved from the ghetto to undeveloped northern Toronto, we were still just scraping by, for I remember deciding with new friends that we would buy a model airplane for which each of us would chip in five cents. But when I told my mother why I needed the money, she refused to give it to me. "Five cents is not to be wasted on *narishkayt* [the Yiddish word for foolishness]," she said. I was deeply disappointed and resentful but later came to understand that there was simply no spare cash, except perhaps on Fridays when, with one oven and no help, Mother would cook Sabbath dinners that over the years increased in size to feed twenty, thirty, and sometimes fifty family members and friends.

In every other way, she was prudently frugal. In fact, I can't remember having a room of my own until my oldest sister married, when I was sixteen. And growing up with three sisters, I had some unusual hand-me-downs.

I also remember that in building a house then, Dad would save leftover wood, three-or-four-inch scraps from the underflooring, sidings, and ceiling, and I would bring my little wagon to his work site after school, pile the scraps into it, and take them home to burn in the kitchen stove.

Once, on the way home, a man stopped me to say, "I'll give you five cents for that wood."

Five cents to me was a fortune, and I figured I could just go back and get more, so I sold it. But when I went back there weren't any more scraps. "Why didn't you do what you were told?" Dad asked. "Now how do you think Mom's going to cook tonight? How do we heat the house?"

I felt terrible, much worse than if he had spanked me. But he didn't, then or ever. It was not in his nature.

That was my first business experience. It taught me a needed lesson: Never take anything for granted.

As we children grew old enough to look after ourselves and help with the housework, Mother took full control of the business. Dad would buy a piece of land and build a house on it, and Mother would either sell it or sell ours and move into the new one. Whichever it was, we always seemed to be moving. Dad would simply hire a trailer, we would load it with what little furniture we had, and within a few hours, we'd be living somewhere else.

Once Mother got an offer she felt she couldn't refuse for the house we were then living in, although Dad was far from having a new one finished. So she called her sister, Sarah. "We're coming to stay with you," she said, which we did. They were a family of six and a dog, as we were, and for six months we all lived together in a small three-bedroom house with only one bathroom, and my aunt never complained of overcrowding.

By the time I reached my mid-teens, we had moved some fifteen times. That meant changing schools: as always, on our own. And being trusted that we knew what to do made us, I believe, independent at a very early age.

After selling a few houses, our parents felt they could now afford a low-rent cottage for the summer. None was available for rent. "We *have* to have a cottage," Mother said, and whatever Mother wanted and asked for was a command.

"OK," said Dad. "I'll build one."

He bought a forested lot at Crystal Beach, a beachless street near a swamp. And very early one Saturday morning, he and I and four of his workers drove out—one hundred miles—with our tools in the old car Dad was still using for construction and everything else.

We worked all day, continually slapping mosquitoes, till after dark. Then we slept in a nearby rooming house, the four workmen in one room, and worked from dawn to dusk, on Sunday as well. After six such weekends, Dad—who lost no time whatever on his current day job—presented Mother with a cottage.

From my early teens, construction became very much a part of my life. I'd often get up with the sun during summer holidays, go to my dad's then-current site and, weather permitting, work until dusk. I dug ditches, carried bricks for the bricklayers to lay, brought plaster for the plasterers, and helped drivers unload their delivery trucks: heavy bundles of bricks, eighty- to one-hundred-pound concrete blocks. And this digging, lifting, and loading was always a challenge. I was always trying to measure up to Dad's workers, very strong and rugged individuals. I never could, of course, but in trying I knew I was earning their respect, and that was then as important to me as anything I was learning.

As I grew older, I laid bricks and drains, built concrete walls, and installed wiring. I even tried to emulate how carpenters hammer a nail, hitting it once dead center, then driving it in with one or two blows. I could never quite do it then, but that, like everything else I was seeing and doing, familiarized me at an early age with construction. And I found construction enjoyable.

Dad, too, taught me in his own inimitable way. I was building two steps for a house, making wooden forms to be filled with concrete. Dad, who was watching, never told me I was building them wrong; and it wasn't until I had poured the concrete that I saw my mistake: the first step was too big and the top step too small. Dad handed me a sledgehammer, and all he said, then or later, was, "Break it, and do it the right way next time." He could have saved a little time and money by telling me beforehand, "Measure twice, cut once." But the method he chose was unforgettable.

Once in a while, hanging around with friends in the evening, we'd go back to the building site. In those days it was not boarded up, and just for fun and perhaps to test my nerve, I would climb up through the open studs and joists to the roof. Once, I fell off and by sheer luck was able to grab the eaves of the roof. If I hadn't swung back into the house, I would have fallen all the way down into the trenches, breaking arms, legs, head, who knows what. Sometimes, looking back at all my youthful injuries—a nail cut off from my finger by a chisel, my thumb crushed by our car door, beatings in football and hockey—I feel I'm very lucky to be in one piece.

During these teenage years, I sometimes summered at the cottage doing odd jobs. I set up pins at a bowling alley. I played horseshoes well and occasionally hustled a few dollars playing for money. One year I made French fries at a drinks stand on the beach, working in a dark back room where the potatoes were dumped in great piles through a window for me to put in a drum to be skinned. Then I bathed them in water and sliced them with a potato-chip machine. That was the summer I came back home looking whiter than when I left.

We may have owned a cottage then, but we must still have been just scraping by, because we had no truck, only the car, to haul things in. And not only did that car break down with insistent regularity, the gearshift had lost its knob, so the bare stick wore a hole in your hand. At age fifteen, when I used Dad's car to get my driver's license, the inspector asked me, with some incredulity, "*This* is what you're going to drive?"

"That's it," I said.

"Kid," he told me with evident sympathy, "if you can get this thing moving, you'll get your license." Which I did.

MY LIFE from a very early age also revolved around sports. In winter we played hockey, at first just on frozen ponds, and we didn't have all the paraphernalia kids have today. We used magazines for shin pads and rocks for goalposts.

At age twelve, I needed a pair of skates to try out for the Peewees, a hockey team for youngsters that we kids considered big time. Dad, when I asked him, said, "You'll take your sister's skates."

"But those are white figure skates," I protested. "I need boy's black hockey skates."

"We'll get your sister's skates dyed black," he told me, and my mom took them to a shoemaker.

Well, when you dye white skates black, they come out a queer shade of blue. And despite my qualms about wearing them, I made the team, in part, I think, because the coach felt sorry for me, perhaps presuming that if I wanted so badly to play, I just might contribute something worthwhile.

Not only did my parents never drive me to rinks or playgrounds as most parents do for youngsters today; they came only once to watch me play, and I had to coax them to do that.

It was a hockey playoff, crucial to win. I remember it well. I was body-checked, did a flip in the air, and landed flat on my back right in front of where my parents were sitting. I looked up at them in the stands, and they

Forest Hill, junior high, Toronto, grade seven, one hundred pounds or less to qualify. I'm in the top row, second from left.

The Ryerson football star, 1952.

Ryerson Rams basketball, 1952.

Ryerson Athlete of the Year, 1952.

looked down at me with an air of incredulity that seemed to say, *"That's a game you like playing?"* But I doubt if they really understood how serious my fall could have been, though my mother might have. More than once she took me to the hospital with cracked ribs after football season.

MY PARENTS never questioned how or what I was doing.

Not only were they totally involved in work, monitoring a child's playtime was not in their tradition when they grew up. My father never took his children anywhere. He never took me fishing or swimming, though he did teach me to swim. He took me and my sisters out in a boat, threw us overboard, and said, "Now swim."

Growing up, I can only recall one entire day that I spent with my dad. This was the day following my bar mitzvah, when I'd delivered a speech the rabbi wrote for me. This was during the war, and the speech was about fallen heroes, a real tearjerker. My mother wanted a record made of it, so she told Dad to take me to a recording studio downtown and have me read the speech again, which I did. My mother loved it so much that she played it for anyone who would listen; the recording eventually became so worn that no one but Mother, who knew it by heart, could distinguish the words.

Leaving the studio, Dad asked me, "What would you like to do now?"

"Go to a movie," I said, and we did. This was so unusual I can even remember the movie: *Arsenic and Old Lace,* with Cary Grant at his best. That was the first and only day I ever spent alone with my father.

Attending various schools as a teenager, I always starred in sports: hockey, football, basketball, track and field. I was a popular guy but a lousy student. School to me was a place to have fun. It wasn't until my last year at Ryerson Polytechnical School, now a university, that I really focused on education.

I went to Ryerson to study architecture, because it related to building and I had every intention of making construction my life's work. In my first year at Ryerson I played all the sports and was voted Athlete of the Year. In my final year, though still playing sports, I discovered, I'm not sure how, that riding the learning curve has its own appeal, and that year I won a silver medal for academic proficiency, gaining knowledge that would later serve me well.

Although my mother was always giving everyone instructions on household affairs, and though Dad was religious—he read the Bible, studied the Torah, and led his life according to its beliefs, though never insisting my mother keep a kosher house—neither parent ever pressured us children to think or do as they did. Nor did they ever sit down with us, as we have with our sons, and give us guidance on sex, love, or success.

What they did was teach us by example, showing, not telling, us the right thing to do, and expecting, not merely hoping, that we would do it, which we all did. And that gave us, I believe, the assurance of self-confidence and the guidance of values that were acquired emotionally and thus they endured.

CHAPTER 2

Max Sharp & Son

On graduating from Ryerson at twenty-one years of age, I went immediately into construction with my father, doubling the size of his company. It's usually difficult for a son to begin work under his father, but for me it was the other way around. Perhaps because I had gone to college and studied drafting and architecture, Dad stepped back to let me take over Max Sharp & Son.

My labor force was immigrant Italian: a carpenter, Vito Pisano, and a laborer, Ciro Rapachietti. Neither had much English, but I'd watched them work, liked what I saw, and trained them to be supervisors. In fact, I had so much confidence in them that every morning I'd jot down all the things that needed to be done that day, tick off whatever jobs I gave them, and simultaneously cross them off, because I had no doubt whatever that they'd do it or that if they didn't, they'd tell me why.

These were my earliest long-term employees; they had come to me in the fall of the year I became a full-time builder. It had rained a lot that autumn, and most builders had closed when it rained, sending employees like Ciro home for the day. Going home on the bus, he passed our building and saw us still at work despite the rain, and one day soon after, he got off the bus and asked for a job. I hired him, and never again did Ciro, nor Vito either, lose a day's work.

Vito worked with me until he retired some forty years later, but Ciro died of cancer in the 1980s. I went to see him in the hospital just before his death, and Ciro, a deeply religious man, told me something I'll never forget. "Mr. Sharp," he confided, "I believe God sent you to me." It was a revelation of how he had felt about his job. Both he and Vito worked hard

Pouring concrete for Motel 27 in 1954—the job that inspired me to get into the hotel business.

I soon promoted Vito Pisano from laborer to foreman.

and saved enough to send their children to college and, when they married, buy them homes.

Max Sharp & Son had little trouble getting contracts that kept both men working. Canada's soldiers were back from the war. And immigration was endowing Toronto with large and growing new communities: Italian, Chinese, Portuguese, German, Ukrainian. And while growing into a cosmopolitan city, it was also fast becoming a financial center.

Dad had begun by building houses, but now we were into apartment buildings. Roselawn Court—the first one, at Bathurst Street and Roselawn Avenue—was financed by Max Tanenbaum, a man who came to Canada with nothing but business savvy, which made him rich by wise investments in various businesses. He would advance the capital required, Dad would do the building, and once he paid Max back, they'd share profits fifty-fifty. It was the trust between Dad and Max that gave us this opportunity.

I found myself with extraordinary and premature authority to build something I'd never done before. Construction in those days was primitive compared with that of today. Construction companies now have huge trailers with air-conditioned offices for secretaries, bookkeepers, engineers, and all the architects it takes to draw up plans so detailed that if stacked they would be two feet high. I, on the other hand, was forced to be a jack-of-all-trades, working alone in a little construction shack with a small sales office in front and an eight-by-twelve work office in the back. And when I wasn't there, I'd be on site, not only giving orders to workers but also doing whatever needed to be done, though not necessarily in the right way.

Roselawn Court, my first apartment building, was a learning experience in which luck played a major role. Portable toilets were not yet in vogue: You just dug a hole and put up an outhouse, changing its location as the building went up. But I once put the outhouse too close to the building, and a big concrete block fell from the roof, smashing the outhouse with someone in it. And this fellow burst out of the shattered privy with his pants down, looking around as if God had saved him; and who knows, maybe He had, for the block missed his head by only two feet.

My second apartment building was Northview Terrace, where my parents lived for the rest of their days. I remember one hot holiday weekend laying out footings so construction could begin the following week. I was working alone, using a transit. The excavation was twenty feet deep. I'd find a corner, climb down the ladder, drive in two pegs, nail a stick across them, then climb back up to find I was almost a quarter inch off and would have to do it again. It was stupid and time-wasting, but I thought I would save money. I only found out later that you never, ever, do that. You bring in a surveyor to position the building precisely to avoid disaster.

This Northview apartment building was close to another one next door, so I figured we'd need steel piles and wood planks to support the structure around the excavation. But when you do that, the vertical steel columns have to be braced as you dig down. And I didn't know that.

In the last stage of excavation, we were hit by a major storm. We were working in the late afternoon with the rain pouring down when suddenly I could see the support walls move. It looked as if the whole building would fall into our excavation.

I panicked and called Max Tanenbaum, our financial backer. Max owned York Steel and—with some trepidation, because he was as tough as he was smart—I said to him, "Mr. Tanenbaum, this is a crisis. You've got to get welders down here with twelve-by-twelve timbers. Unless we reinforce our columns the whole building's going to fall into our excavations."

Then I called the head of the company supplying our concrete. "We've got an emergency," I said. "We've got to keep on working, so it's important you stay open."

Both he and Max came through. And in driving rain that lasted hours, we reinforced our entire series of columns, everyone working like Trojans to save the building. Which we did. If we hadn't, it's doubtful that this book could have been written.

As factual head of Max Sharp & Son, I was not only in charge of construction; I was rental agent, salesperson, and financier. Once, at age twenty-one, wearing rubber boots and work clothes, I went to Dad's bank, the Bank of Toronto, now TD Canada Trust, and explained to the branch manager, Ted Hemmans, how we optioned land, now worth considerably more than we paid. "You know, I could sell that land tomorrow and make a significant profit," I said. "But I don't want to sell it, I want to build on it. And I want you to loan me the money I need. You may say I'm putting no money down, but that wouldn't be true. What I've gained on the land is my

Northview Terrace, Toronto, 1954. Rosalie and I lived in apartment 1001, my parents on the floor above.

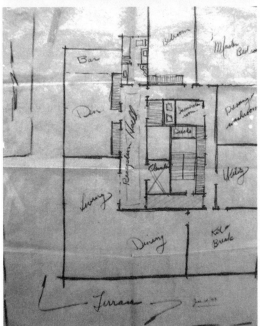

My sketch for the penthouse apartment on top of Northview Terrace, 2515 Bathurst Street, Toronto, residence of Max and Lil Sharp for over fifty years.

The "office" trailer that moved from Northview Terrace to 575 Avenue Road, to the Jarvis Street Hotel, and finally to the Inn on the Park.

equity. And if I had come to you when we first looked at this land and said we'd put up that amount of equity, I'm sure you'd have gone along with it. Well, our gain on that land, easily checked, is exactly the same."

He then gave me some advice. "Why don't you get rid of the rubber boots and start working with pencil and paper instead of pick and shovel?"

I got the money, but not until afterward did the significance of his advice sink in. He was telling me, "You've got a good business mind. Why not stop laying bricks and use it?"

I didn't know it then, but I'd be doing that very soon.

CHAPTER 3

Rosalie

While most of my early days were spent working hard for Max Sharp & Son, sometimes to the point of fatigue, it didn't prevent me from playing basketball and hockey after work nor from leading an active nightlife, taking girls to shows and dances, cavorting, drinking, and gambling, sometimes into the morning hours. Then I met Rosalie.

I went with all our family to the wedding of my cousin, Leonard Godfrey, son of my Uncle Max, who brought so many of our family to Canada. And while dining at the Sharp banquet table, a beautiful young lady at the nearby bridesmaid table caught my eye. After dinner I went over, introduced myself, and asked her to dance. Afterward I asked for her phone number. Without hesitation she gave it. Later I learned she had told her best friend, Merle Shain, that she'd met "*the* man of my life," but was absolutely certain I'd never call.

For a week, she must have been sure she was right, for that was one of my dawn-to-dusk weeks, leaving the work site so beat that all I wanted to do was rest. It was a week before I called and suggested we take in a movie.

She agreed, and we went to see Jerry Lewis in *Sailor Beware*. But the picture had barely begun when I slid down in my seat and slept until the end of the show. I awoke dismayed, thinking Rosalie would be either hurt or incensed, which in either case could end an intriguing affair.

But no, she was impressed, amazed that I could be so cool on a first date. She was then seventeen, and her previous dates were all with what she called nerdy types, academics. She was drawn to me, as I was to her,

In the garden on Green Valley Road, Toronto, 1966.

despite our differences—or perhaps, though we didn't know it then, because of them.

WE CAME FROM SIMILAR BACKGROUNDS, but our lives growing up were poles apart. My parents never questioned what I did away from home. But Rosalie's father, Joseph Wise, who once ran Wise's Dry Goods but was now retired and living off the revenue of his stores and the apartments he had built, was excessively strict with his only daughter, disallowing her lipstick, bare legs, or high-heeled shoes. He expected her to marry someone important, a doctor or lawyer perhaps, certainly not some roughneck in rubber boots.

I began to take Rosalie out, though I was still gallivanting around. Our relationship was not to her father's liking, so when a crony told him he saw me in a bar with a questionable girl, he forbade Rosalie to see me anymore.

She nevertheless accepted my next invitation and then came to see me the following day at my Northview Terrace construction site. "Sorry, Issy," she said. "I didn't tell you Dad forbade me to go out with you, and now he's locked me out of the house."

"Let's go talk to him," I said, and still wearing my rubber boots, I went with Rosalie to their home.

When his wife let us in, he was sitting on his couch, reading the newspaper. I didn't argue, just quietly explained our relationship, and gradually he came around.

Rosalie was amazed. "I saw my father change before my eyes," she told me later, "from self-righteousness to subdued child. And from that Freudian moment when you took charge, I transferred my allegiance to you."

Rosalie and I continued dating for two years, discovering how and what each other thought. Because her parents gave her neither toys nor dolls, her playground from childhood on was the public library. She loved mulling over books, taking her selections home to read, sometimes finishing one in a day, reading while walking to and from school, at meals, or late into the night. I wasn't much of a reader, and her ability to recall so much of what she read amazed me. I believed she had a rare gift, a combination of a creative mind with an exceptional IQ. She maintained that I was prone to exaggerate, but her school marks confirmed my thoughts. Deciding to take Grade 13 German and Latin while still in Grade 12, she studied during lunch hours to make up three years of Latin plus two of German, and without ever taking a language class, she passed her Grade 12 final exam with top honors.

We each learned from the other the little things that bring people together. Rosalie taught me to like Chinese food and movies with subtitles. I taught her to ski and exercise regularly.

The first time I took Rosalie to see my mother, I had not yet asked her to marry me. I only told my mother I was bringing a girl home to meet her. But as soon as I introduced them, Mom threw her arms around Rosalie, lifted her off her feet, clasped her to her bosom and said, "Velkom to de femily." My mother acted on instinct, usually correctly.

Rosalie herself did not believe our relationship would last, and she had very good reason for her fears. I was still irresponsible, taking life a day at a time. But later she confessed that she was smitten, that however long it lasted was good enough.

Rosalie was almost nineteen and I nearly twenty-four, still living at home, when I asked her to marry me. That fall, Rosalie's parents gave a traditional dinner-dance wedding, inviting five hundred guests, though Rosalie said being married at city hall would have been more romantic.

We honeymooned for nine days in New York, Miami, and Cuba, where one night we went on a bus tour of the nightclubs. At El Trocadero, we were seated with an ancient colonel and his wife. But our table was so far from the stage where near-naked girls were dancing that I thought I'd check out their gambling casino.

I told Rosalie, "I'll be right back," and left her making conversation with the colonel, who was quite deaf.

I checked out the casino like the gambler I was, losing three hundred dollars, a large part of our honeymoon money. But Rosalie, who was shouting at the deaf colonel for an hour, made the best of it. "What's done is done," she said. "We'll manage."

After a few days at Veradero Beach, where we had the off-season hotel to ourselves, we came home to the new one-bedroom apartment my dad had built on Eglinton Avenue. We found it not only empty but also filthy.

Our shoes left footprints on the grimy kitchen floor, which clearly hadn't been cleaned since the last tenant left. The kitchen counter was coated with greasy grime, and the bedroom was empty except for a mattress and box springs leaning against a wall, still wrapped in brown paper.

Rosalie immediately took charge. Within a month, our apartment looked like a page from *House Beautiful*. We invited both our families to a Friday night Shabbat dinner. She had no cooking experience but a lot of chutzpah. Following her *Gourmet Cookbook*, Vol. 1, she planned an ambitious menu of French dishes one might find in a three-star Michelin restaurant. At four o'clock on Friday, she was only half-done, so she reduced the number of courses to four. Because it was Halloween, she decorated the table with orange-and-black jelly molds and a lighted pumpkin trimmed with black crepe paper. Halfway through dinner, the pumpkin exploded and hit the ceiling in flames. Days later, small particles of soot, like fruit flies, were still descending.

This apartment was small for a couple who were planning to have children, and we soon moved into a larger one in an eleven-story tower on Bathurst Street that I'd been building. Here Rosalie got deeply into interior decorating, even taking out a nib wall at the entrance. This left the column exposed, giving an open diagonal view to our L-shaped main room, which made the apartment look even larger.

As soon as she'd changed our apartment to meet her creative taste—which in the years ahead would make us partners in more than marriage—she began campaigning for a child. And although we'd agreed to wait until we knew each other better, I eventually gave in. Within four and a half years, we had four children, all boys.

THE BOYS put a considerable strain on our income. But Rosalie, growing up with little money to spend, was a highly proficient economizer. She not only did her own decorating and made her own clothes, she also shopped with inordinate care. Instead of having milk delivered, she would walk with the kids to the store and buy milk by the jug, which gave her one quart free. It was five years before we could afford our first vacation: three days of sunlight and sunburn at the Midtown Motor Inn in Niagara Falls, which we then considered glamorous. Once a year, though, to celebrate our marriage anniversary, we took in Toronto's Canadian National Exhibition, a renowned but inexpensive world's fair.

Three children, a couple still in diapers, in an apartment with only two bedrooms—our situation was not only a drain on income but on time. And I had neither the knowledge, judgment, nor time to become a good parent. I was working morning till night, six or seven days a week, so with few qualms, I left the upbringing of our children, along with the care of our house, to Rosalie.

Rosalie never complained, never tried to change me, though she once left me a note so succinctly pertinent that I still keep the original in my notebook: "Overachievers suffer loss of intimacy. No time for fun. Relationships starve on a diet of self-absorption. Home is the place to express the playful part of oneself."

I doubt if I changed immediately, though I certainly did thereafter, for home eventually became the one place I could leave my problems behind and enjoy the moment. From our first child on, Rosalie considered me a good dad, because before going to work, I always changed the babies' diapers. This was a joy I looked forward to with every child: opening the door and seeing the baby standing in his crib, oblivious to the urine-soaked diapers hanging around his knees, beaming with the anticipation of seeing me. It always put me in a good mood to start a day of work.

Life settled into a routine: on the job by seven and home by seven P.M. No frills for us like vacations or the golf club. Work was my life.

Rosalie and the boys.

A 1960 photo at the Canadian National Exhibition, where we celebrated our wedding anniversaries for many years.

On the French Riviera when we were young and gorgeous, 1963.

CHAPTER 4

A New Kind of Project

E ven on our honeymoon, work was often on my mind. For our wedding night, in fact, I reserved a room at an airport hotel in Toronto. I'd heard that it was successful, and I wanted to find out why. We expected glamour; it was anything but. Our room was small and noisy, people coming and going. Then, in the middle of the night, Rosalie woke me. "There's somebody in our room," she said.

"Don't be silly," I replied.

"I'm telling you," she said, "there's somebody in the bathroom."

I got up and went into the bathroom. No one was there but someone had been, for the bathroom served two separate rooms.

It was an unusual beginning for a honeymoon, though we laughed about it later. But I thought that if a hotel like this was making lots of money, it shouldn't be hard to build a hotel that would make a lot more. And because all the other hotels we had stayed at on our honeymoon were widely considered first class, I had taken endless movies of all the exteriors, lobbies, and courtyards.

This interest was generated by a job I did that year. A friend of mine, Jack Gould, had sold his business so he and his wife could set up and run a motel, which he asked me to build. It would be just an ordinary little motel, seven rooms on each side of an office and storage room, close to the junction of Highway 27 and Queen Elizabeth Way near the southern Toronto lakefront.

I thought it could be tricky for prospective customers to find. "Jack," I said, "this won't work unless people know how to get here."

"It'll work," he said, "I've looked into it. Don't give me advice. Just build it."

The builder on the job at the first Four Seasons, Jarvis Street and Carlton, Toronto.

"Then let me give you a suggestion," I said. "Why don't you build it twice as long. Just exterior with no interior finishes, no plumbing; it won't cost much. But that will give you a big roof you can put a huge sign on—MOTEL 27—so people can easily find you."

He considered the price reasonable. "OK. Do it," he said.

His motel went over so well, he asked me, soon after he opened, to finish the other rooms. And I thought, *If it works so well here, why wouldn't it work downtown?* The more I thought about it, the more intrigued I became.

I was still busy building houses and apartments, of course, but in what little spare time I had, I began soliciting opinions from our current and previous financial backers on building a motel downtown.

I began by calling on Cecil Forsyth, head of Great-West Life insurance in Toronto, using him as my sounding board. Cec was the major backer for our two apartment buildings, and we also had something in common. In his younger days, he had been a semipro athlete—a fine football player, a great golfer. He liked me, but he didn't like this new deal I was proposing.

I typed out, using one finger, a profit-and-loss statement on building and operating a one-hundred-room motel. Then I went to my best friend, Wally Cohen, and asked if he would invest in it. Wally's parents had died young, leaving him and his sisters a considerable fortune.

"Sorry, Issy," he said. "My money is all in a trust, and my trustee won't invest in something he thinks will never work."

I approached Max Tanenbaum, of course; Max was everybody's financier. "You're crazy," he said. "You know nothing about the hotel business. I do, and I wouldn't touch it with a ten-foot pole."

I found a possible center-town site at Eglinton and Yonge, then went back and propositioned Cec Forsyth again. Again he told me I didn't know what I was doing. This went on and on for some three years. Every couple of months I would go to see him. "Cec, I've got a new idea," I would say. "I think it might work. What do you think?" And he would patiently explain why he disagreed. We were forging something akin to a father-son relationship. But one day his patience gave out. "Stop bothering me," he said.

With Jack Gould, center, *and Ciro Rapachietti, Motel 27.*

Cecil Forsyth of Great-West Life, who was the first investor to believe in me. We developed a mutual affection.

"Don't come back until you've arranged to get all the financing you'll need. I'll give you fifty percent if you can get the other fifty."

"Can I rely on that?" I asked.

"*If* you get the other fifty, yes." And I think he figured I'd never get it.

I tied up several sites, none completely satisfactory. And concurrently, in what little spare time I had from building houses and apartments, I was talking about the prospect of a motel to various people, two in particular. My sister Edith had married Edmund Creed, son of Jack Creed, who owned Creeds, a highly fashionable clothing store. Eddie's best friend was Murray Koffler, a pharmacist whose father died, leaving him a drugstore. He now owned two and before long would own many more. I'd built a rental apartment over one drugstore for Murray, and since he and Eddie were always looking for ways to invest in real estate and we all lived in the same neighborhood, all three of us were soon talking frequently about building a motel.

None of us, of course, knew anything about the hotel business, let alone the prospects for a motel within the city. So when Murray read in *Time* magazine about a man named Mike Robinson, who ran a successful chain of motels, one of them in downtown Phoenix, I wrote him a letter. He invited us down, so Murray and I flew to Phoenix.

We lunched with Robinson by the pool in the courtyard of his motel: two stories high, all the rooms facing inward. It was sunny, attractive, and peaceful despite being surrounded by a run-down area with a noisy bus depot. This idea of creating a courtyard oasis without spending a fortune captured my imagination, and when this fellow said we should fly to Los Angeles and talk to a man named Al Parven, who knew a lot about the hotel business, we complied.

Parven was about to leave for Las Vegas. "Come with me," he said, "and I'll show you something."

He showed us a hotel designed for gambling. What I learned of relevance to our mission was that landscaping really enhances the type of low-rise building we were contemplating.

We also learned something about Las Vegas in that era. I'd made money gambling in my later teens, and I said to Murray, "Let's play some dice. I've got a system. You put your chips down, a dollar or two, whatever, and if you lose you double up. As long as you have enough money to keep doubling up, you'll eventually win. Then you start over. Watch."

He watched me make a little money, a little more. Then I said, "Murray, let's not waste time playing together. You play at that table, I'll play at this one."

We soon made two or three thousand dollars and decided that was the business for us. So we called our wives and said, "We won't be home for a while."

Soon a guy comes up to us and says in a low voice, "You better leave, they're going to take you," and walks away.

We ignored him, kept on playing, kept on doubling up. In just ten minutes, we knew we had to go home: We were broke.

Back in Toronto, working overtime, I continued my unsuccessful search for a suitable hotel site. Finally I enlisted the help of a friend, real estate broker Andrew Csepely, a colorful refugee from Budapest whom I'd met when he came to me with a new concept for Canada—cooperative apartments, the precursor of condominiums—and in 1957 we built Toronto's first co-op on Avenue Road. Andrew brought a European sensibility to his view of future Toronto land values, which put him well ahead of his competitors, and he found us a good-sized piece of property on Jarvis Street in the center of the city. All three of us liked it. But almost everyone we talked to about it had the same reaction: "How could you think of building a motel or hotel on Jarvis Street! People will think it's a flophouse!" Jarvis was, at the turn of the century, a major thoroughfare of grand mansions for families such as the Masseys and the Seagrams. Since then, it had slowly gone downhill; it was now a hangout for gangsters, hookers, and street people, with many rooming houses on that street selling drugs or sex. But I believed in our courtyard concept and doubted that land in the center of a fast-growing city like Toronto could remain cheap.

Lack of money was also a major problem. Murray, Eddie, and my dad had each agreed to put up $90,000. I secured $125,000 from the Bank of Nova Scotia, lent not on my credentials but on those of the Creeds, one of the bank's most valued customers. I then got my suppliers and subcontractors to agree to wait for part of their money until the hotel was opened, and

I arranged for Simpson's Contract Division to supply the furniture and equipment on a lease-purchase contract over seven years.

I then went back to Cecil Forsyth. "The last time we talked," I said, "you told me that if I could raise fifty percent on this motel, you would give me the other fifty." And I showed him how we raised 50 percent.

"But that wasn't what I meant," he protested. "I didn't mean for you to borrow more money, I meant for you to raise equity. Real money. This is all borrowed money."

"Yes, but your first mortgage is still secure. And I've raised the full fifty percent. You said you'd give it to me if we did."

He looked at me for a few very long moments. "All right," he said, "we'll see if you can do it."

And that was the one critical decision that determined my future career. I was now, for better or worse, about to become a part-time hotelier.

We needed a name, and someone came up with "Thunderbird." But on checking it out, we found it already taken. We kept looking, leafing through phone books to find a name that stood out. Then Eddie remembered a hotel in Munich he had stayed at during one of his buying trips, the finest hotel he knew, the Vier Jahrzeiten. That translated as Four Seasons. It sounded right. And that was the extent of our market research for a name.

In 1960, still looking for ideas, we took in the annual New York Hotel Show, all three of us. We walked around, collecting brochures, gathering information, and questioning people.

One of the exhibitors we talked with was Tom Lee, a leading American interior designer, who was sitting in front of a display called "The Room of Tomorrow." It was interesting. We approached him, told him how great the room looked, and explained what we intended to do in Toronto. Then we asked if he'd like to do the design.

I showed him our makeshift plans. He considered them and said, "Sure, I'd love to do it." And Tom became our interior designer.

We looked at another room on display: the duo bedroom, designed by Elliott Frey. It had a double bed adjacent to the bathroom wall and perpendicular to it a single bed resembling a sofa. Then between them was an angular desk, which, when the sofa was pulled out on a slant, became its headboard. The room, when you walked in, looked like a living room. It was a fresh idea that we liked and thought we should use.

We sat in on a lecture on the hotel business by Fred Mino, CEO of Horwath and Horwath, a prominent consulting firm. Afterward, we talked to another consultant, Steve Brenner, about our motel plans. We realized we couldn't afford consultants, but I kept in touch just in case I eventually became a hotelier. All in all, our several days at the New York Hotel Show were well spent.

Our plans and funds were now at the stage where we needed an architect. A friend of mine, Peter Dickinson, an ex-Brit, was in Canada at the time. He was the country's foremost architect, but we couldn't afford his standard fee.

I went to see him and said, "I'm building a motel, Peter. But I don't need the usual plans you give a client. Nor do I need specifications. Nor any supervision. I just need plans to get a building permit."

Peter at that time had a lot of smart young people working for him. One of the best was Peter Webb. "I'll let Peter do the job for you," he said. "It shouldn't cost you much."

I told Peter Webb about the courtyard we had seen and why we liked it. So his architectural plans were simple, but his detail was good and his structure quaint—a little gem. And I don't think what Dickinson charged us would pay for the paper Peter used.

In landscaping I remembered what I had thought about in Las Vegas: that as a building depreciates, landscaping appreciates, camouflaging the signs of age in the structure. We landscaped accordingly. But taking the Canadian climate into account, I told our landscape architect, Austin Floyd, "We need to do something interesting in winter."

The motel was designed with balconies for all rooms, overlooking the courtyard. Floyd considered that for a while, then came to me and said, "We'll put Christmas trees on every balcony, all lit up. Create a luminous glow around the interior of the hotel. Then when the season's over, we'll put these trees in the courtyard in front of the dining room, build a sculptural mountain out of them, water it, and freeze it so it looks like a winter castle." That's what we did. And it was stunning. Austin was articulating what we already knew we should have, an ambience that would help make our hotel a winner.

Soon afterward, we began looking for a manager. I went to the Westbury Hotel, now a Courtyard Marriott, to talk to Joe Stanbury, the general manager of what was then considered Toronto's best as well as newest hotel. I told him what we were doing and asked if he knew anyone available to manage our little motel.

"I've got just the guy," he said. "Ian Munro. He's a Scot who came from England to see his brother and wants to stay. He took the first job he could get."

Ian worked in a little place in midtown Toronto, a considerable comedown for the ex-GM of several of England's most celebrated inns as well as the Treetops Hotel in Kenya, where Britain's present queen once stayed. He had every credential we needed, and just then he needed us. Another lucky break.

Ian was a large, good-looking, relatively youthful man whose portly waistline affirmed his love of fine food. He was not only gregarious and funny, he knew everything we didn't know about hotels. But when we first met, he was wearing striped pants, part of a very formal outfit. I said nothing about it then, but when we officially hired him, I said, "I have only one condition. I never want to see you in striped pants in the motel. Just wear a suit."

"What's wrong with them?" he asked. "They look good."

"Not in the kind of hotel we want," I explained. "We want class but not formality."

He agreed, although later, when I suggested that our bellmen stress informality by wearing cardigan sweaters, he said firmly, "That's carrying it too far!"

Because Ian, like me, didn't want the hotel to seem pretentious, we agreed that class for us would be a standard of relaxed elegance. And despite the fact that we had to keep costs down, Ian gave us class: class in the way he made customers welcome, no matter how they were dressed, class in hiring and training his staff to be friendly and efficient, and class in the affluent atmosphere he created with little money. So whenever people would tell me, "You don't know the hotel business," I would say, "I don't need to. I've hired someone who does."

We became good friends. And everything I learned about running a hotel I learned from him, although I was making his job more difficult by saving every dollar I could. For example, I didn't see why his secretary couldn't double as our telephone operator. "She's just sitting there by the phone," I said. "Can't she also take notes when you need them? Why do we need two people?"

"Please," he said, looking around at his office, no bigger than a dining table. "At least give me a secretary."

Often Ian and I would sit there talking, generating ideas, inexpensive things that would set our hotel apart. Because we couldn't afford advertising, we decided to make food our drawing card and establish the dining room as our showcase, something people would come for and talk about, thus attracting others. In the end, we decided to serve only roast beef, make our roast beef the best in the city, and present a customary menu only in our coffee shop. So after some research, with help from Eddie Creed, who also loved food, we found a company in Chicago selling very high quality beef from corn-fed cattle.

I, of course, was checking out hotels for several years, finding that in most of them, the towels were so thin that it took two or three to properly dry yourself. We put in bigger bath towels and thicker hand towels, all 100 percent cotton. And we were among the earliest at our level to do so.

Growing up with three sisters, I'd also learned something of women's habits: I knew that while traveling, because they don't like to wash their hair with soap, they usually carry a small bottle of shampoo. So we put shampoo in all our rooms. And that was a first. Today you can't go into any hotel or motel in the world without seeing shampoo in the bathroom.

It finally came time for our opening, and Murray, always a great promoter, said, "Let's open as a charity event for the Toronto Symphony Orchestra and the opera." He also told me, "When I was in New York; they had this fantastic outdoor art show. Thousands of people came to see it. Well, we've got hundreds of fine artists here in Toronto, and they can't get a place to show their work. Let's clear the parking lot of cars, and they can hang up their pictures here."

The Four Seasons Motor Hotel opened in 1961 and instantly became a popular hangout for the literati and glitterati.

We arranged for our guests to park across the street where a car dealer had a large lot, and several hundred artists hung their pictures in our parking lot—a first for Toronto, and a great draw for us for eight years. The event is now at Toronto's City Hall in its forty-second year, the largest outdoor art show in North America.

Eddie followed up Murray's arrangements by borrowing the Creed store's mailing list, which included most of Toronto's social elite. That gave us the marketing clout of Zena Cherry, the *Toronto Telegram*'s society reporter, and anybody who was anybody showed up at our opening, supporting not only their symphony, opera, and artists, but also us.

We opened in 1961 with elaborate publicity and much more soon to come, for directly across the street was Canadian Broadcasting Corporation (CBC) headquarters, generally known as the Kremlin by its staff. One of its staffers, Elwood Glover, hosted a popular daily half-hour noon radio program called *Luncheon Date*. Murray knew him and suggested that by broadcasting from our adjacent dining room he would have the applause and stimulation of a live audience. That appealed to both him and CBC management, and Glover began broadcasting from a corner table in our dining room, headlining show-business celebrities from Canada, the United States, and Europe.

Glover's program grew better and better, eventually becoming an hour television show and then a simulcast, a TV program simultaneously broadcast on radio. We gave him a place in the lobby with stage and tables, cabaret style. For thirteen years, Glover's program drew some two thousand guests a year, the illustrious of stage and screen, music hall and opera.

Glover was not the only person coming across the street. Many CBC employees and guests made the hotel a popular after-work rendezvous. One day, shortly after opening, a young woman came out of the CBC, strolled across the street to the pool, where guests were sitting around, took off her clothes, swam stark naked one length of the pool, turned, swam back, picked up her clothes, and walked dripping wet through the courtyard and lobby, then back across the street.

It made a newspaper headline: "The Naked and the Fled," a takeoff on Norman Mailer's new book, *The Naked and the Dead*. No one ever found out who she was. A young starlet was the best guess. But she gave us great publicity, and for the next few days, many diners and guests patronized our motel in the hope of enjoying a repeat performance.

This was promotion that no advertising, however costly, could match. And not only did the CBC make the first Four Seasons quickly and extensively fashionable, it also made it profitable beyond all expectation. It was an extraordinary beginning for a small, unknown hotel company.

PART II

STARTING
AT THE
TOP

Never follow the crowd.
—BERNARD BARUCH

Partners: from left to right, *Fred Eisen, Eddie Creed, Max Sharp, and Murray Koffler with me in the courtyard garden of the new Inn on the Park.*

CHAPTER 5

Murray, Eddie, and Issy

O ur second hotel was even more of a gamble than the first. I was putting more scarce capital in a business I didn't really yet know; I was still primarily a builder, constructing houses and apartments. But even before Four Seasons' success rationalized my desire to build a second hotel, I was seeking a suitable site for building another.

Murray, Eddie, and I were still meeting and kicking around hotel ideas, but not to the same extent as before. Murray was planning a chain of drugstores, and Eddie was taking a bigger role in his family's opulent retail clothing trade.

Then one day, as Murray was driving north to a new drugstore he had opened in Don Mills, he saw on the corner of Leslie and Eglinton avenues an empty lot displaying a sign:

FOR SALE
16 Acres
J. J. FITZGIBBON

He immediately made a U-turn that cost him a traffic ticket and raced back to tell Eddie and me. We drove out and walked around, looking it over: sixteen acres of field and scrubland adjoining a park. It rose gently to a small hill, a great site for a hotel. But it had drawbacks: Close behind it ran a noisy railway track, while across the street was a garbage dump. The only building in sight was IBM headquarters.

I recognized the drawbacks while envisioning the possibilities, which created what seems to me now, looking back, a subconscious belief in success. I liked it.

So did Murray. Eddie wasn't impressed. "As far as Toronto's concerned," he said, "that's no-man's-land."

"No way," Murray said. "This is the geographical center of metropolitan Toronto. There's over a thousand industries within a five-mile radius. People call this the Golden Mile. It may seem quiet now, but it's going to be big."

Eddie was still skeptical, with good reason. There wasn't much around this site for miles. Murray was grossly exaggerating, though what he was saying might later be true. My feeling about it was so strong that when Murray said he knew the son of the guy who was selling the land, J. J. Fitzgibbon of Famous Players, I told him, "Go ahead. See if he'll give us an option to buy."

Fitzgibbon, it turned out, had bought the site to build a television station in Toronto but, having lost the competition for a license, had no objection to passing the site on to us.

Eddie was still reluctant to proceed. "Let's do a market survey," he said. "See how well a hotel would do here." So we commissioned a survey that said, in effect, "Go ahead."

I was now envisioning another new type of hotel: a resort within a city, a two-hundred-room hotel with a pool and courtyard surrounded by parkland. But most of the people I talked to about it were unenthusiastic; they figured it was too far out, in more ways than one.

I took Rosalie to the site to get her opinion; I have always valued what she thought. She was supportive, as usual. Not until years later did I find out that when she saw only one neighbor, the head office of IBM in Canada, and a lot of trucks dumping garbage across the street in front and a noisy railway behind, she'd resigned herself to losing our home, the first we'd ever owned, and going to work. Since she was taking care of three young boys while pregnant with our fourth, the prospect was not in any way appealing.

Despite Eddie's skepticism, I decided to go ahead. I foresaw only one difficulty, but it loomed large: How do you build a two-hundred-room resort without any money?

This was literal fact. My earnings barely covered my rising family costs. Murray and Eddie didn't have any more money to invest. And lenders like Max Tanenbaum made it clear that they wanted nothing to do with the hotel business. To build, I would have to leverage, not the usual 70 percent or so, but the total cost, the entire 100 percent.

Raising this money was now wholly up to me. Murray and Eddie had no idea how much money would be required. They knew we could get a mortgage and a bank loan as in the past, and assumed that would give us full financing. They had no conception of the shortfall in money we faced if the hotel should not prove successful, a loss so great I could be in debt for the rest of my life.

I went to the Bank of Nova Scotia and spoke to the man who'd given us a small loan on Four Seasons. He considered my request and shook his head. "I can't deal with this," he said. "This is a big loan. You'll have to go to head office." He set up an appointment with Cliff Ash, deputy general manager of the bank.

I went to meet him. His office was awesome, the biggest I'd ever seen. And he cut to the chase, wasting no words. "What are you here for? How much do you want?"

"Could you give me a chance to explain what this is all about?" I asked.

"I understand you know your business," he said. "What can I do for you?"

I wasn't accustomed to this, and I gave him some background anyway: what I had just done, what I intended to do. "Cec Forsyth of Great-West Life will give us some of the money we need, more if it's working out. So what we need now is"—almost choking as I said it, because I really would have taken anything—"six hundred thousand dollars." (That was the equivalent of over $4 million in today's currency.)

He didn't ask why I was sure that Great-West Life would increase its loan. He didn't ask me how much backup I had. Then, as now, the Bank of Nova Scotia puts character before balance sheets. He just said, "OK."

"Is that it?" I asked.

"That's it," he said. And it was much the same with Cec Forsyth, the mortgage company, and my tradesmen. They all went along with me as they did with Four Seasons, believing I would do what I said I could. They were all banking on faith.

I took my concept of a resort to Peter Dickinson, and again he assigned my project to Peter Webb. Webb designed a Y-shaped building: three stories, two hundred rooms. But I didn't think it said much architecturally.

I called Dickinson again, found him in the hospital. He had just learned he had cancer, but he said nothing about it then.

I commiserated with him on his illness, then told him Webb's concept wouldn't work. "This is a resort. We need something attractive. Something so architecturally dramatic that people in Toronto and nearby cities will drive all the way to North York to see it. And it also must be something we can expand, because we have sixteen acres for future development."

Peter knew I couldn't pay his rates. Nevertheless he said, "Leave it with me." We were friends. He did this as a favor.

When he called me back to the hospital, he showed me on a sketch pad what would become the Inn on the Park: two low wings with dramatic concrete prows like those of a ship, backed by a six-story tower. It was magnificent. Sophisticated. Unconventional.

"This isn't my idea," he said, "It's a concept of Frank Lloyd Wright. Designed on 60- and 30-degree angles. You told me the hotel might have to grow. These angles will give you the flexibility you need in planning for expansion."

"Peter," I said. "It's perfect."

When I saw Peter Dickinson again, cancer had taken its toll. It was exceedingly sad to see this formerly robust six-foot-five man, not yet forty years of age, passing away at the height of his career.

Peter Webb, to whom he had delegated his concept, told me he couldn't continue, that the firm was folding.

"No, Peter," I said, "you've got to go on with it."

"What do you mean?" he said. "I've got to go out and find a job."

"No, no," I told him. "Why can't you and the guys working with you just take over? Be the architects?"

"But I have no office, Issy."

"Just rent an office," I told him.

So Peter Webb, Boris Zerafa, and Rene Menkes formed their own firm, rented an office on the second floor of a small store, laid doors over sawhorses for drafting tables and desks, and went on designing our hotel, for which I paid them weekly, enabling them to keep struggling along.

The footings at angles of 60 degrees and 30 degrees—a simple matter to draw on paper but very challenging and dizzying to build.

By now I was doing some struggling myself. We were $1 million short on building costs, and I really didn't think I could persuade our mortgage holder, Cec Forsyth, to come up with so much more money. But he was my only hope, so I went to see him. And perhaps because Four Seasons was earning more than expected, he agreed to increase the loan.

In building our first hotel, I had been concentrating on customers: What would our customers want most? I had little hotel experience but enough to know what most people wanted: a quiet room, a good night's sleep, and an invigorating morning shower.

Sound was crucial. And knowing what reduces sound, I did what I'd done in my first hotel: ensured that no plumbing in rooms touched concrete and that no two electrical outlets backed into each other, thus making the room as quiet as possible.

I tested foam mattresses, just coming on the market, found them quite comfortable, and put them in all our rooms. I knew that the most important factor for a consistently enjoyable shower is the water pressure and a good showerhead. So I searched for and found a long-lasting, self-cleaning showerhead called the Sloan Act-O-Matic and installed it throughout the hotel.

The completed building by Webb, Zerafa, and Menkes was all I had dreamed of. Exactly like Peter Dickinson's sketch: a six-story building with two two-story impressively original wings partly enclosing a courtyard with a large swimming pool, a separate pool for diving, two tennis courts, flower gardens, and walks that in winter could be flooded to make a skating rink. And all around the exterior, there was plenty of space for free parking.

The wings were intriguing to look at: natural wood, stone, and glass warmed by color; sweeping horizontals; contrasting textures. They were informal but luxurious, theatrical yet restful. Moreover, we could add rooms without harming design or landscaping.

It was also an architectural milestone, the start-up and first building of what is now WZMH Group, one of Canada's leading architectural firms, with offices in Dallas, Boston, Denver, and New York and prize-winning buildings in Holland, France, and China. I still use them on many projects today.

For the opening of our new hotel, I told Ian Munro to hire another Four Seasons manager and come over to manage what we'd decided to call the Inn on the Park. I knew Ian could give it the relaxed but elegant ambience we wanted.

Again, we discussed ideas that would set us apart from competitors. The township had agreed to relocate the dump, and we were surrounded with picturesque parkland. We provided bicycles for rent and maps for walkers.

We discussed smoking, how tobacco smoke bothered a lot of nonsmokers. "Why don't we ask our guests if they smoke," I said. "If they don't, we could designate some floors as nonsmoking and segregate them." And we did: the beginning of what became a worldwide practice.

Murray, Eddie, and I knew a man named Lloyd Percival, a physical training instructor at Don Mills Collegiate. Lloyd was a pioneer who dominated Canadian sport. As a track-and-field coach, he trained more champions than anyone in Canadian history. He produced, in one five-year period, two world champions, two Pan-American champions, and thirty-seven Canadian champions. He founded Sports College, which grew to a million card-carrying members. He became "Mr. Fitness," a CBC radio broadcaster, author, pamphleteer, and nonstop speaker on such novel ideas as aerobics, energy diets, muscle-sense training, and isometric exercises. He was so far ahead of his time that government health officials in the United States, Europe, and Russia solicited his advice.

I exercised to keep in shape every morning and knew others who did or would like to, so we asked Lloyd if he'd operate a fitness club in the hotel. He demurred at first, but by the hotel's opening in March 1963, he was ready to announce that the Inn on the Park would be the location of the Fitness Institute, the first of its kind in the world. "Hotel guests, local residents, and industry executives," he told reporters, "may avail themselves of a scientifically planned, individually tailored program designed to maintain or shape their physical condition."

Percival gave us welcome publicity for several years. But his penchant for bluntly criticizing coaches who didn't meet his standards made him many enemies who accused him in 1966 of giving prohibited drugs to athletes. After holding hearings, the Central Ontario Branch of the Amateur Athletes of Canada made a ruling on Percival's eligibility as a coach that seemed to substantiate these charges, and the branch asked the national executive of the AAU for support. It refused. Percival sued the five-member registration committee for libel and slander in the Supreme Court of Ontario.

In John Smart's *Athletes and Pills: Lloyd Percival and the Crothers Controversy of 1966*, he says that reports vary on the outcome of this case, which was settled out of court after some testimony had been given. Apparently one of the conditions of the settlement was that none of the parties would reveal the terms of the settlement. Most commentators have assumed that Percival was exonerated. I was exceedingly sorry for him but couldn't do anything except sympathize. When you're too far ahead of your time, you need the temperament to handle it.

After moving into the Inn on the Park, Lloyd often claimed to have the only Canadian gym with wall-to-wall broadloom, and he called me "my benevolent landlord." I believed in his theory of fitness, which, as Lloyd explained to me, was less about building strength and speed than mustering coordination: getting one's whole body to work like a coiled spring. He put me on a circuit-training program. The first circuit, some ten exercises, was repeated as fast as possible. When my time of six and a half minutes could no longer be lowered, I moved to the second circuit, which took slightly less than ten minutes, then to the third, which I couldn't get lower than nineteen. That gave me my peak of fitness, from which I can always judge, even now, what shape I'm in.

Another exercise was to quickly climb up, across, and down a pegboard using a one-arm pull-up with a weight around one's waist, strength and coordination working together, consistent with the way the body works.

Lloyd also had original thoughts on medical remedies. He didn't believe in putting a broken arm or leg in a cast, as he claimed that the muscles atrophy. Once when I broke an ankle while skiing in Europe, I didn't let the doctor put it in a cast; instead I followed Lloyd's suggestion to merely tape it when I got home. "Just use it as best you can," Lloyd had said. "The human body protects itself by the level of pain it can withstand." And he was right. My ankle healed in every respect just as he said it would.

Another interesting thing he told me was that if you keep physically fit and mentally alert throughout your life you will never lose your sex drive. What better advice could you give a dutiful thirty-two-year old? Again, at least so far from my experience, he knew what he was talking about.

Now, of course, Percival's views are accepted universally. And no one would think of planning a hotel without a health club or fitness center. But with Lloyd Percival, who later died of lung cancer from smoking, the Inn on the Park was first: another milestone.

Because the township did not allow the public sale of hard liquor, we built a large beer hall, later supplanted by a discotheque where people could drink and dance to records, an idea Eddie brought back from France. It was another first and a great success, if you counted the dancers—but not if you counted what the dancers spent!

The sad truth was that for a hotel catering to holidayers, the inability to serve cocktails with meals was a serious financial drawback. But my partner in Max Sharp & Son, Fred Eisen, who had married my sister Bea, knew his way around city hall, and he and his colleagues organized and finally won a referendum that ended North York's ban on serving liquor.

The Inn on the Park—architect, Peter Dickinson.

We closed the discotheque at the height of its unrewarding popularity and reopened the room as the Café de l'Auberge, a dinner-dance club. Then, on Eddie Creed's advice, we brought in Chico Valle to play Latin dance music, the newest rage, and made our food the best in the city. Soon our Café became *the* place to dine and dance, so popular that tables were sometimes reserved months ahead.

A great migration by car to the suburbs brought homes and commerce to North York. Conveners of business meetings liked a nearby first-class hotel without any city-center distractions. Torontonians and denizens of adjacent cities, mostly Buffalo and Detroit, were glad to have a genuine resort so handy, and out-of-town tour buses added the Inn on the Park to their travel agendas. Then, when a Yorkville restaurant was named the Inn on the Parking Lot, I knew we were definitely in.

The hotel was so successful that Cec Forsyth, our mortgage lender, congratulated me for reaching the pinnacle of success, which seemed to imply that business from here on would be somewhat anticlimactic.

Nothing could have been further from the truth.

Off on our first trip to Europe, August 1963.

At Le Mouton du Panurge, a Paris nightclub.

CHAPTER 6

London

In 1963, now that we had two successful hotels, Rosalie and I decided to take the trip of a lifetime, five weeks in Europe, our first genuine holiday in the eight years since our honeymoon.

We planned the usual circuit: London, Paris, Rome—plus Israel, of course, because we're Jewish and have many relatives there. And because we wanted to stay on budget while vetting some world-famous hotels, we decided to average costs: We spent every other night in the cheapest lodging available. No messing with the in-between.

In London we stayed at the Dorchester, and I was just blown away—everything about it was beyond anything I had known. In Paris we splurged and stayed at the George V, and here, too, the etiquette, luxury, and grandeur made for an enchanting, enlightening experience. So much so that we didn't waste time sleeping.

After Italy and Israel, we returned to Toronto, and I was working in my small, triangular new office at the Inn on the Park when another builder, a Brit from London, dropped in to see me. I told him I'd just come back from London and mentioned my memorable experience at the Dorchester. "The epitome of elegance," I observed.

"That's interesting," he said. "My company owns that hotel." He explained that he worked for the Robert McAlpine Company, owners of a huge UK-based construction firm with vast real estate holdings.

"No kidding," I said. And without thinking, half joking, I told him to tell his company that if they ever wanted to build a hotel better than the Dorchester, I could do it for them.

It was such a flippant remark, I never thought any more about it. But obviously he had passed on my comment to his head office, for a few weeks later, he called me to say, "Mr. Sharp, my people are interested in what you were saying about building a hotel. We've been working on a real estate project in London for some ten years, and we haven't been able to get it off the ground. If you're interested. . . ?"

I couldn't believe it. But maybe the Inn on the Park impressed him. "I'm very interested," I said. "I'll be glad to fly to London to talk it over." And I did.

At our London meeting, they explained that they had a piece of land in the center of the city on which they wanted to build a hotel: 320 rooms, average size, moderately priced.

"I'd like to do business with you," I said. "But I want to build a first-class hotel, something like the Dorchester."

"London has too many hotels like the Dorchester," they told me. "There's the Connaught, Claridge's, the Ritz, the Savoy, Grosvenor House. Even if we could meet their grandeur, which we can't, it wouldn't be profitable."

We had an amiable parting but no agreement on building, and again I put the matter out of mind.

Several months later, I had an overseas call from a man named Gerald Glover. In a crisp British accent, he told me he worked for the McAlpines and asked if I would be interested in coming to London to talk with him.

"Yes sir," I said, "I would," and no doubt my voice conveyed my eagerness.

We agreed on a date, and I flew to London overnight, arriving, because of the difference in time, early in the morning.

I met Glover at his impressively paneled eighteenth-century club. He was a stately gentleman in his late fifties, flawlessly dressed with impeccable manners. Lunch lasted two hours, and our conversation continued in his office.

Glover was a lawyer with his own practice. But he was very much a McAlpine confidant, as I learned later, a man they relied on to negotiate business deals and keep tabs on many of the company's vast real estate holdings. I found him knowledgeable and charming, though a bit bewildering, for he often seemed more interested in getting to know me than in getting down to business. And when I flew home the next day, our business was still where it was when I arrived.

Over the next four years, we replayed this scenario a score of times, and invariably I'd return to Toronto and tell Murray and Eddie that I didn't think I'd be able to cut a deal: the McAlpines just weren't willing to commit themselves. But because they never said no, I would fly overnight for a day with Glover whenever he called saying, "We're still interested."

Our major disagreement was the type of hotel to be built. At one meeting with Glover, I explained why a luxury hotel would succeed. "When I drove into the city this morning, your streets were chockablock with people, people streaming in from all directions, masses

I asked Sir Gerald Glover, "How do you keep your lawn so perfect?" "No problem," he replied. "You just cut it every week for three hundred years."

of them. More people come here every day than come to Toronto in a year. Whenever North Americans travel to Europe what do they want most to see? London, Paris, Rome. London today is like New York in the forties, one of the world's most exciting cities. Now, with business recovering from the war, travel is bound to increase even more, especially for top business people who will want to stay at five-star hotels." And again I proposed to Glover that we build a 230-room luxury hotel instead of the 320-room midrange hotel they wanted.

"With the competition we would be up against," Glover said, "my clients don't care to take the risk you're proposing."

"I believe in what I propose so strongly," I told him, "that I'm willing to pay the same rent for 230 rooms that your firm wants for 320 rooms."

But evidently nothing I said made sense, since all the studies by all the experts and consultants of their company unanimously concluded another luxury hotel wasn't needed. Once again I flew home believing this deal would never go through.

Not long afterward, Glover called again. "I'd like you to come over and have lunch with some of my friends."

"You're asking me to fly across the ocean just for lunch?" I protested, although that was what I'd been doing for more than three years.

"Well, I think before we enter into business relations, I would like my friends to have an opportunity to meet you."

"Your friends?" I asked.

"Yes. The Duke of Westminster and his advisers."

"I'll be there," I said.

I arrived in London at the designated time, keyed up by the prospect of such a novel experience and what it implied. I was picked up at the hotel and taken to a private and historic gentlemen's club at precisely 11:45. Eighteen people were in attendance. Cocktails were served, followed by lunch, at which protocol seemed to prescribe that business not interfere with digestion.

Afterward, everyone relaxed in their chairs to enjoy port and cigars. After a rather long silence, one of the duke's advisers turned to me and said, "Mr. Sharp, I know you have been invited here as our guest. But we're very interested in what's happening in Canada, and we'd like you to tell us your views on some current issues."

He then gave me three topics to discuss: my opinion on Canadian prime minister Pierre Trudeau, the Canadian government, and a few complex business matters.

I was dumbfounded. With no prior knowledge that I would be asked to speak on these subjects, here I was, the center of attention. And because I wasn't politically connected, I had to struggle through these matters with a bit of bravado: around the point rather than to it. And afterward I had no recollection whatever of what I had said.

But I remember what I said to Glover driving back to the hotel: "Gerald"—we were now on a first-name basis—"why would you put me in such a position without warning me what I'd be asked? Surely you must have realized I could have embarrassed you? These are your friends, and while

English gentlemen lunching with the "crazy Canadian" to see if he passes muster. Field Marshal Alexander is on my right. *Sir Gerald,* far right, *always addressed me as "my dear boy."*

I'll probably never see them again, you'll be held accountable for considering to go into business with me."

"My dear boy"—which is how he'd begun to address me—"to warn you would not have been cricket." Smiling warmly, he added, "I had all the confidence in the world that you would present yourself in a manner that would not embarrass me. Nor have I a problem with how you handled yourself today."

That trip was certainly different, but nothing tangible seemed to come out of it. Glover kept calling me, asking me over, and I kept responding as usual, wondering if I'd ever recover expenses.

This went on for another six months or more, and nothing changed that I could see, except my relationship with Glover. This was now becoming similar to the one I had had with Cec Forsyth, a kind of father-son affiliation that I appreciated, as Gerald was a wise and delightful man.

Then one day he called with a most unusual request. "My dear boy, it would please us very much if you could bring your wife over. We'd like to meet her."

So Rosalie and I flew to London. I was glad to have her with me. Not only did it make the trip enjoyable; it added to my security, for Rosalie is a most interesting person. Her facility to retain so much of all that she reads, hears, and sees always amazes me, as does her creativity. And, most important for me at this time, she's an articulate and charming dinner companion.

This was a dinner party at Gerald Glover's town house, attended by a dozen very proper British businessmen. It was a very formal dinner: three knives, three forks, three spoons, a formality we had not yet become acquainted with. But I think we struggled through it without too many mistakes, and Rosalie's presence and answers to questions lightened the mood at the table considerably.

After dinner we adjourned to the parlor where, as usual, port and cigars were passed around.

"A cigar, Mr. Sharp?"

"No, thank you," I said.

"Mrs. Sharp?"

"Yes, thank you," Rosalie said, accepting a cigar.

I looked at her in amazed dismay. She had never smoked, not even a cigarette. Why, when this most important business deal of my life was at stake, was she making such a gaffe?

No one else in the room batted an eyelash, of course; the British are invariably polite. But my hopes of passing this long-awaited test sank as Rosalie held out her cigar for the server to clip. Then, as he went to light it, she put it in her purse, saying, "No, thank you. I think I'll keep it for later."

Everyone in the room burst into laughter, even I, though mine included a large degree of relief.

Rosalie was just being herself, expressing her sense of fun. And because the British, as I've learned through the years, are very down-to-earth, they appreciated her being so natural.

That episode capped four years of flying overnight to London. All those meetings with Glover had served a single purpose having little to do with the contemplated project. The McAlpines simply wanted to know for sure whom they were dealing with before entering into a long-term business relationship.

The deal was cemented shortly afterward. The McAlpines were going along with me on building a 230-room hotel only because I'd agreed to pay them the rent they wanted for ninety more rooms. They still didn't think I knew what I was doing. They called me "the crazy Canadian" and said I'd go broke.

I'd kept in touch with Fred Mino, the CEO of Horwath and Horwath, whom Eddie, Murray, and I had met at the New York hotel show. His company was considered the world's foremost expert on hotels, so I hired it to do a survey for us.

Their survey also found that I was wrong. London's five five-star hotels, it said, left no room for another, especially an unknown.

I still wasn't convinced. I remembered how everyone knowledgeable in Toronto was sure our two hotels there would fail. And here we would not be building in some third-rate district but in the center of London on Park Lane and Piccadilly, next to a beautiful park: a magnificent location. With London growing, business booming, and travel on the rise, I couldn't see why a five-star hotel in such a location could fail.

More important, I believed that the biggest percentage of our customers would be businesspeople and affluent tourists from North America, and I thought I knew better than London's hoteliers what would please them most. So we signed an eighty-four-year lease at £210,000 a year, to be renegotiated every twenty-one years, and I asked McAlpine's representatives to let me bring over my own architect.

They agreed, and I called Peter Webb, who sent me Robin Clark. Robin at that time sported earrings and long hair, looking very much the rebel.

But he was a brilliant designer, and McAlpine's architect, Michael Rosenauer, an elderly, very understanding man, had no trouble working with him to create an outstanding hotel that featured a grand staircase and extra-large rooms with balconies. It would be glamorous yet functional.

For the next two years, I worked with them, negotiating my cost with the McAlpines on every change, for I was trying to save every dollar I could. And as someone who had learned to build from the ground up, with his hands as well as his head, I knew how to direct designers so they didn't put changes on paper in a way that would cost more than necessary.

They did not include air conditioning in their plans. "You won't need it," they told me. "Once or twice a year in summer, maybe."

"We must have air conditioning," I said. "The North American traveler expects it." It was a costly upgrade, but in my view, absolutely necessary. Meeting customers' expectations was my first rule for success.

The man who kept tabs on these costs was Chris Wallis, head of McAlpine's quantity-surveying department. The cost of every change had to be negotiated with Chris. When I wanted to change the usual front entrance doors to revolving doors in order to keep the cold air out in winter, I asked him how much it would cost.

Chris reviewed the drawings and named a price.

"That's far too much," I said. "Forget it. Leave it the way it is." It would have been nice, but unlike air conditioning, I wouldn't be neglecting customers' expectations.

For interior design, I again hired Tom Lee. And again Tom did an outstanding job. He was interested in history, and on the second floor, he decorated half a dozen suites named after various historical notables, including: a Napoléon suite in red and blue with paintings of Napoléon and Josephine; a Lord Nelson suite in Georgian style with a portrait of his mistress, Emma Hart, Lady Hamilton; and a Lord Hamilton suite in the Second Empire period.

Our furniture in a typical room was revolutionary. Opposite the bed was a dresser with kneehole and mirror. Adjacent to it was an armoire unit with drawers, and above that a television set with doors that concealed the TV if no one was watching it—again a hotel first.

Armoires became standard in most hotels, more recently replaced by flat-screen televisions. But what has been seldom copied, even today, was the type of furniture. It wasn't built to meet normal hotel standards; it was residential, like a guest room in a fine home, expensively classical. And while it wasn't built for durability, it remained in our London hotel for thirty-eight years. Currently the hotel is closed for major restoration.

Key to a fine hotel, I believed, was a comfortable bed. Travel can be fatiguing, especially for overnight American travelers to London; they get little sleep on a plane and usually arrive dead tired. So while we opened our first hotel with foam mattresses, the most comfortable type we could find at that time, I searched for years for the world's best mattress, having possibilities shipped to me periodically to test. I finally discovered one in Germany that we felt was probably the most comfortable ever made, and we installed these throughout our London hotel. We were the first hotel company to make beds such an important feature, and since then most major hotel companies have copied that approach.

The beds were expensive, adding to the considerable cost of the long list of expenses that Chris Wallis presented me with on completion of all my changes. He even presented me with an extra cost for the front door.

"What's this?" I said. "We didn't change the front door. You mean you're charging me for changing it back?"

"Oh yes," Chris said, "but you have to realize this is what we did." And he laid out his facts so convincingly that he almost had me believing I *had* changed the doors and should pay for it. Even when mistaken, Chris's confidence was such that one doubted oneself before doubting him.

I settled up, still arguing the cost of every change with Chris, which now totaled £700,000 ($13 million in today's dollars). This was one of Glover's responsibilities. "How are you going to pay for this?" he asked, knowing I couldn't.

"I'll need time to arrange the financing," I said. "Can you give me six months?" Where I was going to raise that much money, I hadn't a clue.

"There's one thing I can do for you," Glover said, "I can change the terms of the lease we have given you and save you quite a lot of money, if instead of negotiating a new lease every twenty-one years, we negotiate a new lease every fourteen years. But I don't recommend it. It's not a good deal for you."

I considered his offer. "It may not be a good deal for me," I said, "but

"Topping-off" ceremony, Inn on the Park London.

since it reduces what I owe you, I'll take it."

"All right," he said, "you asked for six months. I'll give you a year. Make sure you pay me back."

I hoped I could.

The formal opening of the London Inn on the Park in January 1970 was an event in aid of the Red Cross, a McAlpine-favored charity. We had set this date during construction, but as the opening grew near, I noted that our grand stairwell, a major feature of the hotel, featured a two-story window divided by a wide spandrel beam. I called the architect and said, "You know where you've got this big horizontal beam holding a spandrel at the midpoint of the stairs? It looks good from the outside, but from the inside the spandrel breaks your window in half and you lose the grandeur of your staircase."

"Well, it doesn't really matter from the outside," he told me.

"Then let's take it out," I said. And just as the workmen were about to put in the window, I told them to take out the spandrel and the beam.

One of the McAlpines in charge of the building came over and said, "Are you crazy? You're pushing us to get this structure ready for the opening and you're making a change like this!"

"It won't delay the opening," I said, and we took out the beam.

We didn't hold up construction, but it still moved slowly. I went to the head of the company, the most senior of the McAlpines. "Lord Edwin," I said, "you've set a date for Her Royal Highness Princess Alexandra to open our hotel. The invitations are out. But the way construction is going now, we won't be ready in time. That's going to be embarrassing, for you as well as us."

"Don't worry about it," he said. "Go ahead with the opening. If I have to put a thousand men on the job to finish in time, I will. But we will open on the date we set."

And that was what he did: put on a thousand men to finish up—so many that on the afternoon of the day we were to open, you could hardly get into the hotel for all the construction trucks in front and the workers swarming all over the place. It was an amazing madhouse of activity.

The opening was due to begin at 6:00. Early that afternoon, I rounded up all the people in charge. "Look, you guys," I said. "At four o'clock you're out of here. I don't want to see anyone in a construction helmet in here after that hour."

They left on time with everything swept clean. We put flowers in the lobby, turned on music, and Princess Alexandra arrived with her entourage and guests to begin festivities in a lobby gleaming with polished walnut and precious marble. The McAlpines had the power to get us off to a notable start.

What mattered now was how we were seen by potential customers. Ian Munro was now overseeing all three hotels. Ian knew not only what Londoners but also what North Americans wanted, and he trained our employees to deliver it: luxury without formality, service without a class attitude. And whereas none of London's world-famous hotels served meals after 10:00 P.M., Ian ensured that hungry guests could eat any hour of the day—or get their shoes shined and clothes pressed. We would have a caring staff to answer every need.

The first year that London property opened, it was named Europe's Hotel of the Year, and it won that title twice in the first ten years, plus additional awards, something no other hotel had done before. Its occupancy was consistently the highest in the city, and it's still one of London's most successful hotels.

Shortly after the opening, Chris Wallis asked me if I could give him a job.

"I can't hire you," I told him, "The McAlpines are my partners."

"But I'm leaving them, I'm emigrating to Canada."

Chris was a senior McAlpine employee, one of their prized future top executives. "Why are you leaving?" I asked.

"Because the company has plotted my whole life out, what I'll be doing at thirty-five, forty, forty-five. That's the way it is in the UK."

"Well, I think you're exceptionally talented, Chris. I'm sure you'll find a job easily. But I can't give you one. Your company and mine are partners." Chris did emigrate, and later I got him a job with architect John B. Parkin.

London's success gave me the opportunity to to pay back Glover, who had become an enduring friend. Whenever Rosalie and I had spare time in England, we would visit him and his wife, Sue, at their London town house or drive out to his country estate at Pytchley. Sir Gerald was like the squire of the village, his house akin to a castle, the grand manor house of the area. Once, standing at his front door overlooking a lawn that seemed to go on forever, I asked him, "How do you maintain it so beautifully?"

"My dear boy," he said. "It's very simple. You just cut it every week for three hundred years."

Sir Gerald and Sue would also come to visit us in Toronto. Once, we took them to a party at Murray and Marvelle Koffler's farm, where Glover was appalled to see people eating corn on the cob. "In England," he said, "corn is used only as fodder for horses."

Glover was the perfect caricature of a grandiose Brit: pants pulled up almost to his chest and a British accent so thick that his words at times were indistinguishable. But he was always a delight to be with, and his role in my life was critical.

I asked him about it several years after our London hotel had opened. "Sir Gerald, how could you have trusted me with such an important project when you knew if things didn't work out, I couldn't have covered my obligation?"

"My dear boy," he said, "over time you make a judgment about people. You develop a belief and a trust."

Those many meetings of ours were not primarily about business per se. They were about the foundation of business: trustworthy relationships. This was something I'd long believed without giving it much thought. But from then on, in every deal, it would be in the forefront of my mind.

CHAPTER 7

ITT Sheraton

It took four years to win McAlpine's confidence through Glover, and another two years to complete our London hotel. Throughout most of this period, I was also deeply involved in another project, one that seems incredible, looking back, for I can't believe my chutzpah in embarking on the idea of creating a hotel in Toronto five times bigger than our hotel in London.

In 1965, the city of Toronto built a new city hall, so strikingly original in design, by Finnish architect Viljo Revell, that it outshone five hundred other entries. Across from it, the city's leaders expropriated a large piece of land in what had been Chinatown. Then they called for tenders to build upon it a first-class hotel that in elegance and size would harmonize with the new city hall.

This would be one of the world's great hotels, and I don't know why I thought I could build it. I had neither the experience nor the money such a hotel required.

The competition for the hotel was worldwide; the bid solicitation had been sent out in seven different languages. And presumptuous though it was, I hired the architect John B. Parkin to draw up a presentation. He envisioned a big entry courtyard encompassing pools and gardens with a thirty-story tower for accommodating conventioneers and a seven-story building for high-end transient businesspeople, both leading into a central lobby: 1,600 rooms in all. Not surprisingly, we didn't win, though our presentation was admired.

The winner, however, found that he couldn't raise the capital required, and I was once again in the running—except that I didn't have any capital whatsoever, and no prospects for raising any from the people who'd backed

The huge convention hotel Four Seasons Sheraton, which made it clear that we should operate only London-like medium-sized luxury hotels.

me before. I'd pestered them for months, to no avail. I had even persuaded Cec Forsyth to bring some investors and bankers together to look at the architectural model of our huge hotel displayed in a room at the Inn on the Park. They came down as a group, looked, liked it, and heard my spiel, but they still refused to invest or loan me money on it.

"Forget it, Issy," Cec said afterward. "You're reaching for the stars. You're way out of your league on this one."

I knew he was right, and yet I wouldn't accept it. One evening after a workout in Percival's gym in the Inn on the Park, I was relaxing in the sauna when I spotted an old *Time* magazine with a picture of Harold Geneen on the cover.

Geneen was then America's foremost business guru. He headed ITT, the world's largest conglomerate, encompassing fifty or sixty different companies. Curious, I scanned the article. Geneen's next move, it said, would be in the hotel business. Seems he'd tried and failed to buy the Holiday Inn chain, and was now considering taking over the Sheraton Hotel Company.

I called ITT, and spoke to someone on a lower level. "If *Time* is right and you're thinking of taking over Sheraton," I said, "I can give ITT an opportunity to build Sheraton's flagship hotel." I explained the situation in Toronto, told him we now had the inside track on the site, but couldn't, by ourselves, build a $100-million hotel. Would he be interested?

He passed me on to someone higher up, who said, "Yes, we're interested. Why don't you come down, and we'll talk."

I flew to New York. The ITT Building, with its enormous range of offices, was intimidating. I began by introducing myself to someone on a lower level, then managed to work my way up to a senior executive, Claude Fenniger. He told me to come back, and he'd try to get me an appointment with the person in charge of hotels.

I left, then returned to explain my proposal to another senior executive, Howard Miller, in charge of Avis Rent a Car and other businesses, now also in charge of the hotel division.

"Sounds like a good idea, kid," he said. "We're in the process of buying Sheraton. Why don't you discuss it with the Sheraton people in Boston. They'll be running the hotels under my supervision. See if they're interested."

I flew to Boston with Murray and Eddie to meet the Sheraton CFO, Dick Boonisar, and some of his top people, all tough, successful businessmen with worldwide hotel experience. "Who are you guys?" asked Boonisar.

"I'm a druggist," Murray said.

"I'm a furrier," Eddie said.

"I'm a builder," I told him. And as he looked at us incredulously, I went on to say, "We're also in the hotel business, and this is what we've done."

I showed him brochures for the Inn on the Park and the Four Seasons Motor Hotel. Then I gave him the exceptional operating numbers on each, explained the status of the competition, our concept, and how the site could be a flagship hotel for Sheraton.

Boonisar, turning to his executives standing by, said, "If you guys could come up with figures like this we'd have a very successful company." And that meeting, testy in spots, was our only contact with Sheraton until ITT could be convinced to put up all the money required.

My next move, clearly, was to persuade ITT people that this deal would be good for them. Ten of them came up to Toronto in their private jet. We rented two stretch limousines, picked them up at the airport, and drove them north through the city, pointing out apartments I'd built, while heading for the Four Seasons Motor Hotel. The hotel not only looked beguiling but also was a beehive of guests, and that went over well.

Then we showed them the Inn on the Park, along with our architectural model of the city square hotel and Tom Lee's perspectives of its interior. That and our two hotels must have impressed them, for they soon called me back down to New York to discuss a deal.

With Paul Henry, our lawyer, I flew to New York to talk with ITT, two of us at a huge table surrounded by a group of ITT lawyers and executives, some of the brightest New York lawyers and Harvard MBAs.

Negotiations continued into the early morning hours, for ITT employed tier after tier of experts. Here I was, with no money and not much experience, up against the smartest people of one of the biggest and richest companies in the world.

But Paul, as my only support, held his own, making sure our business terms were properly documented. In fact, he was brilliant, though as it grew very late, I began to worry about him, because his legs, partially paralyzed, gave him trouble. "Paul," I said, "I'm sure you're tired. Maybe we should leave and come back."

"No," he said. "I'm OK. When they want to quit, we'll quit."

The discussions went on and on. And eventually we reached an agreement: we would put in $3.5 million for a 49 percent interest in the hotel, which ITT would finance and Sheraton would manage. Its name would be the Four Seasons Sheraton. We would have a put, which meant we could get our money back at 10 percent compounded interest or market value, whichever was greater, for three years and then at market value thereafter.

With that agreement, I went to the Bank of Nova Scotia and had no trouble in borrowing the $3.5 million we needed since ITT guaranteed my payment.

From having no money whatever and very little hotel experience, our little company now owned 49 percent of one of the world's biggest hotels, an extraordinary outcome.

ITT saw it much the same way. During the negotiation of the deal, the company said, "Look, this deal is way out of your reach. You're not putting much money into it. Why don't we just pay you $2 million and all your expenses, anything you've paid or invested up until now, and we'll take over."

"No, that's not what we're here for," I told ITT. "We're here to become a partner."

"I know, but we've rethought it."

"Does that mean you're not prepared to proceed with the deal?"

"No, no, we're prepared to go on, but we don't need you as a partner. We'll give you a good profit for your work."

"No, that's not the deal I'm interested in," I said, and the negotiation came to an impasse.

Paul Henry, sitting beside me, suggested that I consider ITT's approach further.

I knew what he was thinking: $2 million clear profit was a lot of money for a young man.

"I have thought about it," I said. "I'm not here to sell."

ITT agreed to continue, and we concluded the deal as originally discussed.

In fact, later ITT wanted to make our relationship permanent. The company generously gave me support and accolades, even offered to buy Four Seasons and give me a job with ITT at whatever salary I thought I was worth. "You'll earn far more with us," I was told, "than you'll ever earn on your own."

I listened. I don't think the word "tempted" fully conveys my feelings at the time; "overwhelmed" might be more accurate. Here I was with just two small hotels, dealing with a company that owned hundreds. I didn't know what to say.

"I'll give it some thought," I replied.

The following morning, I rose early, between three and four A.M. Nothing stirred. I sat down at my desk with pencil and paper and thought for a couple of hours, not writing a single sentence on paper, just letting my thoughts about working for such a huge organization sink in, making a list of pros and cons as darkness faded. By dawn I knew, without further thought, exactly what my answer would be. Strange as it was, this was the beginning of a generally beneficial habit when facing my most consequential decisions, one that I practice to this day.

I then responded to ITT.

"Look," I said. "I wouldn't be much value to you within your organization. I owe my success to my freedom. I think for me independence has an incalculable value. So I'm honored by your request, but let's just continue as partners."

As a partner and an owner, I attended monthly meetings while this world-class hotel was being built. ITT took control of Sheraton, and Phil Lowe, an ITT executive, was appointed president of Sheraton. He knew it was my concept that had won them the right to build this hotel, and when contrary ideas arose between Sheraton's officials and me, he would usually support me, saying, "I think Sharp knows a little more about this."

I was aiming, in design, for a first-class hotel that would deliver the kind of service that made our other hotels so profitable. But Sheraton's general manager, one of Sheraton's most senior people at the time, did not separate guests who wanted peace and quiet from conventioneers. At one time, he even suggested putting locks and coin machines on our public toilet cubicles.

When he brought up this idea, I said, "You're joking. This is Sheraton's flagship. A magnificent hotel. Not just for Toronto, but also worldwide. And it's directly across from the city hall. What do you think the Toronto newspapers will be telling the country in the morning?"

He backed down on that one. But this was the way he planned and ran the hotel. In planning a hotel interior, you first build a mock-up room. Then you make all your corrections and improvements on that one room, rather than having to change, in this case, 1,600 rooms. Tom Lee designed a mock-up room that I'd seen and approved. But when I looked at it later, I didn't recognize it. "Where's the one I saw before?" I asked.

"This is it," a Sheraton executive said.

I looked again at drapes, bedspreads, furniture. "I don't remember any of this."

"Well," said the Sheraton hotelier, "we decided to make some changes. For example, it's cheaper to print the material using two colors instead of three. And it doesn't make that much difference."

They had changed much more than color, changes that made all the difference in the world to me.

Apart from its first appearance, the Four Seasons Sheraton, by our standards, was not a five-star hotel. But as a convention hotel, it was highly profitable, not only for Sheraton but also for us as a near half owner.

I had a big financial problem: We owed a great deal of money on a hotel we were building in Vancouver, much more money than I could raise, so much that I was literally facing bankruptcy. All in all, it was a good time to let Sheraton buy us out.

I told Jim McGraw, their chief financial officer, that I'd decided to exercise my right to sell Sheraton my shares at their current value.

"I don't know," he said, rather dubiously. "We'll have to negotiate." But I discounted his manner. I felt this was music to his ears; our name on Sheraton's flagship hotel was a constant aggravation.

Negotiations proved I was right. I sold at what I thought at the time was a handsome profit: $18 million for our $3.5 million investment. Immediately thereafter, the biggest hotel I ever built put up a new sign: The Sheraton Centre.

The Sheraton buyout paid what I owed and kept me in business. And dealing with ITT—one of the most powerful companies in the world—was the best business experience anyone could hope to get.

PART III

COMMUNITY AND CULTURE

Do unto others as you would have them do unto you.
—THE GOLDEN RULE,
REITERATED IN EVERY RELIGION IN THE WORLD

All business proceeds on belief: Trying to run a company
without a set of beliefs is like trying to steer a ship without a rudder.
—ANONYMOUS

Christopher Hugh Sharp, 1960–1978.
His plan was to go to work for Four Seasons before he finished high school.

CHAPTER 8

Chris Sharp
and Terry Fox

I was sitting in my office one day in November 1976 when Rosalie called to tell me that our sixteen-year-old son, Chris, had found a growth in his groin the size of an egg. Our doctor ordered a biopsy, but she wasn't too worried about it because Chris was a six-foot-two athlete who looked the picture of health—handsome, wholesome, with a disdain for drugs, cigarettes, and even coffee. He was a street-smart, take-charge person, the only one of our four sons who looked forward to spending his life in our hotel business. But as it turned out, his blond good looks, through lack of pigment in his skin, made him a candidate for skin cancer, and his growth was diagnosed as melanoma.

We consulted the best doctors and took him for treatment to Boston and New York. We did everything we could but finally accepted the tragic reality that Chris had only a few months left to live. Our doctors insisted that he be hospitalized, but we decided to take him home. While I continued going to the office, Rosalie looked after Chris: no nursing routines, hospital tubes, or impersonal institutional atmosphere for him.

The following four paragraphs are taken from Rosalie's memoirs: *Rifke: An Improbable Life.*

Chris slept in our bed and Issy and I took turns sleeping with him, while the other slept in Chris's room. Once, as I was fussing with the sheepskin he lay on because of the bedsores, he asked, "Am I going to die?" and I answered, "We hope you will recover, but it's possible you may not. No one knows for sure."

Once I said, "There can't be a God," and he answered, "Don't say that. There is a God."

Those were black days and black nights: I remember going up the stairs so heavily, with nothing but dread in each step. The night before Chris died, the rest of us ate a chicken dinner in his bedroom. We were chatting normally, hoping to make him feel included. He didn't speak. He just lay there quietly, very still, looking at the ceiling. I marvelled at that stillness that he had maintained during the three months he was bed-ridden—graceful and easy in his body, never a twitch of anxiety—like John Denver's "Serenity of a clear blue mountain lake." That last night he was wearing sunglasses, which he had asked for before dinner. He was removing himself, the way people do when they are ready to leave the world.

The next morning, Friday, March 10, 1978, Chris said, "Dad, don't go to work today." Issy stood by his bed and I lay across the bed and each of us held one of his big beautiful hands.

That was the day he died.

Losing Chris changed my life forever. We must each find our own way to deal with the pain of losing a child, and I continue to include Chris as part of our family. Years have passed, but I still say we have four sons, and every day I say the "Mourner's Kaddish" for Chris. Over time, you build a protective shield to fend off the emotion that a child's absence arouses at family events, celebrations, and weddings. But there are unexpected times when the shield is down and the tears flow. You never get over it.

Two years later, Peter Martin, our western regional vice president in Vancouver, called to ask if we would support a young man who lost a leg to cancer and was running across Canada on an artificial limb to raise money for cancer research.

"Wherever we have a hotel," I said, "we'll supply him with food and accommodation."

The *Toronto Star* carried a story on this young man, Terry Fox, and when Eddie Creed called me about it, Rosalie and I decided we had to do more. I got in touch by telephone with Terry, then running across the Maritimes from his start in St. John's, Newfoundland. He said he wasn't getting the media attention he had hoped for. He sounded discouraged and despondent, ready to throw in the towel.

I told him what we had in mind, that our director of advertising, Doug Hall, had come up with an idea: an ad headlined "Let's Make Terry's Run Really Count." It would challenge companies across the country to do what we would be doing: pledge two dollars for every mile he ran. If a thousand companies did this, our ad would say, we could raise $10 million for cancer research.

His mood brightened immediately. "That's all I need," he said.

But in fact, it wasn't enough. Media and crowd support sagged as Terry entered Quebec. I sent one of our marketing people, Bev Norris, to Montreal to assist the Cancer Society's organizer, and she helped incite public interest by getting football star Don Sweet to run with Terry into the city. For his entry into Ontario, we hailed him with a brass band while sending up thousands of printed balloons reading, "Welcome Terry. You can do it!"

The governor general received him in Ottawa, where Terry won a standing ovation by kicking the opening ball of a Canadian Football League game. By the time he reached Toronto, and we met for the first time in person, his emotional reserves seemed fully restored.

I had no idea then of the public effect this young man would have, but having lost Chris, Terry's youth, sincerity, and resolve had moved me deeply. I felt he was more than admirable; he could be inspiring. And before he arrived in Toronto, I invited five hundred business leaders to a luncheon at the Four Seasons to meet him and hear him speak.

Most of those invited showed up, including Lieutenant Governor Pauline McGibbon—an exceptional response on such short notice.

Terry was dressed in his running clothes—T-shirt and gray shorts cut from sweatpants; artificial leg, as always, exposed—and he seemed a little nervous talking off the cuff to all these important people. But not for long.

He told us how reading of an amputee who ran in the New York marathon planted the thought that a disability need not be concealed. He spoke of how the suffering he'd seen and experienced in a British Columbia cancer ward had steeled his resolve to do something to stop the hurting and of why he felt cancer research was the answer.

He spoke from the heart. He held a paper clip in his hand as he talked, unconsciously flicking it with one fingernail. That room was so quiet you could hear those tiny flicks. It was almost as if the audience had stopped breathing. And you know, one of the biggest mistakes of my life was not having that speech tape-recorded.

Terry later returned to the podium to thank me for hosting the lunch. "Oh, and I would also like to thank Pauline for coming." That wasn't exactly the protocol for addressing the lieutenant governor, but she didn't seem to mind in the least.

From Toronto on, the run was covered daily by national and local media, and Terry's emotional impact gathered force. An artificial leg had been a symbol of weakness; it was now a symbol of strength. Whole families followed his progress day by day, talking about how courageous, tenacious, and uplifting it was.

We didn't know yet, of course, that he was running despite heart problems, refusing to take scheduled medical exams for fear his run would be stopped. He was running twenty-six miles a day on one leg despite exhaustion, a swollen ankle, and a bleeding stump, because he felt he was generating, finally, a great swell of support for his cause.

I was in California when Doug Hall called to tell me that cancer in both lungs had ended the run at Thunder Bay. Like so many others, I was dejected that he'd lost his personal struggle, but I didn't believe his mission was lost. He had run 3,339 miles, the equivalent of 128 twenty-six-mile marathons, against obstacles no marathoner had ever faced. As Prime Minister Trudeau later told the House of Commons, "We do not think of him as one who was defeated by misfortune, but as one who inspired us with the example of the triumph of the human spirit over adversity."

I telephoned Terry at home in B.C. about keeping his dream alive. "What do you have in mind?" he asked.

"What about an annual family run? We could raise more money for cancer research."

"Sounds great," he replied.

We followed up with a telegram of commitment:

> Dear Terry:
>
> *The Marathon of Hope has just begun. You started it.*
> *We will not rest until your dream to find a cure for cancer is realized.*
> *I am asking every Four Seasons hotel to organize, along with the local*

*branch of the Canadian Cancer Society, a Terry Fox Marathon of Hope Run,
to be held on the first Sunday in October. Beginning this year, it will become
an annual fund-raising event for the Terry Fox Cancer Research Fund and
we will not stop until cancer has been beaten.*

*We will also ask every city and town across Canada to join in on the same
day so that you will be running in our hearts and our minds every year until
the battle is won. Your courage and determination is an inspiration to us all.
Our hearts and our prayers are with you.*

With deep admiration and affection.

Isadore Sharp
Four Seasons Hotels

Terry died in June the following year, 1981, but not before he learned
that one dream thought impossible had come true: He had raised one dollar for every person then living in Canada: $24 million.

His death brought an enormous outpouring of sympathy. For many, he
personified self-sacrifice: a hero who gave his life for the greater good.
People commemorated his name in songs and movies, in statues, streets,
youth centers, and playgrounds, in a postage stamp and the name of a
mountain, in a Boeing 747, an icebreaker, and half a dozen posthumous
awards. Two decades later, in 2002, Ty Warner, owner of Four Seasons
New York and Santa Barbara, brought out the Issy Beanie Baby, which
raised $2 million for cancer research.

The memorials helped immensely in getting the run under way. We
formed a Terry Fox Committee with Terry's parents, Betty and Rolly Fox,
the Cancer Society, and Sports Canada, a federal ministry. We enlisted the
help of corporations, associations, and schools. And that September, three
months after Terry's death, we held the first Terry Fox Run.

Four thousand volunteer organizers and three hundred thousand participants put on nearly eight hundred runs and raised $3.5 million. Some
thought our success was due to the emotionalism of the time. But after
dropping off slightly the following year, it grew.

Runs were put on by corporations, day care centers, schools, retirement
homes, even prisons. A run organizer at Walkworth prison near Kingston
told of an inmate who had never finished anything in his life, but he put a

The Issy Bear, created in memory of Christopher Sharp. Ty Warner donated $2 million for cancer research from sales of this Beanie Baby.

forty-pound sack on his back and finished the run.

It became a Canadian institution, a vast and diverse endeavor encompassing people of all ages, from preschoolers to seniors in nursing homes. People of every race and occupation covered the course— walking, jogging, cycling, rollerblading—from diplomats in Ottawa to dogsledders in Yellowknife.

Cancer, of course, knows no boundaries, and in 1981 we originated the run in our four U.S. hotels and our one overseas hotel, in London, England. We solicited support from the Department of External Affairs, the armed forces, Canada's embassies, and Canadian Forces bases abroad. And as we opened new hotels, we gave Bev Norris a full-time job of organizing and expanding the run around the world.

Hundreds of thousands of people were moved by a new spirit of hope: not hope as easy optimism—"Don't worry, things will work out"—but the kind of hope that Terry showed, that is, hope as self-belief, faith in oneself, the inner strength that counters despair. People thought, *If Terry can do it, so can I.* Kids like Tyler Dunn of Santa Barbara, California, who had lost his eyesight and one leg to cancer, read about Terry, then joined the annual run that our Santa Barbara hotel initiated. Seniors like the Reverend Tom Smith of Wingham, Ontario, eighty-four years old, who walked a thousand miles to train for his annual forty-mile grind. Young women like Marianne Moore of Vancouver, a victim of Hodgkin's disease, who found in herself, through Terry, resources she didn't know she had, and became a crusader for cancer research. "Without Terry's gift of hope," she wrote, "I would not be here today."

Other people emulated Terry. Rick Hansen of Man in Motion fame said

Terry inspired his two-year round-the-world wheelchair marathon; this led to his becoming an outstanding benefactor and spokesman for the disabled, as well as an inspirational model for others.

Terry's message was telling everyone you might beat cancer if you try, if you set small goals, meet them step by step, and never, ever, give up. Terry had taken cancer out of the closet. People at the time of his run were terrified of cancer. They didn't want to talk about it. They called it the Bad Thing or the Big C. And Terry did more than anyone to take away the stigma. As I said at the time, "Terry did not lose his fight. He did all he needed to do. He was like a meteor in the sky—one whose light travels beyond our view, yet still shines in the darkest night."

In 2008 we celebrated our twenty-eighth year of the Terry Fox Run. Hundreds of thousands of people in fifty-five countries, widely diverse in race, culture, and creed, responded to a young Canadian's confirmation of very old values. They've given energy, time, and money to help people they've never seen—over $500 million as of 2008—demonstrating that concern for human welfare is universal.

That's the wider implication of Terry's message: that mankind shares a deeply rooted instinctive moral sense, that the ethic of mutual responsibility, caring, and sharing—the goodwill sometimes known as brotherly love—is as universal as selfishness and hate.

To me, that's the central theme of Terry's story, which continues to unfold, thanks to the many volunteers who've played key roles. I have told just a portion of it, the part known to me personally. I just wish our son Chris could have been here. I'm sure he'd have wanted to help advance what Terry's run began.

Terry Fox's living legacy: A quarter-century of inspiration

ABOVE LEFT: *A ceremony honoring the twenty-fifth anniversary of Terry Fox's Toronto stop on his marathon.*

ABOVE RIGHT: *Greg Sharp helped to organize the corporate run at Wilket Creek Park, Toronto.*

CENTER: *Most Four Seasons hotels worldwide hold a Terry Fox Run. In Shanghai, more than a thousand participants were very pleased to do their part.*

BELOW: *With the grandkids, Emily, Julia, and Aaron, and a poster of Terry Fox.*

CHAPTER 9

A New Business Model

W hile helping Terry Fox with his mission, I was still constructing houses, apartments, and condominiums, anything that gave Max Sharp & Son a reasonable income. Neither conceiving, building, and operating our hotels nor conceptualizing and helping build the Four Seasons Sheraton in Toronto made me think of myself as a hotelier. Throughout the 1960s and early 1970s, even though we'd built seven hotels, I continued thinking of myself as a builder, for that was what I had done since my teens.

My projects were a mixed bag. In 1971, Bell Telephone announced a competition to build a training center in Belleville, Ontario, a small city near Toronto. One part of this center would be classrooms; the other part, a hotel with spartan rooms where trainees would live while being taught.

I believe we won the competition because I proposed to Bell officials that they upgrade the hotel. "You're investing all this money in future employees," I said, "people you hope will make a successful career in your company. Instead of a dormitory, why not upgrade their accommodations? Give them a pleasant experience of the company and a good night's sleep, so they wake up fresh in the morning, eager to learn. We can design it and run it in a way that I'm sure will pay off."

Bell bought the idea and paid us enough to build a small Four Seasons hotel, which also accommodated transient visitors, though Belleville was not a place that drew many travelers.

Not all my ideas came to successful conclusions. In Vancouver, on waterfront land known as Coal Harbour, adjacent to Stanley Park, I organized and readied for construction fifteen acres for a thousand apartments and a

Rendering of Vancouver Coal Harbour waterfront development.

two-hundred-room hotel. Our partner was CN Pension Fund. They were putting up most of the money. We only contributed $600,000 for a full half interest.

It was approved, and I was about to start building when Vancouver's mayor, Tom Campbell, came to see me. "We have a problem," he said. "We need to make a change. City council wants you to move the development a little farther from Stanley Park, or they'll hold a plebiscite to expropriate your land."

"Our land's already hundreds of feet from the Stanley Park entrance," I pointed out.

"Just move it another hundred feet," suggested the mayor.

"What's another hundred feet when you've got two thousand acres?" I said. "We're ready to start building. It just doesn't make sense."

"It's not the number of feet that's important. It's the opinion of the city council. A hundred feet will get us around that problem. Otherwise they'll call for the plebiscite."

City of Toronto Archives, Fonds 1244, Item 1946

The original Granite Club, 63 St. Clair Avenue West.

Nobody would do that, I thought, so I made no move.

But that was exactly what they did: They took a vote, won, and expropriated our land, so that Max Sharp & Son ended up with nothing.

That was one of my biggest gaffes, one that might have again altered the course of my life. If that project had gone ahead and I had built all those apartments, I could have made so much money that I might never have become a hotelier.

I was also, in this period—along with my brother-in-law Sigmund Levy, a businessman and developer who married my sister Nancy—a partner in a real estate company called Tengis. Our major investors were Robert and Rickey Burton, sons and heirs of a successful financier, and Francis Hilb, a man of prodigious energy and exceptional skill in negotiating. There was complete trust. Once we shook hands on a deal, there was no need for lawyers and signed documents.

We built various properties for Tengis: residential subdivisions, cooperative apartments, and one building of which I'm especially proud.

The Granite Club in Toronto, a long-established private social and sports club, owned a valuable piece of land on St. Clair Avenue, but its clubhouse was very old. They wanted a new one built and called for tenders, asking contestants what they would pay for the land and what they would charge to build a new clubhouse according to a brief describing the scope and intent of the facilities.

We gave them a proposal: I thought we could pay enough for the land to cover the cost of the clubhouse. That appealed to them, as I knew it would, and we were awarded the job. But I also knew we were taking a bit of a risk: in effect, guaranteeing to build a new clubhouse for a fixed amount of money.

Then the Canadian Jewish Congress heard I was going to do this, and the B'nai B'rith approached me, saying, "How can you, a member of the Jewish community, do something for a group of people that discriminates against Jews?"

"What do you want me to do?" I asked.

"The best thing you could do would be to get them to stop discriminating."

I asked Jack Murray, the Granite Club member with whom I was working, to call a meeting of the club's board of directors, at which I confronted them with this issue.

"It's very embarrassing for me, as a member of the Jewish community," I said, "that your club is restrictive, that no Jews can join. I don't see how we can go ahead with our proposal under such circumstances."

They discussed it, then met with an ad hoc committee of B'nai B'rith and agreed to change their discriminatory bylaws. Club membership from now on, they promised, would never be rejected on the basis of color, race, or creed.

We built the club, despite declarations to the board by some of their building experts that our contract was loosely written, enabling us to build in extras by which, they said, many contractors make themselves a lot of money. "Just wait," they told the board, "these people will crucify us."

They were right about one thing. The contract *was* loosely written. But Jack Murray, the chairman of the club's building committee, didn't believe his naysayers, so we agreed to go ahead, and we finished the club, without making any demands for extras.

The club members were appreciative, and T. Miller Chase, the presi-

T. Miller Chase, president, and I. Sharp break ground for the new Granite Club on Bayview Avenue, Toronto, November 9, 1970.

dent, said to me, "In the light of our commitment to end discrimination, why don't you become our new club's first Jewish member. We'll give you an honorary membership with complete privileges."

"Thank you," I said, "but I'm not a club person, I'd never use it. But if you're sincere, as I think you are, talk to reporters at your opening. Make sure the public knows your new policy."

And that was what they did.

The Granite Club, which until then had been slowly but steadily shrinking, began expanding, and some of these new members were Jewish, including Randy Weisz, an executive vice president of Four Seasons, who became the Granite Golf Club's president in 2004. The Granite Club is now one of the most successful sports and social clubs in Toronto, and I like to think that in helping end discrimination, we played a role as useful in that success as it was meaningful for society.

Our next major building was a four-hundred-room hotel in the heart of downtown Calgary, with a block-long, city-owned convention center that we ran. This also included a 250,000-square-foot museum and art center, making it a perfect hotel location. The Four Seasons Calgary opened in 1974 and was such a winner that we started another hotel in Vancouver that same year.

The Vancouver project was a joint venture with three major corporations—Toronto-Dominion Bank, Cadillac Fairview, and Eaton's Department Stores—on the same terms and conditions that had worked in Calgary. I expected that it, too, would be profitable, but my timing could not have been worse. An unexpected inflationary spiral began, something I'd never experienced before.

I had worked out probable costs, but as the real numbers came in, I saw that the costs would be considerably higher than the existing market could support. I was faced with what must have been a familiar business decision at that time: going broke slowly by lowering quality or quickly by keeping it high.

I confronted my partners and told them: "Costs have gone crazy. But I still want you to build a first-class hotel." Ignoring their lawyers' legalisms, they agreed verbally to change the terms of our deal, then sealed it with a handshake. That providential display of rectitude made the deal less disastrous for us, and I went on building quality in—with money I didn't have. Eventually that made the hotel profitable for us all, but only because our partners had put ethics ahead of profit.

That near-ruinous experience changed my thinking on hotel investment. I decided that in the future we would protect the company financially by capping our share of ownership at a small percentage of equity, no more than $3 million to $6 million per property. This was based on a simple principle: invest no more than our hotel fees would give us over the first five years, an amount we could easily borrow on our management contract, and if more money to invest was required, we had the option to reduce our equity or put up our share.

Besides limiting risk, it established a new business model: Four Seasons as a management company, not a real estate developer. Now, just as bankruptcy loomed, I thought of the ITT-Sheraton contract, which gave me $18 million, as my most consequential as well as most productive business deal. Until then, I was a builder engaged in development, a hotelier only part time. But the contrast in comfort between running a huge convention hotel in Toronto and catering to the carriage trade in the finest hotel in London made me realize what I would really like to do: create a group of the best hotels in the world. And what we really want to do is usually what we do best.

Murray and Eddie disagreed with my vision of building the world's best hotels. They felt I was getting delusions of grandeur. "You're narrowing your market," they said. "How will that ever work? Who's going to pay the kind of money you'll have to ask? More money for a hotel room than anyone's ever paid before!"

Most of my senior people agreed with them. "No other company does that," they said. "Look at Westin, Marriott, and Sheraton. They've got hotels in three-, four-, and five-star categories, and look how well they're doing."

But my mind was made up. "We will no longer be all things to all people," I said. "We will specialize. We will offer only midsize hotels of exceptional quality, hotels that wherever located will be recognized as the best."

I resolved to sell any hotel that didn't meet our new standards. We soon leased our first, the Four Seasons Motor Hotel, to another operator, sold the Four Seasons hotels in Calgary and Belleville a few years later, and discontinued management of the Four Seasons Netanya.

The Four Seasons Netanya was a fourteen-story apartment hotel, cooperatively owned, on a two-hundred-foot cliff overlooking the Mediterranean Sea, twenty-five miles from Tel Aviv, Israel. It was built in the late 1960s, primarily by my dad, with some financial support from a few well-off friends who wanted to do something for Israel.

It was a handsome building, an emotional commitment by my father to encourage tourism and immigration to Israel and to give him a second home in the land he loved. It was reasonably successful; every apartment was sold. But it didn't quite measure up to our new standards.

Dad never mentioned my giving up management and taking our name off his favorite building project. But it was his joy, his love, and I know it hurt him, though neither he nor my mother ever said a word. I felt terrible about it afterward. Too late, I realized I should have said, "This particular hotel doesn't have to measure up." But I didn't, and I've never forgiven myself.

That was a lesson painfully learned. One has to be accountable. We can't make judgments and decisions in isolation; we always have to judge their effect on others. Although I could never undo that particular mistake, it taught me to make decisions and judgments with a little more thought.

But my feeling about that mistake had no relevance whatever to my decision to try to create a group of the world's finest hotels. I no longer thought of myself as primarily a builder; I was now a hotelier with a clearly

Four Seasons Hotel Netanya, Israel.

defined objective. I believed that what we had done in London we could do anywhere in the world: be the best.

The strength of that conviction overrode doubt, bolstering my self-confidence to press on with an idea that no one else thought would work. But that raised an immediate question: How, precisely, could it be done?

CHAPTER 10

Building Our Culture

My midseventies decision to create the world's best hotel company was not taken seriously by most of my staff. I couldn't blame them. We had just one hotel abroad and only four that were not up for sale in Canada, where our name was far from being a household word. We'd be competing with world-famous companies, each with hundreds of hotels, and here I was saying that ours were going to be the best. No wonder they laughed behind my back.

I knew how it looked to them. But to me it made perfect sense. Because the hotels we'd beaten in London were among the world's best, the logic was clear: If we were going to specialize and operate only one class of hotel, we should surely be better than companies that didn't. So at a meeting with our head-office executives, when they asked how we could do it, I told them, "We are going to win on quality. Quality is far and away the chief factor in competitiveness."

"But how are we going to control it?" someone asked.

"We are not going to try," I said. "I think quality control is a misnomer. Quality can't be installed through elaborate appraisal systems, inspection systems, or quality training. Look at all the companies seeking quality by distributing books and tapes to employees, by running motivational or communication programs. They invest a lot of money, time, and energy in quality improvement and end up, most often, with little to show for it.

"I think a lot of these firms are failing with what they call quality control because they're not considering how the customer sees it. And customers think primarily in terms of value. They buy whatever gives them the most value for their money.

"So what do our customers value most? Well, we know why they're making us number one in London. According to all our studies and feedback, it's because our building gives them beauty and comfort. Because we give them amenities no one else does. But most of all because we're giving them better service than anyone else.

"Service, I'm convinced, is key. Through service we can do, over time, what we're doing now in London in any equivalent city in the world."

"But every hotel company sells service," they argued. "Look at all their ads: smiling employees, great service."

"You're right," I said, "they all say it and often do it. By *their* standards. But we're going to do it differently. Do it so it's something we'll become known for."

I turned to McDonald's for some lessons in service. Through quick, pleasant servings of French fries and hamburgers, always made to specifications, thus always meeting expectations, McDonald's had become the world's biggest success in the fast-food business. They didn't just sell hamburgers; they sold value.

I called my friend George Cohon, president of McDonald's Restaurants of Canada, and asked if I could sit for a day with his new hires undergoing orientation. I wanted to see how they integrated their service component.

He agreed, and I spent a day at his training school watching their films and listening to their lectures. But what intrigued me most was the difference between their training and their advertising.

Almost every month, McDonald's changed its TV advertising, but the film they were showing new entries must have been at least fifteen years old. It struck me then that when you have something people can identify with, you don't have to keep reinventing it; once it's rooted, it sticks. Our service problem, though much more complex than McDonald's, could nevertheless adhere to that pattern.

The next day, I told our senior headquarters people, "I want you to come with me to McDonald's and see how they train people for service."

So they came, looked, and listened, then laughed and joked about it. As one of them said, "Look, they're selling hamburgers and we're selling filet mignon. How can you even compare it?"

"I know what we're selling," I said. "I'm talking about *how* we sell it.

Quality doesn't necessarily mean luxury. It means giving customers what they expect, meeting customers' expectations every time. That's performance, value."

I didn't go into it further then; this group and I didn't think alike. But at our next weekly meeting, I said, "I have a thought I'd like to pursue. In order to manage our employees so they give our customers personalized service, we should be treating employees the way we expect them to treat our customers. Treat them with the same understanding we want them to give our guests." And I came up with an expression that embodied what I meant, something I had heard, I don't know where: "We are only what we do, not what we say we are."

Well, they joked about that, too. I could see they weren't taking me seriously. Like all hoteliers at that time, they thought our primary purpose was profit. They considered employee performance a function of rules and supervision. Actually I couldn't blame them too much. That's the way it was then in just about every sector of business. Most managers had been trained under a system that assumed most employees don't work harder than they have to; they had to be driven by the carrot or the stick. Now I was turning that prevalent style of management upside down, saying people who were considered expendable had to come first. It was a complete turnaround in attitude, theory, and practice.

Giving our customers more value than anyone else, I figured, would ensure that in return they would give us profit. And our London hotel had proven conclusively to me that what our type of customer valued most was superior service.

Unsurprisingly, not all our managers in all our hotels went along with this. So at all my visits to all our hotels, I kept restating our aim of superior service, focusing employees at every level—and, I hoped, management— on one simple compelling purpose: pleasing customers.

We had some customer response, at least enough to give us growth. In 1976, we opened a hotel in Montreal, Le Quatre Saisons, built in partnership with Bernard Herman of City Parking. In 1977, with one of the world's largest real estate developers, the Reichman family, we bought a hotel in Ottawa, then, the following year, hotels in Toronto and Edmonton. We already had hotels in Vancouver and Calgary, so there were no more

Canadian cities big enough to support a five-star hotel. To continue to grow without lowering quality, we would have to go for broke in the major leagues: an American market led by competitors several hundred times our size.

Looking back, I guess I should have been intimidated. We were just an obscure little company heavily weighed down with debt, taking on the Goliaths of our industry on their own turf. We could have been squashed like a fly. Though the United States was the world's biggest market, easy for Canadians to enter, and receptive to new ideas and products, it could also be merciless to losers.

But hotel history and recent experience bolstered my confidence. Two years before our decision to enter the American market, Jack Hodgson, a friend of one of our senior executives, had called us from Seattle. "The Clift in San Francisco is coming up for sale," he said. "Are you interested?"

Though I hadn't seriously contemplated the American market then, a single hotel is always worth considering. "Yes," I said, "we're interested." Then I flew down and looked it over.

The Clift was badly run-down, but it had a good location. And San Francisco is a great city. I thought the deal had potential, so in partnership with Bernie Herman, we bought the Clift and began to restore it, though a restoration can cost as much or more than building from scratch.

Then the following year, I heard of another possible U.S. deal, the Ritz-Carlton in Chicago—a new hotel but financially a problem. When the word got around that its owners intended to change its management, most of the major hotel companies went pounding on their door. As little upstarts from Canada, I didn't think we had much of a chance, because this would be the most prestigious hotel built in America in three decades. Nevertheless, I went down for what turned out to be a kind of interview. And perhaps because of a personal rapport with Tom Klutznick, the CEO of Urban Investment and Development Company, and perhaps because we offered to buy a 25 percent interest, we got it.

The Ritz-Carlton gave us some recognition as hotel operators, and hotel developers began to bring us deals. So it forced us to consider what our competition was offering.

Holiday Inn had created an empire on U.S. highways, first through stan-

The Ritz-Carlton in Chicago.

dardized rooms, then by becoming "the host with the most," the first to offer free cribs, dog kennels, soft drinks, and ice machines. Marriott had found a profitable niche in suburban complexes, between the new roadside motels and the older downtown hotels. I believed we could do as well, maybe better. All we had to do was stand out from the clutter, be distinctive.

Checking around, I found that many luxury hotels were owned by independent operators. They'd had it fairly easy, but most had not kept up with the times. Our big-name rivals operated a mix of first-, second-, and third-class hotels. And this meant that we would become the first hotel chain in the United States to focus exclusively on the top end of the market. It seemed to me we were coming in at the right time.

In Canada, we'd been operating hotels of various sizes with various price structures in markets where incomes varied. In the United States, we settled on one size: big enough to meet upscale needs, small enough to give personal service at all times. And each hotel would be consistent in its standards, each different in reflecting its regional atmosphere.

We initiated many more ideas to enhance customer appreciation. We introduced fitness centers and no-smoking floors. We anticipated trends in food with low-fat, low-salt haute cuisine. We put shampoo, hair dryers, makeup mirrors, and bathrobes in rooms for guests who prefer to travel light.

Each room was slightly larger than our competitors' regular rooms, with quieter plumbing, a better showerhead, and a bed with a comfortable custom-made mattress. We offered all this, plus an abundance of carefully chosen details, from the right pillow to the softest toilet tissue to bouquets of fresh flowers daily.

Not all my senior people agreed with all these decisions on quality. "Why don't you use vinyl instead of leather?" they asked. "Polyester instead of silk? Most people can't tell the difference."

Four Seasons Management Conference, 1994. These are held every two to four years.

"A lot of the people we hope will become customers can," I told them. "They're wealthy. Discerning. They know quality. And quality to them is value."

Well, they thought I was either wasting money or didn't care about profit. And when I would tell them that profit was not a guide for a business decision but merely a confirmation of its result, I knew they were figuratively shaking their heads.

Service, I believed, was our win-or-lose area. We had researched our market segment: affluent Americans, mostly top business executives. They were often under pressure, fighting jet lag, stress, and the clock while trying to make deals and decisions involving not merely thousands but millions of dollars. They obviously needed service they could count on: service to replace support systems left at home and the office; time-saving service that gave them assurance and productivity; problem-solving service, fast, personal, unobtrusive, and consistently error-free. That's the ultimate in value for these specific customers. And the more I thought about this, the more convinced I became that exceptional service was the advantage that could eventually make us the best hotel company in the world.

But if service was to be our second winning strategy—and to me it clearly followed from the first—I was facing perhaps the most difficult job of my life.

CHAPTER 11

Selling Our Culture

Conceiving a winning strategy of service had been relatively easy. Selling it internally—getting it across to all the hotel managers and supervisors, design staff, purchasing people, and engineers—was proving exceedingly difficult. We needed to get it down to the front line: clerks, bellstaff, bartenders, waiters, cooks, housekeepers, and dishwashers, the lowest-paid and in most companies the least-motivated people, but the ones who would make or break a five-star service reputation.

At a meeting of all general managers, I told them, "Our customer–front line relationship is crucial. Customers seldom see or talk to you. They interact almost solely with our front line, three to seven junior employees. If that contact disappoints the customers we want as lifetime patrons, they become ex-patrons. But when our employees remember them, greet them, know what they want and provide it quickly, they create a loyal customer whose referrals and long-term repeat business can often run well into six figures. That's a cycle of success, dependent entirely on junior employees.

"That's going to be your managerial challenge: reaching our goal of being the best, down to the bottom of our pyramid—motivating our lowest-paid people to act on their own, to see themselves, not as routine functionaries, but as company facilitators creating our customer base.

"So we can't go on mechanizing service through rules or controlling it by supervision. We need employees able and willing to respond on their own to whatever comes up, employees who can spot, solve, and even anticipate problems. That means delegating authority as well as responsibility."

I sensed that didn't go over too well, and I realized more clearly what I was facing: a giant management turnaround, one that would overthrow the century-old concept that a company is a machine: that management is a profession based solely on logic sans emotion, that labor is a cost to be controlled, not an asset to be enhanced, and that an atmosphere of fear and anxiety is more productive than one of enjoyment. For most of our managers and supervisors, it was less a process of learning than unlearning, which is much more difficult.

That meeting brought home to me the magnitude of what would have to be done to tap the full potential of junior employees: the top levels of management at most of our hotels would have to change some deeply ingrained habits, for like managers almost everywhere then, most thought bosses were made to give orders. They might talk about teamwork, but what they really wanted was a workforce that did what it was told, referring any problems to them. Yet what was needed was a workforce that willingly and immediately solved its own problems as they arose.

For several years, I toured our hotels, telling management at every level in various terms, "Remember, we can't change employee behavior without changing ours. We have to have employees who think for themselves and act on it, who can remedy service failures on the spot. We're asking them to see the company's interest as their own and to voluntarily take responsibility. We're asking them, in effect, to be self-managers.

"So keep your egos in check, and let the people who work for you shine. Because they're the people who know our customers best, the people we depend on to lead the way. It's no longer 'Do as I say.' It's 'Do as I do.'

"That means every employee," I emphasized. "A doorman can please the customer with a smile and a few words of welcome, but one surly waiter can kill the effect. Or if we keep an executive waiting in his suite in his underwear for his only suit to come back from a one-hour pressing, we could lose a lifetime customer worth hundreds of thousands of dollars. No hotel, however splendid, looks good to someone whose day it has ruined."

Some managers went along because they agreed and believed my methods could yield results. Others thought difficult goals would dishearten and frustrate employees. But I was sure from my experience that the opposite was true, that usually people try to live up to expectations. Working closely with people from all walks of life, people at the bottom as well as at the top, I had found that people, emotionally, feel much the same about work: They derive the most satisfaction from doing the best they can.

"Sure," I told our managers, "our employees may have to stretch a bit, accept risk, and learn from mistakes. But if we believe in them, they will believe in themselves, be happier and more productive, and therefore more successful.

"Almost every employee," I also pointed out, "knows more about some part of our work than we managers do, and if we build good relations, they'll let us know when they think we're wrong. And the more top performers we can develop, the more chance we have of winning. The fast track for self-development includes helping others develop."

But some GMs and supervisors didn't like that idea, either. They didn't want to develop hotshot subordinates who might become rivals. Others still saw employees as a cost.

"That's just an accounting mirage," I told them. "The books may show that employees represent the largest share of expense. They don't show that they also earn the largest share of revenue. Or that long-term service employees are storehouses of customer knowledge, role models for new hires, and advisers for systems improvement—all in all, our best source of added value. If employees are really doing their job, they're not a cost, they're an asset, our primary asset."

Many of our managers paid considerable attention to our public image, but few considered our image within the company: how our employees saw their managers, which I considered equally important, for without complete rapport between top and bottom, complete rapport with our customers was impossible.

On visits to every hotel, I met and talked to all our managers, trying to judge how well each was developing and motivating staff. I also visited the back of the house and talked to their employees, people who often think in terms of "us" and "them"—and "them" doesn't mean our competitors or our customers. These were the people whose actions would decide if we won or lost customers, and I didn't get the feeling that all of them cared as much as they should.

I talked to some of our older hands who'd been with me for years. They confirmed my belief that I wasn't getting through to all our managers. Some managers, they said, were giving employees instructions, as I had requested, to act on their own. But in practice they were still exercising control. And because of this conflict of interest, some of these employees were still acting the way they always had.

I eventually had to admit that my pep talks weren't working. I didn't know how many managers were choking off staff motivation and the vital bottom-up flow of information, but even a few delinquents were too many. Full effectiveness meant getting through to everyone. All our five-star competitors gave excellent service some of the time. But we'd never be able to establish a world-class reputation without consistently superior service every day in every hotel. And we'd never achieve consistency with a mix of good and bad employees, the inevitable result of good and bad bosses. Everyone had to have a common purpose.

Management credibility was my single biggest problem. I remembered as a young builder working side by side with my crew, digging ditches, pouring concrete in the rain. And when I had to leave, they would go on working as if I were still there, knowing I had faith in them and trusted their common sense.

This was the attitude that had to be established throughout Four Seasons, an attitude based on mutual values: respect, fairness, honesty, and trust. Unless we could cultivate these values, some employees wouldn't have much concern for the company; they'd become self-concerned and self-protective. How many I couldn't guess, but even a few was too many.

Trust throughout the company was imperative. Actions speak louder—and much clearer—than words. I could tell employees how deeply we cared about them, but it wouldn't go over unless confirmed by their managers. Employees are natural boss-watchers. Everything their bosses say and do tells employees their real concerns, their real goals, priorities, and values. And within a day or two, those disabling concerns are known throughout that hotel.

To compete, we'd all have to feel about service the way Ray Kroc, head of McDonald's worldwide, felt about hamburgers. Explaining why his company led competitors around the world, Kroc had said, "We take the hamburger more seriously than they do."

That meant that not just some but all our managers had to be role models, had to show belief in action by everything they did: the decisions made on quality and customer relations and the time given to frontline versus bottom-line concerns. We all had to commit ourselves to walk the same line we talked.

And although service was slowly improving, we weren't doing that yet.

CHAPTER 12

The Golden Rule

For years I endeavored to create within the company a climate conducive to top-grade service, an attitude and atmosphere that would give junior employees some stimulus to act on their own, become self-reliant, self-motivated, and self-controlled. Some hotels were improving, especially those run by the new young managers we had brought in, but certainly not all. And even one lagging hotel would tarnish our reputation.

I hoped we could influence all our people, especially those at the top, but now, in 1980, I ran out of time. Excellence in service could not be an event; it had to become a companywide habit. To build a unified team giving consistently superior service, I could no longer tolerate some managers saying, "These are the values we live by," and others saying, in effect, "Forget it."

We couldn't have role models sending down mixed signals. Values, as I saw it, were a company's psychic core. Without values in common, we couldn't develop companywide trust. And without trust, we couldn't communicate. We wouldn't be believable.

My first move was obvious: implant throughout the company, top to bottom, a sense of purpose. But first we needed a written code of values that would bring us all together, spell out to everyone how we expected them to act, something to give us a reference point from which all our people could ask themselves, "Does this deal, this decision, this action, square with our values?"

I realized, of course, that some 80 percent of all companies had ethical credos that rarely factored into their actual operations. Every year in their annual reports, they'd declare, "Our people are our most important asset," then ignore their people the rest of the year.

I had, however, someone knowledgeable who really believed as I did, our director of advertising, Doug Hall. Doug formerly worked for the marketing and advertising agency we hired at times. Now he alone was our advertising and public relations branch. And whenever I needed to send an intelligible message, I'd turn to him with confidence—as I was doing now.

"Doug, you know we have an implicit operating policy. I want to make it explicit, ensure it gets across. All it's really about is the Golden Rule. It's as simple as that. But I want to expand it so people will understand what it means and talk about it." (See the Four Seasons Mission Statement, page 284.)

Working with me, Doug summarized our goals, beliefs, and principles in a formal credo based on the Golden Rule: "Do unto others as you would have them do unto you."

I discussed this with Rosalie and my sons, who were supportive. Next, I took it to John Sharpe, second in command at our corporate office.

I'd met John at the Four Seasons Sheraton, where he was manager under Lloyd Carswell. I liked him, admired him, and hired him to manage our Calgary hotel. Then I put him in charge of our latest, most important acquisition, the Ritz-Carlton in Chicago. John was bright and forthright, even outspoken, and because I felt he'd be of great use to me at headquarters, I promoted him to vice president of operations. If he didn't like what I was doing, he wouldn't hesitate to say so.

John approved, but he asked, "Who else will buy into this? Certainly not all our managers—though they might say they do."

"That's OK," I said. "We don't need everyone's opinion. We're not going to circulate it yet, we're just going to talk about it."

So John and I took it out to our hotels, starting with the Inn on the Park in Houston. Every hotel had a planning committee, and these were the people I met with, about eight of us sitting informally around a table.

"I've got an idea," I told them. "It's just an experiment, and I'm starting with you."

I handed each of them a copy. "Read this," I said. "Give it some thought."

When they'd all read it, I tried something unusual, grade school stuff. I said, "Would each of you read, out loud, a part of this, then tell us what you think it means and what you feel about it."

They all looked a little embarrassed, but they each took a turn. When they'd all read it aloud, I said, "Now let's talk about it. What do you think? Is that something you can live with? Something you would prefer?"

So they talked about it, and I could see it was hard for some to answer. Because what we were talking about was supporting their fellow workers, treating everyone below them with integrity and respect, which some of their superiors didn't do. When I pressed for answers, some of them admitted, "No, you really won't be able to do that. Our bosses and the people we work with—that's not the way some of them act."

"I know," I said. "But can *you* do it? Are *you* prepared to work this way?"

When most said yes, the talk loosened up, and someone asked, "What happens to people who don't live up to this?"

"I guess they'll have to leave," I replied.

"You mean anyone who doesn't go along with this will be out?"

I said, "This is what we stand by. Anybody who doesn't believe in it—anybody—doesn't fit in." I went through most of our hotels like that, and John Sharpe went through the ones I missed.

I had no illusions about all that would have to be changed. Commanders who believed that bosses are made to give orders would have to learn to advise and support employees who act on their own. Autocrats who depended on position for authority would need to earn the personal authority of respect. Number crunchers would have to consider feelings as well as facts. And although we made some headway on all this, we still had a long way to go.

In every area, we pushed responsibility downward, from our corporate office to our GMs to department heads to our front line, the hourly employees to whom we gave authority to make most decisions they felt were needed to satisfy guests.

Simultaneously, I became an evangelist, preaching the gospel of service every hour of every day on every trip to every hotel, continuously restating it, clarifying it, developing it. My job was getting employees at every level to focus on one priority: pleasing customers. And it was also getting managers to focus on the obvious corollary: pleasing employees.

We treated these frontline people as members of an elite team. We set challenging goals. I didn't want a complacent "good enough" attitude creeping in. So we ordered them to aim high: zero mistakes. Not that we didn't expect mistakes to continue for quite some time, but our aim had to be perfection, or we couldn't keep getting better. We'd either keep getting better or fall behind.

Inevitably, mistakes were made, but there wasn't any finger pointing. We couldn't chew employees out for exceeding their authority and then expect them to continue sticking their necks out. And the efforts they made in responding to mishaps beyond their control turned complaints into new service opportunities, so that what the customer remembered was not the complaint but the outcome. In that sense, we aimed for and often achieved 100 percent in customer satisfaction. As I told our managers, "We either trust them or we don't. We can't hedge our bets with penalties." Empowerment was synonymous with trust.

It took most of the first half of the 1980s to clear out all the obstacles that stood in the way of improving service: to part ways with every executive who believed my "kooky" credo should be confined to the PR department, to part ways with every executive whose actions contradicted policy and sabotaged our credibility.

I had to make cuts at the very top: hotel general managers and head office senior executives. Some were competent technically, but we protected our values above all else. If we didn't define values positively—encouraging pride and satisfaction in work—employees would define them negatively: sloppy work, absenteeism, goofing off. What we believe about people, positive or negative, is self-fulfilling, and it's fundamental to workforce attitude and motivation.

Enforcing our credo was the most far-reaching decision I ever made, a painful process, often personally distressing. It's perhaps the hardest thing I ever did. But the fastest way for management to destroy its credibility is to say employees come first and be seen putting them last. Better to not profess any values than to not live up to them.

The trust generated from living by the Golden Rule became the core of

*With John Sharpe,
who was to become
president of hotel
operations. John and
I were the first
messengers to go on
the road with the
Golden Rule dictum.*

what we would later call our culture, a belief system we did our best to live by. It began to shape our attitudes, corporate and individual, setting a standard of trust and resultant behavior within the company. And as employees saw us continually confirming the company's values, they slowly began to trade self-protective self-concern for concern for the company as a whole.

Enshrining the Golden Rule as our primary working guide was the most fundamental decision in shaping our future.

Skiing in the Monashees, British Columbia.

CHAPTER 13

A Competitive Edge

The essence of leadership became clear to me in the midseventies when I went helicopter skiing with Hans Gmoser, the best-known guide and mountain climber of his time. He was a Canadian from Austria who began this exciting new sport around 1965 in the Canadian Rockies. He would fly groups of experienced skiers to the top of the highest mountain ranges.

Once, skiing across the top of a mountain in a remote, steep, and rugged range with endless rows of trees below, Hans told us to halt. "Pick a line and a buddy," he said. "We're going down, and you should be with someone if you fall. Some trees have big wells around their roots. Fall into them, and you could be lost forever."

What line? I thought, as I looked down a hill so thick with tree trunks that there was little space between them. If I'd been alone, I wouldn't have thought this area skiable. But we all believed in Hans, and although we had no way of knowing which trees had openings, we immediately followed him unquestioningly.

Skiing down a high, steep mountain through virgin snow on an overcast day, circling trees, and raising snow that was momentarily blinding impelled us to rise well beyond our previous abilities, creating an exhilarating rush of adrenaline: the essence and ultimate joy of deep-powder skiing.

Hans Gmoser not only pioneered helicopter skiing, he also founded Canadian Mountain Heli-skiing, a company that later built lodges in select areas of the Rockies, some of the world's finest skiing areas. He was also one of the nine founding members of the Association of Canadian Mountain Guides, and I submitted his name for the Order of Canada, which he received in 1987. Sadly, he died in 2006 after a cycling accident, an incongruous death for a man who'd so long survived the dangerous life of a mountain climber and heli-skier.

Coming back to work from that heli-skiing experience, I thought about how the trust and belief Hans Gmoser had had in me and my comrades pushed us to ski beyond our previous best. It was true leadership, as applicable to my business as to my skiing. Our managers had to know more than their job; they had to understand their people, be influential as well as efficient, and earn the respect and trust of those who work with them, the way Hans had. They had to be more than bosses—they had to be leaders, bringing out the best in our staff by building up their confidence.

THE GOLDEN RULE became our company touchstone, and most of its doubters were replaced by a younger group, all receptive to what I was doing.

"Our competitive edge is service," we told our new managers, "service delivered by frontline employees we expect you to develop."

This was a process, beginning with a goal. It was not one of the usual goals of management: increased sales, market share, profit, or growth, not even a goal of service quality. Our goal was to add continuously to the value customers put on our service, nothing else. "That means," I emphasized in talking to our managers, "that your success depends upon the success of your employees. So your number-one priority can't be what you as managers want. Your priority has to be, as far as possible, an environment and a structure that gives your employees what *they* want.

"Your role, then, will be a leader, not a boss. Your job will be to bring out the best in all individuals and weld them into a winning team."

Getting employees to do their jobs without managerial supervision is now generally known as empowerment. This was a process that began with the employees our GMs were hiring. We didn't want people who thought servicing others was demeaning—we wanted people with high self-esteem. Not people who said in a crisis, "That's not my job," but people who'd say, "How can I help?" People who'd never answer a customer's question by saying, "I don't know," but rather, "I'll find out."

In hiring, then, we gave more weight to character and personality than we did to traditional résumés and technical expertise. We can upgrade technical skills with training, but no amount of training can change in-grained attitudes or create responsibility and initiative. And we were hir-ing not only for immediate job openings; we were hiring for positions of future leadership.

Admittedly, it's harder to hire on subjective judgment than hard data. Before opening Four Seasons Chicago, we screened over fifteen thou-sand applicants for five hundred jobs. And all the prospects we picked were interviewed four or five times, the last time by the general manager personally.

All employees hired were put through orientation on their first day— usually a Monday at 8:00 A.M. The general manager and his senior team would spend time explaining the company's operating philosophy, struc-ture, and aims, then they'd tell them about the hotel they'd be working in, its staff, and their methods, strong points, and goals.

It was a rigorous, highly selective, costly procedure, but it paid off. Our rates of retention and productivity were rising, and by hiring well, we sel-dom had to fire anyone. It also sent a morale-boosting message to all em-ployees, long-term and new, that we realized how important they were. And because as a builder I'd created a climate that induced my workers to motivate themselves, I had no doubt whatever that we could do the same with our hotels.

We had already done various surveys that told us what our employees wanted. They wanted open and honest communications, so I put that first, because nothing goes right unless it's clearly communicated. "Communi-cation," we told our managers, "is vital to outstanding service. And in or-der to communicate, you'll first have to win trust. Managers live, as you know, in a glass house, every action noted, judged, and discussed on the company grapevine. If what we do doesn't agree with what we say, we lose credibility. Our communications will be questioned, our persuasiveness impaired. So you'll have to live up to your word at all times, operating al-ways by the Golden Rule."

Communication, of course, is a two-way street. We made our GMs re-sponsible, not just for educating employees but for letting employees edu-cate them. Each department in each hotel elected a representative, and these nonsupervisory workers met with the GM monthly and quarterly. The

GMs shared with them their hotel's numbers and told them how well or poorly they were doing. Then the reps would tell the GMs how their co-workers thought their jobs could be done better, tuning us in to potential crises, customer likes and dislikes, suggestions for streamlining systems, and whatever else helped or hindered them in their work.

The GMs passed on what employees told them to their departmental managers, who gave their employees preshift briefings, so there wasn't much chance of employees' feeling they were working in the dark or of managers' being out of touch with employees.

We rewarded extra effort in many ways: we gave feedback on perfor-mance in relation to our goals. Figures on scores are a motivating force for any team. We celebrated every goal we met, recognizing every outstanding effort. Unless we recognized extra effort, we weren't encouraging repeti-tion. We had each GM send a personal letter of commendation to every employee who merited praise, and we honored an Employee of the Month and Employee of the Year at each of our hotels. And no matter how busy we were, we observed such tribal rituals as retirement and holiday parties, which serve as symbols of togetherness, strengthening employees' sense of family.

We didn't talk about values; we acted them out. On hotel tours, I spent as much time with the front line as in the front office. I gave employee complaints as much attention as guest complaints. When upgrading a ho-tel, we first upgraded employee facilities. When a survey at our London hotel showed dissatisfaction with workers' areas, we installed new floors, lockers, and showers within three months.

We passed on quarterly results at a general meeting in each hotel. Dur-ing cyclical downturns, we gave all staff members the hotel numbers and the big picture as we saw it—we didn't try to cover anything up. We said, "These are the problems, and this is what we're going to do about them." When times are tough, employees tend to assume the worst, but by being open, we cut off worrying rumors.

We backed up employees with a network of systems. In each hotel, for example, we installed centrally located hotlines so our frontline people could record their comments on customer problems as they arose. On one of my regular visits to the Four Seasons Boston, Robin Brown, the general manager, told me that on coming into work that morning, he had first, as always, listened to the hotline tape and heard his doorman advise him, "It's seven A.M. Mr. Smith [a pseudonym] just left the hotel. He seemed upset. I overheard him say he'd waited twenty minutes for his car."

The GM immediately phoned Mr. Smith at his office. The swiftness of his response, his frank admission of error, and especially his genuine concern, restored our hotel and its general manager to favor.

Now, after five or six years of operating by the Golden Rule, a new type of manager had evolved: a communicator, not a commander; a coach, not a cop. Our leaders showed their concern for employees by involving them in decision making, which polls said eight out of ten employees wanted. They set up career paths; they were up-front and supportive. An old Japanese proverb put our managers' role in a nutshell: "If they work for you, you work for them."

In this climate of trust and respect, performance rose to meet expectations. We now looked on our service employees as members of an elite team, and living up to that image fostered alertness, judgment, and initiative. The resulting customer satisfaction made employees feel good about themselves. They felt their opinions counted, that their work really made a difference. Our employees began to realize that helping the company grow furthered their own personal growth.

PART IV

A FRESH
APPROACH

Start out with what is "right" rather than what is acceptable.
—PETER DRUCKER

Four Seasons Washington.

CHAPTER 14

Washington

We needed managers to replace those we had let go following our adoption of the Golden Rule. One of the most promising candidates was Wolf Hengst, manager of the Shoreham, a large hotel in Washington.

I interviewed him, and we had a lovely conversation. But at its conclusion, Wolf was puzzled. "You know, Mr. Sharp, you didn't spend much time asking about my professional knowledge," he said.

"Wolf," I said, "you're thirty-two years old, and you've already been a general manager for four years; you're already running an eight-hundred-room hotel. I assume you know what you're doing. You've been successful in your career. What I want to know is who you are as a human being and how I think you're going to treat and manage our people." This was now my first priority in hiring managerial staff.

We were within a year or so of opening our own hotel in Washington, and Hengst's experience in that city made him a natural for the job.

Wolf later told me he just hoped that *I* was the genuine one. After the interview, he said to himself, "If this guy is for real, I've found the perfect job. This could be the place where I want to work for the rest of my life." His viewpoint was typical of the young executives we were now hiring, people who believed in treating employees as they themselves would want to be treated.

Washington was our first U.S. hotel to be called a Four Seasons. It came to us through a partnership with an eminent property developer, William Louis Dreyfus, in affiliation with a Washington company headed by Ben Jacobs, a very bright, talented, and successful real estate developer. Jacobs approached Dreyfus with a concept of building a three-star hotel.

Dreyfus bought into his concept, then decided he wanted something better, so he sent his two senior people, Ernie Steiner and Jeff Sussman, to see if we could give them what he wanted.

We worked out a deal that would turn their three-star into a five-star. This was in stark contrast with the hotel that Ben Jacobs was developing. He and I, of course, locked horns on this, and throughout our entire reconstruction, he vehemently and articulately opposed almost everything we did, continually appealing to Mr. Dreyfus, whose word was final, for Groupe Louis Dreyfus S.A. was one of the world's largest family-owned conglomerates, with major interests in grain, gas, and oil, as well as property development, controlling more than eight million square feet, mostly office space, throughout North America and Europe.

My business relationship with William Dreyfus was one of the most pleasant and satisfying of my career. William was most receptive to the changes we proposed and always sided with me.

Finally, at one meeting, Ben Jacobs, frustrated by all his rejections, said, "What happens if Sharp wants to paint this building purple?"

And Mr. Dreyfus said, "Then we'll paint it purple."

But we had more pertinent issues. We were building in Georgetown in an area many considered a poor location for a hotel. It was the site of maintenance sheds for Washington's bus system, and on the other side of the street was a power plant, so some of our people asked, "Why are we building here?"

Although we were on the last block on that street, it was still Pennsylvania Avenue, known worldwide as the neighborhood of the White House, and I thought such a district might soon attract the attention of prominent business companies or upscale retailers, for in print, 2500 Pennsylvania was an outstanding address, a big, big name.

A more challenging problem was our making over the existing hotel. Major changes were required to make it a five-star property. But the Georgetown area of Washington was at that time a difficult sector in which to make changes. We couldn't alter the footprint or the configuration of the design, and therefore we couldn't change the exterior elevations.

We did what we were now becoming adept at in such circumstances. We reduced some 300 bedrooms to about 210. But our most inspired innovation was in the public area. We turned the entire ground floor into a grand entry, lobby, and lounge with a flower garden so big and beautiful that most visitors came away with a very glamorous first impression.

Some months before we opened, a lady approached Wolf. She introduced herself as Anna Chennault and asked if we would donate $10,000 to help elect California governor Ronald Reagan, who was running for president. Wolf talked to her for some time, pointing out that we weren't the owner and couldn't contribute $10,000 (the equivalent of $100,000 today) but that when Governor Reagan came to Washington, we would give him a suite at no cost, and he could hold his interviews in the hotel.

Anna Chennault, we later learned, was married to General Lee Chennault, founder of Flying Tiger Airlines (a major military cargo carrier). Just before we opened the hotel, she came back and asked Wolf if he remembered her and whether our offer of a free suite for Governor Reagan still held. He answered yes to both questions.

What we didn't know was that Anna Chennault and the future president were holding a three-night fund-raiser, and for those three days the wealthiest, most influential business leaders in America—chairmen of Chrysler, Ford, IBM—stayed at the hotel to meet with Governor Reagan, all of them paying for suites and rooms, many becoming future customers as well as influential Four Seasons promoters. On becoming president, Mr. Reagan always recommended us to his guests, and Wolf thought he was indeed fortunate to have met Anna Chennault.

Washington's outstanding start was further enhanced by our introduction of the concept of a concierge, derived from our experience of the special customer service given by the concierge of our hotel in London, where, as in every good hotel in Europe, the concierge was an invaluable resource. The position had become more widespread since 1929, when an association of concierges, called Les Clefs d'Or (The Golden Keys), was founded in Paris by Ferdinand Gillet.

In bringing the post of concierge to America, it was important to get the right person, someone very familiar with Washington. That was Wolf's job, and he was fortunate. He found a young man, Jack Nargil, who knew

Wolf Hengst is the epitome of a Four Seasons leader. Here Wolf welcomes Ronald and Nancy Reagan to the Washington hotel.

Washington well, for he worked on Capitol Hill for a senator. Moreover, Jack's father was a hotel manager, so he knew what service was all about, as well as the ins and outs of hotel management.

We positioned him in the lobby near the desk so he'd have instant eye and voice contact with every guest coming into the hotel. Nargil was soon proficient at handling difficult requests: hard-to-get reservations for plays, concerts, sporting events, or shows sold out for months, meetings with politicians, plus all manner of exceptional requests, such as the Arab prince who wanted to record a song and take it with him on leaving the hotel in just two days. Jack lined up an available studio, found musicians and a producer, and booked both rehearsal and recording time, and within forty-eight hours, the prince left with a tape of his song.

That concierge service soon was so valuable and popular that we put it in all our hotels, making us the first North American hotel group to employ concierges companywide. Other companies quickly followed, and Jack Nargil was elected as the first president of Les Clefs d'Or in the United States and Canada.

The range of our concierges' activities soon widened to such an extent that we had a booklet written about it, describing a concierge as a combination of personal secretary, aide-de-camp, tour guide, travel agent, social director, best friend, and flat-out miracle worker at the service of every guest in the hotel.

Within a few years, the number of guests utilizing concierges impelled us and other top hotels to employ up to four, almost all speaking two languages, some as many as five.

Our concierge was also a significant factor in the unusually early success of Four Seasons Washington: Thomas Peters, coauthor of *In Search of Excellence*, the best-selling American business book of the century, began the book's introduction with a paragraph on the hotel:

> We had decided, after dinner, to spend a second night in Washington. Our business day had taken us beyond the last convenient flight out. We had no hotel reservations, but were near the new Four Seasons, had stayed there once before, and liked it. As we walked through the lobby, wondering how best to plead our case for a room, we braced for the usual chilly shoulder accorded to latecomers. To our astonishment the concierge looked up, smiled, called us by name, and asked how we were. We knew in a flash why in the space of a brief year the Four Seasons had become the "place to stay" in the district. . . .

Within fifteen months of opening, *First Class* magazine selected Four Seasons Washington as "the best first-class hotel in North America," and our company as "the most outstanding North American hotel chain." Equally gratifying were our financial results: Even as the economy declined in the eighties, Four Seasons Washington continued to be a success, averaging two hundred dollars a night, at that time a record-high room rate, nearly forty dollars above its closest competitor. And when too many newly built luxury hotels began pushing down occupancy levels, they didn't put us in the red like so many others.

Our hotel owners shared our satisfaction with the results. This was especially gratifying to me, for I held William Louis Dreyfus in high regard. He was a man of good humor and fine taste, owner of a vast art collection that he shares with the hotels, and we remain close friends to this day. Even Ben Jacobs was generous in his approval, admitting he was wrong, calling me and saying, "Why don't you and your wife come down to our house, play some tennis and have dinner with us." He continued as a successful Washington real estate developer, and he occasionally called me, but, to date, we have not had the opportunity to do business together again.

Some six to eight months before we opened Four Seasons Washington, Wolf Hengst became seriously ill, requiring intensive care. I called his wife, Caroline, and told her that her only concern should be for Wolf and her children; Wolf's job would still be there for him when he recovered— which he did, going on to become an exceptional asset to our company. My telephone call became a story that Wolf would often tell.

Wolf also helped make the opening of Four Seasons Houston a huge success, thanks to the presence of Luciano Pavarotti and a Canadian jumping horse.

In 1978, when Wolf was still in Washington, I asked him to come to Edmonton and see how Four Seasons opens a hotel. At the time, we were still in the mode of creating a big event for the opening of our hotels. We try not to do it anymore, because it puts enormous pressure on the staff and because it's very difficult to stick to a precise opening date and time with something as large and complicated as a five-star hotel.

On the day of the Edmonton opening, I was in jeans and a T-shirt, using an industrial-size vacuum cleaner in the ballroom, and Wolf was cleaning windows . . . as guests began arriving in black tie! Les Brown and His Band of Renown were there to entertain and we were still cleaning. The next day was the *first* time we decided to end the policy of doing big openings. But four years later, we were doing so in Houston.

In 1982, Wolf went to Houston as vice president and general manager. He had lived there and run a small hotel during the early seventies, so he was a good choice for our entry into the market. He immediately immersed himself in the social life of the city to position the property as a high-society hotel and as a supporter of the arts.

An avid tennis player, Wolf joined a tennis club and soon made the acquaintance of the then director general of the Houston Grand Opera, David Gockley. They played together at the club, and one thing led to another, and Gockley said, "Do you want to join the board of the Houston Grand Opera?"

There was a catch, of sorts: the opera was preparing to open its own new facility and was looking to host an appropriately grand preopening fund-raiser.

"Why don't we combine?" Gockley said. "You're opening a hotel, we're opening a new opera house. Maybe we can find some synergy."

That's when Wolf committed us to the Houston Grand Opera's opening fund-raiser. That was simple enough, but then a woman Wolf met on the board told him she had a connection to Luciano Pavarotti, "and maybe you could talk to him about performing at the opening."

"I'd love to do that," Wolf said, and a meeting was arranged at the Essex House in New York where actor and conductor Carlo Ponti Jr. maintained an apartment. It was Ponti, Pavarotti, his girlfriend, and his biographer, plus pasta and Chianti. The tenor said he would consider performing with the opera at the Four Seasons but that he could not accept any money for the performance because of taxation issues.

Two days later, Wolf was still in New York, staying at The Pierre, and Pavarotti called to invite him back to Ponti's apartment for more pasta and Chianti. By the time the two of them finished a bottle, Pavarotti said, "I looked at the dates when we could do this . . . but I'll need a horse."

Wolf looked at him, befuddled.

"A horse, Luciano?"

"I need a particular type of horse, a Canadian jumping horse," he said.

Wolf was speechless. "I'll see what I can do," he said, actually having no idea where he could find a Canadian jumping horse, whatever that was.

Back at The Pierre, Wolf called Arnie Cader, our executive vice president of finance and development, and said, "I'm stuck with this thing. What should I do?"

Arnie said, "Talk to Murray Koffler."

"Murray Koffler? Issy's partner?"

"Yeah," Arnie said, "he's into horses. I'll have him call you."

An hour later, Koffler called, and Wolf told him the story.

"Don't worry!" he said. "We can do that."

"But, Murray, it has to be delivered to Modena, Italy!"

"Don't worry," Murray repeated.

He went back to Pavarotti and said, "I can get you the horse," and they struck a deal.

Planning for the opening night fund-raiser for the Houston Grand Opera continued apace, but Wolf encountered a nightmare getting the hotel ready in time. He expected five hundred people for a very special seventy-five-minute concert night in the ballroom. We raised $450,000 for the opera that night. Pavarotti sang. It was an incredible concert. And the horse arrived on cue.

Afterward, everyone filed outside, and Wolf and his staff had forty-five minutes to transform the ballroom into a nightclub and restaurant. Rosalie, the Kofflers, the Caders, and I shared a table with the great Pavarotti, and he patiently posed for pictures with everyone.

Photographs and stories about the evening appeared in local and national magazines and newspapers, and all of a sudden, the Four Seasons was the center of Houston's social life.

Wolf Hengst went on to win ever-higher status as a leader, becoming, in 2000, our president of worldwide hotel operations.

CHAPTER 15

The Pierre

Within three years of entering the United States as a little-known Canadian company, we had four hotels, though only the one in Washington bore our name.

What we needed, above all, was a hotel in New York, the most important city for a hotel company on the continent, probably the most important in the world. For several years, we searched unsuccessfully for a suitable New York property. In late 1979, however, the directors of The Pierre hotel called us for management proposals.

The Pierre, if we could sign it, would be an extraordinary coup, well beyond anything we had hoped for, a historic luxury hotel and residence catering to a very sophisticated international clientele, including Richard Rodgers, Yves St. Laurent, and Audrey Hepburn. It had a prime location, at Fifth Avenue and Sixty-first Street, where its forty-one stories towered over Central Park.

The Pierre was built by Charles Pierre Casalasco, a Corsican financed by Walter P. Chrysler, founder of Chrysler Corporation, along with two prominent Wall Street financiers, E. F. Hutton and Otto H. Kahn. Its opening in 1930 was acclaimed by the *New Yorker* as "a millionaire's Elysium," which still applies today. The 1930s depression put it into bankruptcy, after which it fell to various owners, including oil magnate J. Paul Getty, who in 1938 bought it for $2.5 million, less than one fifth of its building cost. In 1959 Getty sold it to a group of wealthy New Yorkers, who turned it into a co-op with seventy-six owners, a Who's Who of the entertainment and international business world. Thirty of them now lived there in very luxurious apartments interspersed among its 201 hotel rooms.

On hearing that the owners were considering a change in management,

Hotel Pierre New York on Central Park—
a typical art deco wedding cake structure.

we immediately approached The Pierre's board with an offer. The board was led by its chairman, Serge Semenenko, and two other prominent members, Matthew Rosenhaus and Arthur Bienenstock. Our proposal was structured in a way that gave the board significant savings by reducing operating costs, and we organized it so that it could also become a tax benefit.

Over time, we gained the support of most of the board. But Trusthouse Forte, the company we would displace, was determined to hang on to this valuable contract, and at the last moment, offered to fund a relatively significant amount for improvements at the property if the board would leave things as they were. Perhaps with a board less affluent this might have worked.

I was quite optimistic that we would get The Pierre. In discussing it with my family one evening during dinner, our boys asked why I was so confident.

I don't usually talk about a deal until it's completed, but I was so sure of this one that I said, "We're nearly there now. We've got the support. We're almost certain it's going through." Then, jokingly, I added, "Only one thing could go wrong. An impossible scenario. A board member could die."

But that's exactly what happened. The two main supporters of our proposal, Chairman Serge Semenenko and Matthew Rosenhaus, both died suddenly, and Arthur Bienenstock, our third proponent, wasn't prepared to push it through alone. We eventually convinced him that The Pierre needed his leadership, and again he brought owners around to our side. Soon I was told that one of the hotel's most prominent owners, Joseph Mailman, would like to see me before agreeing to assign us the management contract.

We met in his New York office, where recognizable French impressionist paintings graced the walls. He greeted me cordially, then said, "If we give you this opportunity, will you agree to be here once a week for the first year?"

"Mr. Mailman," I said, "if I have to be here every week, you've got the wrong company. But I will be here whenever I need to be."

We shook hands on that, and he pointed to a portrait on the wall behind him. "That's my father. He's Mr. Mailman," he said. "I'm Joe." And that began a very long and respectful relationship, for shortly afterward, in late

1981, we assumed management of the most important hotel of that time. As *Report on Business* noted, it was "a stunning coup."

Renovating The Pierre—the guest rooms, the suites, the lobby, the dining rooms, the ballroom—cost us $20 million. But our rates were the highest in the city; suites ran $1,300 a night. And every year The Pierre took in about $20 million—gross, not profit—from many special events: weddings, which started at about $200,000, receptions, debutante parties, and bar mitzvahs.

The Pierre was a hotel unlike any other, a haven for the higher ranks of entertainment celebrities, such as Charles Bronson and Michael Caine. It was the New York choice for heads of state and government dignitaries from around the world, including Canada's Pierre Trudeau and Brian Mulroney, whom, like all world leaders, we put on the top floor, where terraces offered awesome views of New York and Central Park.

But our guests were primarily the business elite, some 40 percent from abroad. Most of the others were people traveling for pleasure or private business, often demanding the same room on every trip over, sometimes delaying overseas passage until assured of their room.

To ensure that we satisfied the rich and powerful, we hired more employees than usual. The average hotel has one employee per guest, sometimes fewer. But to serve the patrons of The Pierre, which included both travelers and residents, we needed three times as many, more than at any other hotel we had managed before or have managed since.

Our service staff, as usual, pleased the hotel's previous customers and brought us new ones: presidents and chairmen of world-renowned companies who kept coming back time after time. Many others liked it for its location and its splendid view, but primarily because the friendly staff remembered their foibles and anticipated their preferences. Within three years of our takeover, *Institutional Investor* magazine, which polls globetrotting financiers yearly for their opinions on hotels, rated The Pierre among the top fifty in the world.

We made the hotel more successful, but it was a difficult job, the most arduous task among all the hotels we ever managed. We had problems with the physical plant, with the divergent views of our owners, and with the staff.

Unfortunately, the union called a citywide hotel strike in June of 1985. We saw it coming, and forewarned the owners, apologizing in advance.

"We don't know what's going to happen," we said. "We can only tell you that all the services you've been accustomed to are going to be cut back dramatically. But we'll do the very best for you that we can."

Four fifths of The Pierre's employees walked off the job. The GMs of our other hotels sent staff to help out, staff they themselves badly needed. The Pierre's maître d' waited tables. Department heads made beds. The front desk manager carried bags. The GM hauled out garbage. Every executive worked long hours, doing menial jobs they had never done before.

Afterward, the chairman of the board of shareholders called me to ask, "How in the world do you get people to work the way these did?"

"By treating them well," I said.

We ran The Pierre for eighteen years, continually persevering to keep service levels high despite the daily complications of sharing authority with so many owners. And obviously we succeeded, as far as customers were concerned. Then in 2007, with a New York hotel under our own name, we passed on The Pierre's management to Taj Hotels, a large hotel company from India.

John Sharpe, our now retired former president, who on his visits to New York always preferred to stay at The Pierre, told me, "You know, of all the hotels in the company, I can say without hesitation that I'm more proud of The Pierre, how much we improved it from where it was when we got it, than of any other hotel in the company. Yes, it cost us a fortune. But the transition we made was the greatest of anything we did."

CHAPTER 16

Bumps in the Road

The good times that had given us growth throughout the later seventies continued into 1980 and early 1981. And even as we were ridding ourselves of people who wouldn't or couldn't change management styles, we were getting calls from all over the United States from financiers and developers offering us deals.

This was a period of change and uncertainty: new employees, new managers, less control. And I was concerned about our ability to handle so many new deals, so I told every financier and developer who wanted us to build a hotel, "I appreciate your coming to us, and I'm sorry to turn you down, but right now we wouldn't be able to give you what you expect from us."

Most of them understood, appreciated our candor, and approved our refusal to compromise, later confirming those opinions by coming back to us again. But internally I had a mini uprising. People said, "We'll stagnate. We came here thinking there'd be promotion. What's going to happen to our future?"

"Our strategy," I told everyone, "is to grow on strength. And that strength is you, our people. I've looked around at our senior managers, our backroom staff, and our front line, and I've visualized opening new hotels and who would staff them and run them, and we just don't have enough people who know what Four Seasons is all about to expand any further at this time."

There was grumbling, but our key strategic factor was service, and I didn't intend to compromise it by overloading the people providing it. Japanese accountants have a saying, "Over is the beginning of under," meaning that growth can become addictive, adding volume without value. I wasn't hooked on momentum or quarterly results. I agreed with Peter

Drucker, the world's most respected management consultant, who said, "Doing too many things at once is the most common mistake in business."

Recession, as it turned out, was just around the corner, silencing all my critics, for if I had gone along with them, it would have been disastrous. Not that it was great foresight on my part; it was just plain common sense. If quality is your edge, you can't compromise it.

But sometimes common sense isn't enough to avoid a disaster. On the night of Friday, January 17, 1981, fire broke out in the tower of the Inn on the Park in Toronto. The front page of the *Toronto Star* on Sunday morning reported that six guests had died and another sixty-five were being treated for serious smoke inhalation.

Other deaths and injuries would certainly have occurred if some of our staff had not been alert and caring. Gladys Draxler, a night switchboard operator, the only one on duty at the time, was told by a clerk at the hotel's main desk to get everyone down to the front lobby. Minutes later a fire chief came in and said, "Tell the guests to remain in their rooms." Fortunately, Rhonda Warlow, assistant manager of our hotel's disco, joined Gladys. Rhonda knew that the smoke was thick in the lobby directly below the tower and, upon checking with a night manager in another part of the hotel, was told that the fire chief had it right.

Room by room and floor by floor, starting at the top, the two women and another volunteer, Linda Fauteux, a cocktail waitress, began a barrage of telephone warnings to the twenty-three-story tower, calling each room twice, almost certainly sparing quite a few people serious harm or death.

Off and on for four months, while the province collected facts for a month-long inquest on the fire, hotel fire prevention was news. It was also continually on my mind. In fact, just before the blaze, we called in fire-safety consultants to develop hotel safety standards, an issue raised by a rash of fires in North America's highest buildings, including hotels—in particular, the MGM Grand Hotel in Las Vegas. But such studies take time to set up, and ours had not quite begun when the Inn on the Park Toronto fire broke out.

This was our first major hotel trauma. It compelled me to act immediately. I contacted a friend with experience at one of the airlines and asked for advice on handling catastrophes.

"It's important," he said, "to be up-front and open. Make senior people available for comment. And make sure you're candid about the cause of the problem as far as you know it."

The cause, according to an investigator working under authority of the Ontario Hotel Fire Safety Act, was a hotel cleaner whose vacuum picked up a live cigarette butt. The cleaner stored the vacuum, the butt still burning, in a closet, eventually setting the closet paneling on fire. From there it spread to the adjacent Tower Room, turning it into an inferno.

I was determined that nothing like that would happen again in our hotels, and I gave exceptional attention to the inquest, considered by some experts on fires to be the most detailed probe into fire safety in hotels and high-rise buildings in Canada. But even before the inquest, we hired two companies, Rolf Jensen & Associates Ltd. and Custom Fire Protection Services, to design and install a new state-of-the-art fire alarm system. And while we were installing all these new features, our seven hundred Inn on the Park employees received in-depth safety and emergency training.

The new safety system cost us some $2.5 million. But as Eber Rice, then chairman of the Ontario Liquor Licence Board, which at the time shared responsibility with the Ontario Fire Marshal's Office for safety standards at hotels selling liquor, told a reporter before the inquest on our fire, "The Inn on the Park will probably be the most fire-safe hotel in all of North America."

Nothing could nullify my sadness about the lives that were lost, but it gave me much-needed satisfaction to know we'd done the best we could to ensure that this would never happen again, that from now on every Four Seasons Hotel would be an exemplar of fire safety.

THE RECESSION IN the latter part of 1981 dropped prices, including those of hotel rooms, while interest rates began heading the other way. Airfares climbed by 32 percent in a single year. Company executives traveled less frequently and entertained less while traveling, an additional impact on our food and beverage operations, which already were suffering from a falloff in company banquets and waning attendance at major conventions.

Most hotel companies responded by cutting costs right and left. "Cut staff, forget the doorman, don't replace carpets," their managers ordered.

"No employee perks, no turkeys at Christmas." They cut basics to the bone.

Some of our people thought we should follow suit. I listened to all their comments, but getting into a price war was a no-win situation. Layoffs might drop costs for a time, but revenue would fall even more and take much longer to come back. True, luxury was no longer in vogue for middle managers and executives, but for most corporate leaders, the people who made up the bulk of our customers, reliable time-saving service was not a luxury but a necessity. And with travel more fatiguing and work more demanding, it was needed now more than ever.

Rather than cut back on service by laying people off, senior managers took a pay freeze and asked their employees to vote on flex hours: working four days a week instead of five. Employees in almost every hotel voted nearly unanimously for it, so all of them would keep their jobs. They knew through the company grapevine that managers' salaries had been frozen and, knowing what other companies were doing, they felt our decisions were more than fair. And sharing a common purpose created a camaraderie that made trying times not only pleasurable but also profitable, for as most of our rivals dipped into red ink, we remained in the black by delivering the quality service that our fledgling marketing division had begun promoting.

I didn't know how long the recession would last or how deep it would go, but I felt that travel and tourism had a great future. Since 1960 it had grown at 10 percent a year or better. In twenty years, it doubled, quadrupled, then doubled again. It was now the third-largest industry in the United States, and the American Hotel and Motel Association concluded that by 1990 it would be the biggest industry in the world, with total spending reaching $1 trillion.

Considering past growth, I, too, assumed that spending on travel eventually would start climbing again. I saw the recession less as a mishap than an opportunity, and I shared my views with our corporate office executives.

"While our competitors are dropping standards, we will raise ours," I said. "And we'll hold firm on pricing." The directive I gave to all our GMs was summed up in one phrase: "Control without compromise."

So we didn't lower prices, though dissenters had reasons for their views.

By year-end, our long-term debt had soared to more than $200 million, most of it at the year's highest interest rate of 21 percent, so to tide us over until the market recovered, I went to see Gordie Bell, our long-term major lender, soon to be president of the Bank of Nova Scotia.

It was a difficult time. Banks were closing down companies, and we already owed our bank an enormous sum that it was pestering us to reduce.

Bell was incredulous. "I thought you were coming to tell me how you would pay me back. And now you're asking me to lend you more?"

"Our business is cyclical," I told him. "I just need more money till the end of the year. Then I'll start to pay it down to what it is now."

"How can I go to my board of directors with this when you have no collateral? You'll have to use your stock in the company to guarantee the loan."

"But I'm asking you to loan the *company* money, not me."

"I know that. But I have to have collateral. And if you've got so much confidence that you can pay back this loan, why haven't you got the confidence to pledge your stock?"

"You're asking me, alone, to risk everything I have?"

"But look at what you're asking me! Not only to extend the loan but to increase it!" he exclaimed.

I discussed it with our new executive vice president of finance and development, Arnie Cader, a brilliant lawyer, close friend, and helicopter-skiing companion. I gave Arnie Four Seasons shares to leave his law firm and join our company. He was an excellent negotiator. We had worked together on many deals. But the downturn was making our business much more difficult than he expected, and now his advice to me was to sell the company. "We could walk out of this a big winner," he said.

In my mind, there was absolutely no question of selling. I went back to Gordie Bell and pledged all my Four Seasons stock, knowing I had to succeed or I'd lose everything. It's strange, but I can't recall being deeply concerned, perhaps because of my depth of involvement and belief in what I was doing.

CHAPTER 17

Partners

To create the world's best hotels, as I so brashly declared we would, meant being best not only in service but in all that we offered our customers, which of course included the hotels we were building in the United States. Fortunately, we had every opportunity we could wish for.

Our reputation was getting around, and many hotel developers offered us deals. Although many were rejected—some because neither the site nor city was suitable for a five-star hotel—we soon attracted many desirable partners, including, among the earliest, development and financial leaders like Aetna Life & Casualty, Urban Investment and Development, Olympia & York, Cadillac Fairview, Equitable Life Assurance, Massachusetts Life Assurance, CIGNAC Corporation, Southland Financial, Galbreath-Ruffin, Louis Dreyfus, and B. S. Ong.

I met B. S. Ong by chance when we were selling our Montreal hotel. He was an interested buyer who asked if I'd come to New York to discuss it. I agreed, flew down, and walked into his office wearing a Columbo-style trenchcoat. He was reviewing photographs of women weight lifters for a promotion he was working on. Looking up, he said, "Hi. Come in. Which one do you like?"

"They're not my type," I said.

"You know, when you walked into my office you looked like Humphrey Bogart in *Casablanca*."

I took this as a compliment, and we were soon on such friendly terms that although he had a very good relationship with one of our rivals, Hilton, he bought the Montreal hotel and confirmed us as its manager, the beginning of a lifelong friendship that would later be extremely important.

While talking of sports at one of our meetings, B.S.—which was what I'd begun to call him—said, "My favorite is scuba diving. I've got a hotel in the Maldives, the finest place in the world to dive. Why don't you come down with me?"

"I don't dive," I said. "I don't even snorkel."

"Come down anyway," he said. "We'll just sit around and chat. Maybe I can teach you to dive."

So I took Roger Garland and John Sharpe—both avid scuba divers—and John Johnson, general manager of Four Seasons Singapore, down to Ong's little two-star hotel on a coral atoll in the Indian Ocean. It was a truly magnificent site. And the following morning, while he, John, Roger, and some of his friends went diving, his diving master taught Johnson and me the basics of the sport.

That afternoon I went diving with B.S. and his group. We swam to the entrance of a cave, and the diving master gave me a flashlight and signaled me to direct my light into the cave. Out of the darkness came an eel—huge, dangerous, scary. But it just looked at me and withdrew. That evening, watching the video they had taken of their morning dive, I saw the same eel come out of the cave at lightning speed to grab some meat they'd thrown out. So they had known it wasn't hungry and wouldn't have attacked when I tempted fate. That was my first diving experience. And my last.

B.S. had other hotels in the Maldives, most managed by his wife, Christine. But he also had one that was going nowhere. Some years later, he asked us to take it over. And because it wasn't up to our standards, he agreed to make all the changes required to upgrade it to a five-star Four Seasons.

So we brought in our people and renovated, making it into a fine hotel with a spectacular spa in one of the world's most enchanting sites. The Maldives then were still known mainly by divers. Tourists were scarce. Jobs paid little. Natives were poor. But Four Seasons was now well known. Our brand brought customers, who raved about the setting. Other hotel companies considered that what was good for us would be a fine site for a three- or four-star hotel. Within eight years, almost every hotel company had built there, making the Maldives world-renowned as a tourist destination.

My first and last time deep-sea diving, at the insistence of B. S. Ong.

"The Maldives government," I told B.S., "should give you a medal. You've brought industry to the country. Great wealth and a good life for the islanders."

"No," he said. "I was always there. It's what your brand was able to do."

"Well, you brought us there," I said. "We can both feel good about it." As I still do.

B.S. and I became partners in many hotels: London, Singapore, Bali, Kuala Lumpur, Shanghai, Phuket, the Seychelles, and many more, some currently under construction. He is one of the smartest and most interesting people I've ever met, and a valued friend of both Rosalie and me.

AS WITH B.S., almost all my partnerships were personal as well as working relationships, based on mutual advantage and mutual trust, which I now considered the emotional capital of a company, an often overlooked component of success. And as each new partnership opened doors to others, it added yet another link to what I hoped would eventually become a worldwide network of influential connections and foreign properties.

No other hotel company has ever been able to duplicate the contracts we signed with these partners. They usually began with a thirty-year term, plus an option on our part to renew on the same basis, giving us contracts that averaged sixty years, typically adding a percentage of gross revenue as well as some participation in net profit. Then we took sole responsibility for deciding and approving the appearance and function of each hotel. That didn't mean everything had to be done our way, for prior to building, there was much discussion with our owners, and their desires and opinions were always carefully considered and if possible incorporated in our planning.

We also checked out the other hotels, who and where our competitors were and what they were offering. A couple of really big chains were then creating flamboyant lobbies, while some of our major competitors were building hotels, some of which, although good, tended to look the same. We felt that people who could afford to travel to different regions or countries did so, in large part, to experience variety, so we tried to make each hotel distinctive, give it a local flavor incorporating regional art and furnishings.

In Texas, we used local materials: native stone, leather chairs, antlers on the lounge wall, strong colors in tiles and in painted stucco walls that reflected the prevalent Spanish influence. In California, we leaned toward a more open design. In the northwest, we might use more wood and give it a rich texture, while in the northeast, the color of our wood might be lighter, the design more contemporary. Or we might decide to ignore all these factors and build something entirely unique.

Concurrent with considering location, we prepared a conceptual design brief. Whatever design we chose, we wanted each new hotel to be better in some respects than the one before, and we wanted every one to have a consistent tone and ambience, a feeling that it was welcoming, that the lounge, which in some hotels comes across as a traffic area, would in ours convey a feeling of tranquil comfort.

We didn't want too formal or imposing a design, implying how people should dress or behave, for we thought that was inappropriate for our type of customer. Nor did we want to be too fashionable, for fashions can quickly come and go.

We spent a good deal of time on the design brief, which decrees the building's size and the number, size, and placement of bedrooms, dining rooms, restaurants, kitchens, and bars, everything from the ballroom down to the pool and fitness center, even the size of the sidewalk in front of the hotel.

Design is glamorous; building is just hard work, calling for careful attention to thousands of details, for unless we inspect every item, we can end up with an operating problem. That includes the mechanical and electrical functions, which are just as important as smart finishes. And we continually looked for ways to make our clientele more productive and comfortable. In our first hotel, we put telephones not only beside the bed; we installed, for convenience, a second line in the bathroom.

Another innovation was to turn two standard rooms into a mini-suite. We separated, with fine French doors, a spacious bedroom from a living room big enough to allow a corporate executive to work, entertain, or hold small-scale business meetings in privacy. It was intimate but less expensive than a full suite. We called it a Four Seasons room, and it soon became so popular that we put it in all our hotels. It wasn't long, of course, before our competitors were copying it.

IN BUILDING, I often made changes that tested the patience of our architects and designers, though it usually worked out for the best. In Boston, we introduced a new kind of building, financed in a novel way. On top of the 290-room hotel, we built eight floors of luxurious condominiums, 100 in all.

We sold the condos at $300 a square foot, then a premier price, for they proved appealing to well-off buyers. It gave them access to room service, fitness facilities, and a fine restaurant without leaving home. Other options included twice-daily maid service, round-the-clock valet service, and all the other features of a Four Seasons hotel. So the condominiums sold well, opening up a new area of profitable building.

A hotel was finally finished when we considered that this could be the best we'd built to date. Our partners usually agreed, for most of our owners take the long view. They know that if a hotel is built to Four Seasons specifications, they'll have a property their grandchildren could be proud of.

CHAPTER 18

Amenities

A large factor in Four Seasons' success has been its commitment to lead, not only in service and structure, but also in everything a hotel offers, primarily amenities, fitness facilities, and food.

We gained an early head start back in 1961 by offering shampoo in bathrooms, then bigger bars of soap and large cotton towels. These were soon followed by bathrobes, overnight laundry, and shoeshines. But an amenity's popularity, we soon found, can depend on its presentation.

When we first offered complimentary overnight shoeshines, we put the bags for the shoes on the toilet tank. We realized they weren't being used much, which could mean they either weren't wanted or our guests were not aware of them. So we told housekeepers, during evening turndown service, to reposition the bags at the foot of the bed. That one small change boosted usage by more than 50 percent.

These earliest amenities were not quickly copied at first. Some hoteliers considered them trivial, not worthy of their employees' time. In some cases, they could have been right; in others, entirely wrong. For example, a certain politician, who for years had been our guest whenever he had to be in Toronto, suddenly stopped coming. Months passed. He still didn't show. So our front desk clerk called his office to find out what was wrong.

He learned that the politician liked our hotel but not our pillows; he liked the pillows of a competing hotel. The front desk clerk called our executive housekeeper, who arranged to get four pillows that were the same as those of our competitor. We then invited the premier to try us again, and he has stayed with us ever since.

We didn't let this little experience end there. We checked all our pillows; they weren't as good. As a result, the pillows at all our hotels were replaced by much better ones. Excellence is often just a capacity for taking pains.

Over the years, we continued to refine and improve our mattresses, and this gave us the best publicity we ever got when Oprah Winfrey interviewed Julia Roberts on travel some years later.

"Favorite thing to sleep in for you?" Winfrey asked her.

"A Four Seasons bed," the movie star replied.

Winfrey went on to say, "Four Seasons' bed is the only bed better than my own; now that is not an advertisement; that is the truth!"

When we noted the increasing number of women executives, we offered them hair dryers and padded hangers, both of these also a first. We knew that time and transportation were priorities with all businesspeople, so we put a device in our new and renovated hotels that allows them to come downstairs at, say, two A.M., tell our desk clerk or concierge, "I need an airline ticket to L.A.," and have that ticket in their hands within five minutes.

Later, we led the way with digital clocks that light up at night, clip-on lights for reading in bed without annoying your partner, lighted makeup mirrors, and the softest toilet paper.

We encouraged our employees to keep notes on guests' preferences, so that when the vice president of a national organization checked in to a room at Four Seasons Ottawa, she was greeted by a flower arrangement in her favorite colors. Not only was this a pleasant surprise, she also felt recognized and special.

We made this a common experience by setting up, early on—far ahead of other hotel companies—what we called a guest-history system. The first time guests stayed with us, we computerized their preferences—in rooms, food, drink, and anything else our employees noted—so that when they returned, we could give them, without their having to ask, whatever they wanted and liked best. And these files, as we added to them, kept us abreast of changing tastes.

The results were effective, and many were brought to my attention. I learned that one world-class crooner liked a room with morning light, because the morning after a nightclub performance, he wants to paint. A classic film star, I was told, liked soda pop in cans, and though we normally stock it in bottles, we could now serve it as he preferred. Each successful amenity extends our service reputation.

In the late 1980s, disposable incomes rose abroad, especially in Asia, and the forecast for global air traffic was a yearly 5 to 7 percent rise. We ensured that all our hotels in prominent business centers had people who spoke a few of the most-used European languages, as well as someone who spoke Japanese, for more and more Japanese big-company executives had begun flying west on business, and more were certain to follow.

We told the general managers of the hotels that Japanese travelers would most likely use to provide them with kimonos and slippers, a Japanese daily newspaper, the telephone number of their consulate, the names and addresses of the best Asian restaurants, and instructions in their language on how to use all our hotels' facilities. We asked them to put out doorknob menus for an authentic Japanese breakfast, explain that guests only had to tick off what they wanted and hang it on their doorknob, and they'd have it delivered at the time they had specified.

These were simple amenities, but many ideas were problematic—minibars, for example. When we first considered introducing minibars to North America, everyone told us we couldn't control the cost.

This was true. If we reached for the new too quickly, we could lose money; but too slowly, we'd lose momentum. We took a chance, went ahead, and when minibars proved popular, our rivals, as usual, soon followed suit.

Creativity—originating or adapting new amenities—could be risky. What seemed novel might be only novelty, and what seemed timely could be premature. In the early 1980s, we tested teleconferencing to see if we should offer it as a service. We decided not to and didn't regret it. At the end of the decade, customers still preferred face-to-face contact.

By then, we were the undisputed leader in hotel amenities. There was nothing outstandingly dramatic, just continuous minor improvement, always from the customer's point of view, until over time it added up to major creative change.

The eighties also brought in a new attitude toward health. About half the population was now exercising in some way, and some of our most important customers were among them. For many, exercise had become a habit, a necessity for both body and mind.

I was well aware of this, for my relationship with Lloyd Percival, one of the world's top fitness mentors, made me something of a savant on how to stay in shape. In those early years, you would seldom see a senior corporate executive coming down to our health club for an early-morning workout. Now, in the eighties, John Sharpe, no fitness nut, was complaining that sometimes the club was so crowded at seven A.M. that he couldn't get in.

We had foreseen this. For several years, we kept the lead in this trend, as we had in everything else. In our recently developed and renovated hotels, we had fitness centers with treadmills and StairMaster machines equipped with TVs or recorders for executives who wanted a workout. We also had videotapes of aerobic routines, which many businesswomen preferred.

Now we were considering something else: the final step in completing the modern hotel. In 1980, Rosalie and I took a brief holiday at Canyon Ranch in Arizona, a resort with a spa specializing in health and fitness. Afterward, I thought a spa might be something we should include, and I asked Chris Wallis and Wolf Hengst, then a vice president overseeing our six Texas hotels, to go down and check it out.

They looked over several spas and agreed that they could be a promising adjunct to fitness clubs. In Dallas at that time, we were building an urban resort with a top-of-the-line fitness and sports club. It had fitness instructors, a tennis center with indoor and outdoor courts, and two golf courses with a membership club of two thousand plus. At the last moment, less than a year before opening the hotel, we convinced the owners, Ben and John Carpenter, to make it the first hotel to include a spa. That spa proved, very quickly, to be a huge success, and spas are today an important and expected facility in all our hotels.

While developing the spa and fitness concepts, I was well aware that engendering good health didn't end with exercise. In 1968, Rosalie had come home from her first spa experience campaigning for spa food. It was not only healthier, it tasted better, she said.

I asked Alfons Konrad, our vice president of food and beverage, about the food habits of our customers, and he said they were cutting down on calories.

"What about our competitors?" I inquired, "How are they handling this?"

"More fruit plates and salads," he said. "Same as us."

In my opinion, that just wasn't good enough. We consulted an expert on diet and nutrition, Jeanne Jones, world-famous author of thirteen medically and publicly acclaimed books on food, including *Jet Fuel: The New Food Strategy for the High-Performance Person*. We hired her, and one year later, she came up with what we called Alternative Cuisine.

It took little time for our chefs to shed their doubts. Our low-calorie specials included appetizers, entrees, and desserts, identified on the menu by an asterisk. They were virtually indistinguishable from regular menu items in quality, taste, appearance, and price, but a two-course lunch totaled only 500 calories or fewer; a three-course dinner, no more than 650. And some people even preferred the light taste.

Remembering that César Ritz made his hotels world-famous by hiring some of the foremost chefs, we decided to do something similar. We hired, as executive chef for the Café Pierre at The Pierre in New York, Gerald Gramzay, a French-trained American who had made Le Bec-Fin in Philadelphia and Le Français in Wheeling, Illinois, into prominent, award-winning restaurants. At the Clift in San Francisco, we installed Kelly Mills, who'd been named top apprentice chef in Canada by the Canadian Federation of Chefs. Mills lived up to his reputation by soon making Four Seasons Clift the premier place to dine in San Francisco.

At the Four Seasons Los Angeles, in 1987, Lydia Shire opened Gardens, and her innovative cooking made her and Gardens what one newspaper called "the hottest culinary topic in town." In Chicago, French-trained executive chef Fernand Gutierrez, who played in the popular TV series *Great Chefs of Chicago,* made our Ritz-Carlton the city's favorite for French-style fare. And a Gutierrez protégée, Susan Weaver-Flori, the first female finalist and the only American in the 1989 Prix Culinaire International Pierre Taittinger culinary contest in Paris, became executive chef of our Inn on the Park in Houston.

Many travelers wanted local color, a sense of place, in their food and surroundings, and prior to opening any new Four Seasons hotel, Alfons Konrad would work on and off for a year or so with its designated general manager and executive chef, ensuring that the restaurant and menu, upon opening, would reflect the unique character of its region. And by the mid-eighties, we had completely demolished the long-standing stereotype of a hotel restaurant as a mediocre, overpriced trap for tired travelers.

On average, some 30 percent of our restaurant sales came from Alternative Cuisine; in some hotels it totaled as much as 50 percent. But whatever extra income it brought us was not its primary importance. What really counted was doing the right thing in the right way—what should have been done long before, when Rosalie first mentioned it.

By the late eighties, some of our restaurants had become the social focus for all diners yearning to see and be seen, the gathering spot for local celebrities, socialites, and politicians. And by 1989, a cover story in *Restaurant Business* noted, "This luxury chain has become a leader in each of its local fine-dining markets. . . . And the company is frequently cited as having upgraded the standards of the entire industry."

CHAPTER 19

The Early Leaders

Four Seasons had many leaders who were pivotal to our early success, for no one person creates an exceptional company alone, especially one such as ours, where dishwashers stay because they're treated with respect and, like vice presidents, contribute by giving their best.

I had been lucky with our first three hotels in hiring Ian Munro, who continually gave his employees a perfect example of how to treat customers. Ian, a first-rate professional, got us off to a fine start. He not only taught me the business; he was such a delight to work with that I came to enjoy my role as hotelier.

But Ian changed, and I can recall when the change first caught my attention: our very successful opening of the Inn on the Park in London. Everyone had gone to bed except Ian and me. We were having a quiet drink in the dining room when Ian began to say things like, "This is the world I come from, but I can't do it. I can't deal with royalty. I'm not in their class."

I made light of what he was saying. "This is no big deal," I told him. "We're not dealing with royalty as such. When royalty is staying with us, they're just guests like anyone else."

Ian at that time was dealing with personal matters that were taking a toll on his work. He stayed with the company until 1976, and soon afterward he died. He was the most important person in Four Seasons' early success. It's a shame he couldn't be around to see the final results.

Our next most essential leader in our early days was Michael Lambert. I had hired Michael as Ian's successor several years before, when I first realized Ian's problem was serious. Michael was highly qualified. He had more hotel experience than any of our people, and as vice president of hotel operations, he brought in numerous members of his previous company, Westin Hotels, setting up the beginning of our organizational structure. In 1983 I sent him over to Singapore to work with B. S. Ong in selecting sites for hotels in financial centers of Asia and Europe. But nothing came of these ventures. Michael then left Four Seasons, and was succeeded by another lifelong hotel professional, John Sharpe.

John was exceptional. In his two years as general manager of our Ritz-Carlton in Chicago, he turned a 1978 operating loss of $3.5 million into a profit of $6.5 million in 1981. And John was already establishing the systems and controls that a highly efficient hotel business requires.

John and I made a good team. He was always concerned about what might go wrong, and I was sometimes a little too optimistic: a nice balance, since we shared similar beliefs and values. It was John, with whom I worked closely, who helped lay a rock-solid company foundation, not only in operations but also in

With Ian Munro, who taught us how to take care of guests in first-class style.

hiring the type of managers we needed to train employees properly.

In 1982 we hired several people who have also played an important role in our growth. One was John Young, executive vice president of human resources. With twenty-eight years of professional experience in Europe and North America, John brought us badly needed expertise in his field: training manuals, policies, and systems. In each of our hotels, he personally ensured that all staff members understood their roles. I often refer to John as our architect of the human resources department.

That same year, we had the very good fortune to employ Roger Garland as our chief financial officer. Roger was outstanding, putting in place the financial structure needed to properly control and manage our business: the knowledge and expertise we previously didn't have.

Three years later, Arnie Cader left us to begin his own consulting business, and I asked Roger to take his place as executive vice president in charge of development and finance.

"You're asking the impossible," Roger said. "I've no idea how to do Arnie's job. I'm not a developer, I'm just an accountant, a finance guy."

I explained that Arnie was not a developer either at first. "It's not something you learn in college," I told him. "It's something you learn on the job."

When he still objected, I said, "Look, Roger, I'll be here to help you deal with it. By working together, I'm confident you'll gain the insight you need."

With some misgivings, Roger accepted and soon excelled in development as he had in finance. The new position gave him authority equal to that of John Sharpe, the two working hand in hand as partners rather than rivals.

Roger then promoted Doug Ludwig to be chief financial officer. Doug joined Four Seasons in 1984, having worked on our audit while at KPMG, and when we went public in 1985, he handled our affairs with great capability, representing the company very effectively. After twenty years with us, he resigned to pursue other options.

Two years later, we brought in John Richards and Barbara Talbott from the celebrated Royal Viking Cruise Line, where in just three years John built a marketing organization that substantially increased Royal Viking's revenues. Our previous experiences in marketing and sales had been disappointing. When Richards heard this on joining us as senior vice president of marketing, he revamped the department, installing new systems and staff, and created a marketing organization highly respected within the company.

John left in the late nineties to go to Starbucks, where he became president. Barbara Talbott took over and, working with Susan Helstab, continued to build our sales and marketing department to what is now recognized as the best in the luxury hospitality industry. For this important achievement, Barbara was awarded, in 2007, the prestigious Albert E. Koehl Award, which recognizes individuals who have made significant contributions to advertising and marketing in the hospitality business.

An important early member of our team was Chris Wallis, hired in 1972. Chris had never built a hotel until he worked with me in London, so I took him under my wing, passing on to him everything I knew. He learned so quickly that he was soon a one-man hotel construction department. From 1973 on, as senior vice president of design and construction, he supervised, with exceptional competence, the design and quality of every hotel we built during the remainder of the century. He blended knowledge, diligence, creativity, and common sense, setting a standard that raised the performance of everyone he worked with.

Chris died of cancer in May 1999, a grievous shock and a major loss. For more than thirty years, he and I had worked together. Great hotels in a score of countries bear his imprint. These will be his tangible legacy, but he left us something of more consequence: what some of us called "the Chris Wallis way," a style of leadership so quietly efficient, so devoid of ostentation, so considerate of others' opinions that he was a positive influence on all who worked for or with him. He was a highly important contributor to making us the best.

I can't think of anyone else who has worked around the world with so many types of people in so many different cultures and won so much esteem and affection. As I told Chris before he died, "You will not be forgotten. Your influence on those you worked with will go on and on indefinitely." That's Chris's real legacy.

The last but by no means least meaningful of our people at this time is Nan Wilkins, my administrative assistant. I was very fortunate in hiring previous assistants. Her predecessors, the capable, energetic Carol Cruikshank and the bright and proficient Patricia Moore, were both invaluable to me before they left. Carol set up her own business. Pat went on working for Arnie Cader, for when Arnie first joined the company, I reluctantly lent him Pat to acquaint him more quickly with Four Seasons. Incidentally, she's still with him, his strong right hand.

Just after Christmas of 1981, I needed someone equally good. Michael Lambert had a secretary who worked for him at Westin International Hotels. Someone with hotel experience, I felt, could be useful, and I asked Michael to call her and set up an interview.

He called and was told that she'd just begun a new job, secretary for a

Nan Wilkins, my loyal helpmate, whom I can't live without. Friends and associates have said, "The person you need to know at Four Seasons is not Issy; it's Nan."

Fred Eisen, 1930–2007, one of the original Four Seasons partners, was married to my sister Beatrice. Fred had a genial, willing manner and patience in dealing with bureaucracy. He organized a plebiscite to bring liquor to North York, which was important for the success of the Inn on the Park.

senior partner at KPMG. And although she wasn't interested in leaving it, she said she'd come in for an interview.

This lasted two hours, for it was important to me. I wanted not only to know her; I also wanted her to know me, for unless she enjoyed her job, it wouldn't work out. So I told her about the company, what we were doing, where we were going, about my family, my philosophy, what I believed in. Then I asked about her.

She was British, with no desire to leave Canada. She was obviously intelligent, well mannered, and an excellent listener, never interrupting, talking only to answer my questions.

"What are your goals in life?" I asked her. "What do you most want to do?"

She said she loved her secretarial role and intended to make it a lifetime job.

"Well, one thing you must understand," I told her. "This is a dead-end

Edmund Creed is married to my sister Edie. He built up the reputation of the famous ladies' department store Creeds in Toronto to the highest degree of luxury. Eddie has always been a great adviser and supporter of me and Four Seasons. He is a measured thinker and a cultivated man, so luxury and quality came naturally to him. Recently he brought us a deal for a hotel in the Dominican Republic and is enjoying watching its construction near his home there.

Murray Koffler, best friend of Eddie Creed, has had a life of great success in both business and philanthropy. He founded Shoppers Drug Mart and invented the mega drugstore. At Four Seasons he had great ideas and was a solid partner.

job. There's no promotion from here to anywhere else in our company. So if sitting here working with me will satisfy your career aspirations, you've got a job if you want it."

"That will suit me fine," she said.

I believe it has. It's certainly worked for me. Nan organized my life with new-to-me professional office systems that now I can't operate without. For twenty-six years, she has been an integral part of my success.

Entrepreneurship often breaks down when a company starts to expand. I believe one of the reasons we've been able to make such a move with only minor mishaps is because I've had people like all those I've just men-

*Max Sharp, 1902–2004, the most tolerant man
I've known, kind and loving to the end of his
102 years.*

tioned. They've brought experience and innovation, filling in any gaps I might have left, enabling us to keep things running smoothly.

But in getting the business started, our original partners—Murray Koffler, my brother-in-laws, Eddie Creed and Fred Eisen, and my father— were very much a part of our success. Their early financial support, participation, and influence were a primary contribution to our progress. It was a business affiliation sealed only with a handshake. There was never a written contract—nor a meaningful disagreement.

First and foremost, of course, was the influence of my father, for he taught me how vital people are to success in business. Dad was the most tolerant, kindest, and most positive-thinking person I've ever known. His example and his unquestioning and unconditional faith in me are the underlying reasons for whatever I have achieved.

Michael Lambert, an Englishman of taste and wit, followed Ian Munro as vice president of operations.

John Sharpe rose from general manager to president. He was bright, funny, and very popular. Every administrative assistant wanted to sit at his table at the Christmas party. In another life he could have been a doctor or, with his outrageous sense of humor, a stand-up comic.

John Young, executive vice president of human resources, was the architect of a department that was new to the company. As sensitive as a therapist, he identified with the needs of his staff.

Roger Garland, deputy chairman, was a solid link in the company chain. He traveled the world and stood for Four Seasons as if the company were his own.

Arnie Cader is very bright, personable, and a canny negotiator who did well for us in deal making.

Doug Ludwig became chief financial officer. He was great on his feet, identifying the company's strengths for shareholders.

John Richards, executive vice president of marketing, was an MBA who won us all over with his affable Wharton know-how. He put Four Seasons on the map.

Chris Wallis headed up design and construction with loving care. He followed my example with dogged faithfulness. He was very tall and Cary Grantish, yet he wrote out scrupulous details in a tiny hand on each set of plans. He is still remembered with love.

The extended family, 2002.

CHAPTER 20

Family Developments

As the Four Seasons family grew, my own family was busy with some impressive accomplishments of their own.

From the time that I had resolved to make hotels my primary business, Rosalie had decided to join me as a designer. Knowing the artistry and taste she'd demonstrated in decorating our first two homes, I was all for it. But her children still came first, and after all these years, I remember exactly what she said: "When they come back from school at noon, I want to be home to hear them say, 'Mom, what's for lunch?'"

She had put her career on the back burner until Tony, our youngest, was three, old enough to attend nursery school. Then she applied to take some courses part time at the Ontario College of Art, but the school, at that time, accepted only full-time students.

Rosalie was distraught. For years, she had been looking forward to a professional education that would make her an accredited interior designer with Four Seasons. But she wasn't about to neglect the children by attending school full time.

I took her out to dinner to try to comfort her, suggesting she pay the full college tuition and go to school on her own schedule. "Nobody fails for attendance," I said, "but you'll learn design."

She decided on a tighter schedule. For four years, she drove the kids to school every morning, went to college every day, and was home at four o'clock when the boys arrived. She describes her first three months in *Rifke: An Improbable Life* as "frenetic and fractured . . . between homework and homemaking there were many days when I almost quit. But I would say to myself, just hold on for another week, maybe it will get easier."

Surprisingly, it did. Four years later, in 1969, Rosalie graduated with two medals, the Lieutenant Governor's Medal and the Art Gallery of Ontario Medal, coming in second in marks and awards out of 240 graduates. I was happy for her, as well as extremely proud, but I wasn't at all surprised. She had always been an exceptional student, first in her class at school, and I looked forward to seeing her talents embellish our hotels.

Yet even after graduating, she reluctantly decided not to go to work for me yet, still believing she should stay home for the children. But there was nothing to stop her working at home.

She set up Green Valley Workshop in a design study we built adjoining our house on Toronto's Green Valley Road, and she began screen-printing color fabrics commercially, eventually supplying the contract division of Simpson's, a Toronto retailer.

Then, in the early seventies, she opened Rosalie Wise Design (RWD). Her first job was for my company, which was still doing real estate projects as well as hotels. She designed and decorated several model apartments in a new condominium in central Toronto. A buyer liked one of the model suites so much, he bought the condo, including her furnishings.

In the beginning, while learning our business, Rosalie worked alone, going along with my requirements even though she didn't always agree. Where I decreed wallpaper, Rosalie would have used paint. I wanted a quilted bedspread; she would sooner have had a duvet. And when I ruled that we would use curtains and a valance, she found the valance too fussy. Rosalie was generally somewhat ahead of her time, so it usually took me a while to catch up to her ideas.

But not always. In Four Seasons Washington's model guest room, she varied our typical layout by replacing the two lounge chairs with one chair and a footstool, putting our standard desk at right angles to the wall with a chair on either side. This became not only a Four Seasons standard, but a standard of many other hotel companies.

Rosalie's first big design job was in 1982, for Four Seasons Houston: guest rooms, corridors, and suites, the decor a mixture of antiques, with crystal and modern glass tables and lamps. Her work had begun to express her own ideas.

Rosalie designed many, many hotels for us. And we were not the only company that hired her. One client, the Prince Hotel, flew her five times in one year to Nagasaki in Japan, where she designed the interior of a large hotel: four hundred rooms with five restaurants. Restaurants and ballrooms were Rosalie's favorite projects because, she says, they can be "capricious, whimsical, or theatrical."

In the restaurant of Le Quatre Saisons in Montreal in 1994, she displayed swivel office chairs on wheels. She wanted the floors to be polished cement, which I vetoed. Now both of these design ideas have become fashionable.

In the nineties, Rosalie came up with a winning idea for one of our restaurants at Four Seasons Toronto, which she named the Studio Café. Glass as an art had come into vogue, and Rosalie wanted to support Toronto's glass artists, as well as come up with something novel and elegant for the restaurant. But her restaurant budget was much too small to buy preeminent work, the best of which was selling for thousands of dollars.

Rosalie telephoned a group of artists, brought them into the hotel and showed them her drawing of large glass-shelved display cabinets, one for each craftsperson. "I will pay you twenty-five hundred dollars," she said, "just to fill it with your work, preferably your best. Put your name and telephone number on the bottom and we'll put it up to show and sell your glasswork. All you'll need to do is deal with your customers and replace sold items to keep the cabinet looking good."

"It will never work," I said. But I was wrong. One of the best of the top-priced artists, Toan Klein, who had been skeptical of her idea, sold two pieces in the first week, and for each sale, he sent Rosalie a bouquet of flowers.

Ten years later, artistic glass is still selling well. It has not only given glass artists much-needed support; it's been a boon for our restaurants, because the cabinets are always changing, giving the restaurant a fresh look.

As the nineties ended, after eighteen years of interior design, Rosalie lightened her schedule to write a memoir and a book on ceramics. But she still continues to take on new projects from time to time, including a restaurant in Four Seasons Toronto.

As our business expanded, I sometimes regretted that none of our sons would be taking over. But I think that was because, as they were growing up, I didn't have much of a business to tell them about, and they were encouraged to follow their own inclinations. They often came to see me at my office at the Inn on the Park, but since they'd always known me as a builder, they didn't understand what my business there was all about. One Saturday morning, I was in the office, meeting with an executive from the Rouse Corporation, a major Chicago construction company, when the door flew open and the four boys burst in. Without so much as a hello, they rushed to the corner cabinet, took out their bathing suits, peeled off their clothes, left them in a heap, and ran out the door, all within a few minutes.

For several moments, my visitor was speechless. Then he said, "I was impressed by your clean desk when I came in, thinking all your papers must be in that corner cabinet, but I see you keep more important items there."

By the time I had a thriving business, the boys were well into their teens, and I now believe that if you want your children to follow you, you have to talk about it and interest them in it at a fairly early age. Having said that, however, I really have no regrets. Our sons are following their feelings, doing what they want to do, which I consider much more important.

Our oldest son, Jordan, never even considered joining Four Seasons. If there's an afterlife I'd like to come back as Jordy. He has had the adventures I only fantasized about. He once drove from London to Athens across the French Alps on a motorcycle. Along the way, one rainy night in Dubrovnik, he slipped on greasy black pavement crossing a busy intersection. He thought the end had come as honking cars screeched to a halt in a circle of headlights all around him.

Jordy was always fond of dogs. He had picked up a mutt at the pound, named him Okanagan, and raised him to become one of the family. Being with us weekends, then watching me go to work, Okanagan developed a

ABOVE: *Okanagan at his Monday morning management meeting. Some of Four Seasons' best guests are dogs.*

CENTER: *Okanagan with a dog's best friend, Jordan.*

BELOW LEFT: *With Anthony,* left, *and Gregory,* right. *Both worked for the company for more than ten years, then moved on to follow their dreams.*

BELOW RIGHT: *The Sharp boys, from* left to right: *Anthony, Gregory, me, and Jordan.*

habit of visiting our company's office on Mondays. He would sit at our boardroom table and soon became a regular member of our committee. Once, after a meeting, I remember John Sharpe remarking, "Okanagan was the only one who didn't say anything stupid."

Jordy, a musician who formed a bluegrass troupe, was adjudged in 1992 the best banjo player in central Canada. He now lives in Hawaii and Salt Spring Island, where he's the music producer for his company, Dog My Cat Records. He has also owned and operated restaurants, including the trend-setting Santa Fe Bar & Grill, and with his uncle, Stan Wise, the Brunswick House Tavern in Toronto, which under their management enjoyed a revival.

Gregory, our second son, has an ingenious mind. Even as a youngster, he devised labyrinth games and flying machines with ropes and pulleys, persuading his six-year-old brother, Tony, to take an inaugural flight, which luckily landed him in a bush. After studying architecture at Toronto University, he joined our company in 1985. Four years later, he became director of our fledgling Management Information Service, dragging everyone kicking and screaming into the computer world. Jim Brown, our vice president of operations, was one of Greg's biggest critics. "I don't need a computer," he said, "I've got everything I need on paper."

"Jim, the mind is like a parachute," Greg told him. "It only works when it's open." And Jim eventually became the computer's greatest advocate.

Greg designed two software programs, Hansard and Plan-it, which served us well for many years. After eleven years with the company, Greg left to start his own software firms, continuing to experiment.

Our third son, Christopher, wanted to quit school at sixteen and start working for Four Seasons forever: "What do I need school for? It has nothing to do with being an executive." We thought he was wrong, but in retrospect it wasn't a bad idea. Sadly, Chris's dream was not to be, and I think of him every morning when I recite the Kaddish prayer in front of his photo.

Anthony, our youngest, taught himself from how-to books to play chess, work an abacus, and write Pitman shorthand. At Yale he made the dean's list, and he made valuable contributions to our company's growth in Europe and with vacation ownership.

In 1999, after nearly eleven years with us, he came to me and said, "Dad, now that I've learned the business, I'd like to get into real estate development on my own." I was disappointed, but I understood how he felt.

Tony is doing well at what he wants to do, with time-share resorts in Niagara Falls and in Breckenridge, Colorado, where all his vacation ownerships have sold. And as his business experience deepens, he's becoming an ever-more-useful asset on Four Seasons' board.

Through the years, I have valued my boys' opinions, and I am grateful for their respect and candor.

PART V

WORLDWIDE EXCELLENCE

Having a positive mental attitude is asking
how something can be done rather than saying it can't be done.
—BO BENNETT,
businessman, author, and philanthropist

To accomplish great things we must first dream,
then visualize, then plan . . . believe . . . act!
—ALFRED A. MONTAPERT,
American author

Four Seasons Maui.

CHAPTER 21

Hawaii

In the mid-1980s the prevalent business view in America was that the economy was going nowhere and that prospects were bleak.

I didn't believe it. It might be true for the present, but I didn't think it would last. Research by the World Travel and Tourism Council had indicated that travel over the next ten years could double. I believed we had reason to look forward to the nineties as the most fruitful decade we'd ever had.

Eventually the opportunity came to expand the number of resorts, because we had customers who liked what we were doing and were loyal to us for business and leisure. We started hearing a familiar refrain from them in our hotels: Could you do this in a resort setting?

We realized it was time to go abroad, time to enter the world resort market. Corporate leaders also go on holidays, but our only resorts were in Minaki, Ontario, a little-known, barren wilderness area, and Santa Barbara, California.

For years we had been trying, with many false starts, to complete a deal for a resort in Hawaii, America's most popular vacation area. In the late 1980s, Takeshi Sekiguchi, president of a major Japanese development company, TSA International, which had many land holdings in Hawaii, approached us. Mr. Sekiguchi and his partner, Chris Hemmeter, an architect, were developing, on the island of Maui at Wailea, two resorts: a thousand-room megaresort and a four-hundred-room five-star resort. The megaresort concept was then so popular that Hemmeter was considered Hawaii's most successful architect-developer.

Takeshi Sekiguchi asked us if we would team up with them to make one of his Wailea resorts a Four Seasons. He showed me the land we would build on: fifteen acres fronting a huge, beautiful, white-sand crescent beach. This was exactly what we wanted: a world-class beach resort. It took us little time to say OK.

Mr. Sekiguchi first visualized our resort as a "palace." I wasn't exactly sure what he meant. This was a period when the megaresort was nearing the peak of its trend, everyone trying to out-spectacle everyone else, even in Hawaii. I had a different view.

My concept of our resort was unlike that of all the other hotels built or being built in Wailea. The main roads leading into them were about seventy feet above sea level, so their main lobbies and entrances were usually at this level, and access to beach and sea was either down long, winding stairs or by an elevator that cut off the view of the sea. I suggested to our architects that our driveway should curve down the hill to beach level so our guests, on arriving at the hotel, would have a striking first impression of the sparkling Pacific. Our architects complained that blasting through the lava would be difficult, resulting in delays and increased costs. But Mr. Sekiguchi agreed with our concept.

Maybe a megaresort wasn't what Sekiguchi meant when he asked for a palace, but soon it didn't matter. Our Honolulu designer, architect Kevin Chun of Wimberly Allison Tong & Goo, didn't want a high-and-mighty look any more than we did, and he toned it down to a more acceptable "palatial villa."

And palatial it was. We lined the driveway into the hotel with lush landscaping that led to a grand porte cochere opening onto a broad lobby with a panoramic view of the beach, the West Maui Mountains, and a vast expanse of Pacific Ocean with islands in the distance, and peach-colored sunsets at dusk, and sometimes a performance of flirting whales.

Four Seasons Maui was the first step in a new direction for us, and the man we picked to head a smooth beginning was Peter O'Colmain, then the young GM of Four Seasons Houston. As usual, we notified all our hotels of the opening coming up, so employees could apply for a possible transfer, and Peter picked fifty experienced people, some from our competitors, whom he paired with those from Four Seasons so they could learn how we handle things, especially service, which was still different from that of any other company.

As opening time neared, we advertised for local labor. More than three thousand applied, many with hotel experience we *didn't* want—we find that expertise is easier to learn than bad habits are to unlearn. Instead, we hired a lot of people who'd been doing backbreaking labor in the sugarcane and pineapple fields, people who we felt would appreciate clean work and nourishing meals in a healthy, attractive, air-conditioned environment. We were right. These were people with positive attitudes who soon learned their jobs and took pride in sharing their "aloha spirit" with guests.

Four Seasons Maui opened on February 9, 1990, Hawaii's most expensive hotel: $325 to $5,000 a night. But as Peter told a reporter, "Once you're here, we don't nickel-and-dime you to death." Guests got more for their dollar, with such complimentary amenities as bicycles, astronomy tours, golf clinics, hula lessons, lei-making classes, windsurfing courses for beginners, and Kids for All Seasons (our nursery school).

Within fourteen months, the resort was making money—unusual in so short a time, especially in a period when the number of hotels was doubling, occupancy rates were declining, and the average length of stay for U.S. visitors was shortening. But we had a highly superior product, and despite our high prices, we were rated number two in occupancy. *Touring & Travel* magazine called us a leader in innovation.

This confirmed our decision to create more resorts, and to make each, as always, even better than its predecessor.

CHAPTER 22

Japan

Two years after we teamed up with TSA president Takeshi Sekiguchi in Hawaii, he introduced us to the top officials of the Industrial Bank of Japan (IBJ), with whom he personally had close connections. Over the years, I had had many meetings with the bank's top executives, including its chairman, Kisaburo Ikeura.

At one of my earliest luncheons with Mr. Ikeura, I had an amusing conversation (as always, through an interpreter, although I secretly believe he understood English). He explained some of the history of Japanese warlords and shoguns, describing how, when they ventured from their protected palaces to meet rivals, they would exchange wives to be held as hostages to ensure each shogun a safe return. Later in our conversation, he said he would like to meet my wife. Would I bring her over on our next visit?

"I'll bring her," I said, "providing you don't keep her as a hostage."

He burst out laughing, jumped up, grabbed both my hands, and told me, "We will do much business together."

And we did, teaming up with Sekiguchi again to build several other hotels: on the Big Island of Hawaii, as well as in Puerto Rico and Aviara in California. (Unfortunately, when the bubble burst in 1990, TSA was unable to proceed with these projects.) But what was probably our most important deal with the Industrial Bank of Japan was in 1987, while we were still building in Maui. The bank's director and general manager, Shuichiro Tamaki, arranged for us to meet the president of Fujita Tourist Enterprises Company Ltd.

Fujita was a major holding company, one of Japan's foremost travel and hospitality organizations, with fifty or more budget hotels. They came to us

Four Seasons Chinzan-so (camelia), set in a beautiful old garden, in Tokyo.

because Four Seasons was gaining recognition as one of the best hotel companies in North America, and they wanted us to build them a top luxury hotel to raise the quality and earnings of their lucrative wedding business, which already brought in sales of about $100 million a year.

Such joint ventures were becoming the wave of the future, the fastest, cheapest, and sometimes the only way to penetrate cultural and political barriers abroad. It was obvious that Japan was where we needed to be. A first-class hotel in the financial center of the leading region in Asia would give us a springboard for development, something we could never do on our own. Even though we had several people who spoke Japanese, there were just too many cultural problems: finding the right suppliers, hiring employees, advertising. For all these reasons and more, the prudent way to enter such a foreign market was through a local partner.

We sat down with Fujita's people to negotiate, with a clear idea of where we could give a little and where we couldn't. Each of us made concessions on minor points, but when it came to the crunch, it turned out they were offering us only a ten-year operating contract.

We weren't about to invest several years of work in a learning experience for Fujita. We told them we couldn't make a deal for what we considered the short term. "We've never done business that way before," I said. "We only take long-term contracts. That's our history." And on this basis, we turned down an opportunity that would probably never come again.

They let several months go by before they got back to us again, and we finally agreed to a contract they considered extremely long: forty years. But as I told them, "That's the shortest contract we've ever signed."

Partnering for the first time with one Japanese developer in Hawaii was an amicable and profitable experience. Now, for the first time, we were working with a Japanese company, and we were told how different and difficult this could be, because nothing could be accomplished unless we reached a consensus.

But the Japanese management approach, we soon found out, was much like ours. Like us, they made quality their major strategy for winning markets. Successful like us, Japanese companies shaped that strategy not on theory but on strength; there wasn't a single business school in Japan. They cooperated as intensely as they competed. They have a saying, *"Ichi-gan to natte,"* which translates roughly as "Be united." And, as we did, they put commitment to people first. Their relationships with partners, employees, customers, and suppliers were akin to the feelings and attitudes of a family.

In North America, some companies rotated purchasing agents so they didn't get buddy-buddy with suppliers, for fear of kickbacks. I found company relationships in Japan to be so close that a Japanese manufacturer might have only one supplier for any one part. And their trust in each other was such that when parts were delivered to a loading dock, they were sometimes not even counted. Japanese contracts were vague; they wouldn't stand up in Canadian courts, for in Japan they didn't have to. If an agreement wasn't working out for both parties, company managers would just talk it over and settle any differences.

If a partner was in trouble, they didn't take advantage of him. They asked, "How can we help? Can we give you a loan? Change the terms of our deal?" Their relationships were cooperative, based on trust and on comfort levels of mutual credibility. This was obviously why, compared with North Americans, they had so few lawyers: a handshake was honored; a breach of trust was a loss of status. And after working with Fujita, I finally understood why Mr. Sekiguchi waited so long to introduce us to his contacts at the Industrial Bank of Japan. If we let him down, he would have lost status, which is very important to Japanese businessmen.

Although Fujita was like Four Seasons in terms of business ethics, they didn't see that space equals luxury. In Tokyo, where space was limited, small rooms were customary and acceptable—Japanese could be seen sleeping while standing up in the subway—and Fujita expected us to cut costs by building as they did.

I studied our building plans with Chris Wallis, architect Don Fairweather of Newport Beach, California, and interior designer Frank Nicholson, our guru of space planning, who has done more of our hotels than any other designer, beginning with Calgary in 1972. The land on which we would build was a good half hour from central Tokyo, so it wasn't the best of sites for businessmen with no time to waste. And while the outer-city location could put off a few of our major customers, a recent survey had shown that the average American business executive traveled with a spouse or partner once every five trips, and for that, the site of the hotel we'd be building had no peer.

It overlooked a five-acre historical garden called Chinzan-so, the nineteenth-century home of a Japanese prince. He had brought in a ninth-century pagoda tower from a mountain temple prefecture in Hiroshima, then constructed a waterfall and a shrine to create a camellia garden so exquisite that now it drew as many as forty weddings a day. Fujita owned a huge facility there for receptions, weddings, and the sale of everything associated with nuptials, including gifts and holiday clothing. There were also a travel agency and a photographer's window featuring brides in kimono or traditional Western white wedding dress. But there wasn't anywhere for couples and guests to stay overnight.

Our research had told us that in Japan, especially in Tokyo, a hotel's food and beverage sales accounted for up to 70 percent of revenue, while in North America it was about 30 percent. And where our city competitors had the best location for bedroom business, the heavy volume of wedding and banquet business at Chinzan-so made it by far the best location for high-profit food and beverage.

The more we considered this, the more obvious it became that by building as Fujita wanted, we were building the wrong type of hotel. So working late one evening, I said to Chris and our designers, "We have to redesign this project, and we have to do it tonight."

We sketched out our ideas and presented our drawings the following morning to our local partners and their board members. "You're competing with five-star hotels on rooms here," I said. "And your location isn't as good as your downtown competitors. But if you build facilities that will bring you travelers on vacation as well as on business, we can compete head-on with the best hotels in Tokyo and come out a winner."

This wasn't what they expected to hear, especially when we recommended reducing the number of bedrooms and increasing the food and beverage facilities. That took the board by surprise: the changes we were suggesting seemed counterproductive to them because our fees would be based on bedroom revenue, not food and beverage sales. We had to do a lot of explaining to convince them that our intent was to make Four Seasons Chinzan-so the most prestigious hotel in Tokyo, which would earn much higher returns for both of us. Granted, it would cost them more than they had intended to spend. But when we assured them they'd have a hotel that could never be duplicated, that would give a higher investment return and outstrip our two Tokyo rivals, they gave us the go-ahead.

The structure still had to conform in size and height to the design originally presented, or it would have taken years to get another building permit. But we changed the interior to create a more effective and lucrative use of space.

We reduced the number of rooms from more than 500 to 283 with 51 suites, and we made them the largest and most luxurious hotel rooms in Tokyo, all with splendid views of the garden. And we priced them slightly under our five-star competitors.

More than a year before the hotel's completion, we considered staffing. This would be, for the first time, a joint procedure, so we brought over John Young to collaborate with the local human-resources people.

It was traditional for the hotel's general manager to be Japanese, because if one of Fujita's people were put in second place, he would lose face and inevitably some proficiency. We agreed that the hotel's GM would be Yuji Odagiri, a graduate of Cornell University's School of Hotel Administration, a man well equipped to bridge the cultural gap. We also put in, as second in command, one of our rising stars, William Mackay. As John Young said, "William is insightful and sensitive enough to willingly accept second place, because he knows this is our best chance to make things work."

Japanese managers were then the product of a culture different from that in the West. Their labor relations were consensual. Employees identified with their company, not their trade or profession. Their system, in fact, was much the same as the one we had created at Four Seasons. It delivered a dedicated, self-disciplined workforce.

But there were differences. In general, the Japanese worked more by rote, making employees more quickly proficient in well-defined tasks but less creative in coming up with service solutions for guests with problems. Young sent about fifty Chinzan-so staff to our North American properties for three months to a year to learn how we train our service teams to attend to all guests' needs and desires. Then we brought in about twenty of our most experienced executives, including a few familiar with Japan, to help with what Young called the final polishing.

We opened Four Seasons Chinzan-so on January 16, 1992, a city hotel with the ambience of a resort. And within a year, the Japanese-based business journal *Nikkei Resort* gave it top ranking among all Japanese hotels, ahead of Tokyo's famed Imperial Hotel.

Our Japanese partners were most congratulatory. While building their hotel, we had grown very close, and they had offered to make me an honorary director in a new and exclusive golf club, asking if I would inaugurate the club's opening by playing its first round.

"I don't play golf," I said, "but I'll bring my father to play that opening round." And because it is Japanese tradition to revere one's elders, they were quite pleased by that.

Shortly before the hotel opened, at one of their many very elaborate receptions, one of the bank's advisers, a Japanese American, said to me, "Do you realize they included you in what they call the inner circle and that very few non-Japanese are recognized in that way?"

I was touched by this recognition, and despite the many industrial and corporate changes in Japan, I retained a relationship with the people we met at that time, especially Shuichiro Tamaki of the Industrial Bank of Japan, with whom I had such rapport that I asked him to join the Four Seasons board. He agreed, and for fourteen years, we had the benefit of his experience in a part of the world he knew well, helping us expand in Hawaii and the Far East.

Four Seasons Chinzan-so quickly attracted widespread attention in Asia, where we had been largely unknown. "What these two partners have done," Hiro Yamanake, executive director of Y.B.S. Travel Agency Ltd., told *International Business Communications,* "is very, very smart. They have combined their strengths. Four Seasons brings in international business travel and the upscale overseas vacation traveler, while Fujita handles domestic reservations and provides a steady flow of guests from their wedding activities."

For both Fujita and Four Seasons, it was a great deal. They could never have built such a hotel, and we could never have built it alone, for the price of commercial land in Tokyo was exorbitant: ¥35.3 million per square *meter.* At the time we formed our partnership, the value of land in central Tokyo on which the Imperial Palace stood was commonly considered to be equal to all the land in California.

With Chinzan-so, we expanded our brand name in Eastern Europe and the Pacific Rim, now the fastest-growing market in the world.

CHAPTER 23

The Caribbean

I was at dinner at Four Seasons Istanbul with its owner, Mr. Osman Berkmen, and his wife, Nuteyra. "Where," Mrs. Berkmen asked, "do you get all of your employees?"

My answer was that I was sure that 99 percent of them came from local villages and the community.

"No, *these* are not Turkish people," she said, referring to the restaurant's waitstaff. "I have Turkish people working for me, and these are *not* Turkish people."

Our general manager, Marcos Bekhit, was with us, so I asked him where the employees came from.

"Of course they come from the local villages and community," he said.

I explained to Mrs. Berkmen that this is typical when we open a hotel and that we are careful in the hiring process to hire people who have the right attitude. We then create a work environment that allows them to be very natural in their behavior. This is typical in most countries: people respond when given an opportunity. Four Seasons Nevis is one of the most striking examples of this.

While building hotels in Japan and Hawaii, we were also working in the Caribbean on what became one of our most important hotels of that period—because it showed us how to develop hotels in parts of the world we knew little about.

This was a deal that began in Paris in the mideighties. We were partners with the Dumez Corporation, one of the two biggest construction firms in France, well known for having built the Chunnel between London and Paris. They owned property on Le Bois de Boulogne in Paris, a fine site on which we hoped to build a hotel we urgently wanted. Unfortunately, it was

Four Seasons Nevis, voted best hotel in the world in 1995 by Condé Nast Traveler.

close to a school that didn't want a hotel nearby, and because of that and other complications, the deal, on which our company had worked for several years—and Rosalie's company for a year on the interior design— eventually fell through. But one of the Dumez partners also owned land in the Caribbean, a coconut plantation on the former British West Indian island of Nevis. They suggested this could make a good site for a Four Seasons resort.

We knew nothing of Nevis, nor did anyone we asked. So John Sharpe flew down and looked it over. It's a small island, thirty-six square miles, two miles southeast of the larger, affiliated island of St. Kitts, where many Canadians went for holidays. "Only three or four places in Nevis take in tourists," John told us, "small, family-run operations, each only ten or twelve rooms." Actually, I learned later, these were old historic colonial buildings, and the largest, up on the hillside, had fifteen rooms and a stunning view of cloud-wreathed Mount Nevis. This small hotel was built with a remarkable wood called lignum vitae, which doesn't float, burn, or rot, actually becoming harder over time.

But John was right in saying there was nothing to do in Nevis but swim, fish, read, take a walk, or laze in the sun. John disliked sun and heat. He perspired so much that he broke out in a rash. He didn't think much of Nevis as a site for a resort.

Wolf Hengst, in charge of our Texas and East Coast hotels at that time, flew down with John on another trip, and, as Wolf explained to me, "We had to change at Anguilla to a little four-seater plane, which landed amid chickens and roosters on an unpaved Nevis runway, then taxied up to a one-room tin-roofed airport."

The Dumez construction foreman picked them up in his jeep and drove them over narrow old roads to the Dumez site. "It was like stepping back in time," Wolf said, recommending that we build a Nevis resort.

It was not a popular opinion. Most of our corporate team weren't sure that Nevis was a wise choice. "No one knows it," they said. "It hasn't even got an international airport." But Roger Garland, who also made a trip down, thought it had great beauty and potential, and he convinced Rosalie and me to go to Nevis with him and check it out.

We did, and as the three of us walked barefoot along a beach bordered by acacias, we agreed with Roger. The island was certainly beautiful, and we were made to feel most welcome. We signed a deal with Dumez and the lieutenant governor of Nevis in ninety-degree heat, surrounded by enthusiastic islanders, in an ancient building that gave Nevis a historical claim to fame, as the birthplace of Alexander Hamilton, the first U.S. secretary of the treasury. Nevis was also known as Admiral Horatio Nelson's operational base in the war with France, during which time he married a Nevisian girl, Fannie Nisbett. At that time, Nevis was a headquarters for the slave trade, with ten times the current population.

With the governor's approval, we could now begin building, but we needed a manager. John Stauss, assistant general manager at Four Seasons Newport Beach, expressed an interest in managing a resort. He was due for a promotion, so we asked if he'd like to be GM of a tropical resort in Nevis.

"I'd love to," he said. "Where is it?" This from a man who knew the Caribbean well and had worked for years in Mustique and St. Lucia.

John, of course, had to get an OK from his wife, then expecting their second child. "We'll go," he said, repeating what she had told him, "if we can have a goat."

This amused our people at the head office. "How many goats does he want?" someone asked. But in a place like Nevis, it was simply common sense for parents to ensure that their youngsters would have fresh milk.

We sent the Stauss family to Nevis as soon as we started building. They found it undeveloped: electricity, totally unreliable; roads, deficient; cars, few. Many people used donkeys, the most practical transportation. Others carried parcels balanced on their heads.

The population had been steadily falling for years. Nevis was not only little known, it had little employment to offer its young people. Most of them left the island before or just after finishing school. The population had dropped to nine thousand people: three thousand too old to work, three thousand too young, and three thousand from which the hotel could build a team of about five hundred employees for the opening.

Stauss began teaching classes after school: accounting, food service, golf maintenance, and other functions, noting the capabilities of each student. He explained to each class the structure of a hotel, describing every position, and as they graduated, he selected groups of as many as twenty, sending them to our hotels in Canada and the United States to learn their jobs in anticipation of the opening.

"I'd never seen potential employees so willing, so caring," Stauss told us, "young people in their late teens and early twenties who really wanted to learn and train, eagerly looking forward to a job."

John was now doing his best to see that we got off to a good start, which included dealing with the government and improving the infrastructure. And after his visits to the high school and hospital, the school principal, the hospital matron, and several government employees all asked, "Can I get a job at the hotel?"

"Doing what?" John asked.

"Anything" was the usual answer.

John told Premier Sim Daniel, "You should know that some qualified people from your public institutions have asked for a job in our hotel."

"Give them a job," Daniel said.

"But what will that do to your infrastructure?" John asked.

"If they are looking, then they are planning to leave," Daniel said. "If they want a job, give them a job and keep them on the island."

So John started hiring and training some of these people, some as mid-level managers and some to be the first department heads. Before long, he was told that seven such people wanted to meet with him. Wondering what had gone wrong, he asked them to come to his office.

They came in and closed the door. "Look, Mr. Stauss," their spokesman said, "we realize what you're trying to do but we're not interested. We don't want to be managers. We just want work."

John now understood. The community was closely integrated. They all knew each other. Many were interrelated. If anyone, as a manager, reprimanded someone, that person's wife or husband would be on his doorstep right after work, saying, "What makes you think you're better than anyone else?" His staff would first have to learn to live as managers.

We began work on the site in August 1989, and on September 7, John, who was using a renovated ruin behind the Bank of Nevis as a preopening office, hired our first employee, Fay Walters, from a secretarial college in St. Kitts. John told her that as his preopening receptionist, she would have to be a role model for subsequent employees, always coming in at 8:00 A.M. on the button, always looking professional and attentive, always coming across as someone who enjoyed her work. All of this she promised to do.

Ten days later, on September 17, Hurricane Hugo swept across Nevis. Many of the island's homes, small hotels, farms, and commercial buildings in Charlestown, the tiny capital, took a destructive battering.

The following Monday morning, when John went to check on his office, Fay Walters was there. It was 8:00. She was sitting at her desk, immaculately dressed and attentive, surrounded by debris in a room with no roof, no electricity, and all her files blown away.

"What in the world are you doing here?" John said he asked her.

"Well, you told me if you hired me, I'd have to come to work on time looking smart and happy." She demonstrated an admirable sense of duty typical of many Nevisians John would hire during the following year.

John had been up all night. He and John Sharpe had known for a week that Nevis was on Hugo's path, and Sharpe asked Stauss to travel around the island compiling a list of those items most needed if and when the hurricane struck. With the help of the hospital matron, doctors, and others, Stauss sent Sharpe the list.

And so Sharpe began, early on Monday the week before, to mobilize our corporate staff and our two Toronto hotels to collect food, clothing, and everything else vital to people in Nevis. Our company parking lot was used as a staging area where transport trucks brought in what we asked for, so that our volunteer headquarters' staff could sort everything out, packaging and clearly labeling children's, women's, and men's clothing, loading it on trucks, and dispatching it to Pearson International Airport, where Air Canada agreed to fly it down free of charge.

Tuesday, our staffers worked all day and evening, a response so quick and generous that by Wednesday those Nevisians who most needed help received their first four tons of necessities.

On Sunday, Sharpe and his corporate team went out to the airport and personally assisted loading the goods on the plane. And when these boxes arrived in Nevis, Stauss told us, "It was a very emotional moment to see hundreds of boxes with labels from our sister hotels. So much caring from so many people."

We also got the Royal York and other Toronto hotels to contribute aid. All told, we sent down forty-five tons of relief supplies: water purification tablets, food, generators, axes, flashlights, lanterns, blankets, bathrobes. Years afterward, driving through Nevis, you could see Four Seasons bathrobes hanging on the local clotheslines.

That was the first aid to reach the Caribbean area after Hugo, coming in well in advance of relief supplies from FEMA, the U.S. emergency agency. And because we sent in so much, we were able to leave a portion in Antigua and St. Kitts, which were hit equally hard.

Our prompt response to Hugo was a major factor in correcting the negative opinion of expatriate business leaders then held by some politicians on Nevis and St. Kitts. As we later learned, they first considered us just another set of investors who for decades had come down with promises of developments that never came to pass. When, after Hugo, the prime minister of St. Kitts was asked by FEMA, "What do you need?" he replied, "A Four Seasons hotel."

Hurricane Hugo held up construction on the Nevis resort for some six months, but John Stauss made good use of this time, continuing to train the Nevisian staff.

I don't think many hoteliers could have achieved what John accomplished in his two and a half years of work prior to our opening. Most of his restaurant servers had no understanding of how to set a formal table or even the purpose of multiple cutlery. When John told them to ask a customer who wanted tea, "What kind would you prefer?" most admitted they hadn't known there *was* more than one kind. Few kitchen employees had ever seen, let alone used, an electric dishwasher, and the housekeepers were not used to electric clothes washers.

We had other unusual problems. As the hotel's opening grew near, Premier Sim Daniel asked Sharpe and Stauss to have dinner with him, during which he announced that we couldn't have a dock.

"Yeah, right," Sharpe said, thinking the premier must be joking, for a dock was essential for bringing over people flying in from Puerto Rico to St. Kitts, from which we would bring them to Nevis by boat.

But the premier wasn't joking. Throughout the Caribbean, and certainly in Nevis, taxi drivers had a very powerful lobby, and they wanted our guests arriving by boat to disembark at the old dock in town so they could drive them to the hotel.

We then declared that unless we could bring our guests by boat directly to our beach, we'd stop construction. The contentious matter of the dock was then taken to parliament, whose members duly voted in our favor.

In the end, the taxi drivers still did well. Many visitors wanted to see the island and hired cabs for long trips. The drivers then earned much more than ever before.

By the beginning of February 1991, the resort was almost ready to open, a half mile of cottages and a large main building low enough to be sheltered by the palms on Pinney's Beach. This was something we'd never designed before: a hotel that blended completely with its natural environment. Our architects and interior designer Frank Nicholson built it in keeping with the low-slung old plantation houses, and our lobby and the 196 rooms had only an expanse of ocean and white sand beach on one side, Mount Nevis on the other, and in between a dense tropical rain forest. This would be the first new luxury resort in the Caribbean for many years, and it would set a new standard for the entire region.

Our research, both before and after Maui, told us that people choose a resort with sport options. In Nevis we included things then rare in the Caribbean: an eighteen-hole golf course designed by Robert Trent Jones Jr., ten fully equipped tennis courts, including a Peter Burwash instruction program, courts for volleyball, croquet, and shuffleboard, even a field for cricket, as well as all the best beach equipment and boats of various sizes for deep-sea fishing and special cruises.

As opening day neared, John mustered the people he would need, including some eighty experienced employees from other Four Seasons hotels. Each of the expats and local managers were employed on one condition: that they sign a commitment to community service that would benefit the island as a whole, such as volunteering at the hospital or coaching Little

League baseball teams. Becoming good citizens, we felt, would not only help the island but also counteract the negative images of some previous U.S. and British companies.

The resort opened on February 15, 1991, and although the opening was the same week as the first Gulf War, which had a substantial impact on all international travel, it still was a very successful beginning. Travel writers enthused about it, our service in particular.

Four Seasons Nevis was open about a year when I asked John Stauss, "To what do you attribute our success in creating such a competent workforce? Most of your people had never worked in a hotel before, and many others had never worked anywhere."

"I think I can put it in two words," John replied. "Patience and understanding."

At the time, I was staying in one of our cottages along the beach, and I ordered room service. A young lady came in with my order and set it up on the terrace. "Where did you learn to do this?" I asked her. "What job did you have before?"

"Oh, I never worked before," she told me. "This was my first job, sir."

"Then how did you learn to do this? There are a lot of items, and everything's here, placed exactly as it should be."

"Well, sir, they taught me everything."

"That's interesting," I said. "How did they do that?"

And she explained, "They let me take everything home for me to practice with my family."

I began to realize what John had meant by patience and understanding. He had put in place a training program for people with absolutely no conception whatever of international hotel service, let alone how to achieve it. He had done this through judging, by attitude, whom we should or shouldn't hire, then patiently helping them understand how and why we did things, and doing this in a way that wouldn't make them reluctant to go on asking questions until they got it right.

The resort's success brought many positive things for Nevis and its citizens. The local government enhanced its electric and telephone companies. It expanded the water supply, built new roads, new schools. With the salaries they now earned, more Nevisians could build new houses and buy cars. With these developments, the government was also eligible to receive support from international aid programs, which financed an airport, further construction of roads and bridges, and a large deep-water seaport.

On November 19, 1999, Hurricane Lenny did so much damage that it closed the resort for a year. That was followed by a third hurricane that closed us down for another six months. We lost money on the hurricanes, but Nevis gave us much more—not only pre- and post-hurricane profits year after year, but also a hotel and a wider accomplishment of which we will always be proud.

Our success in Nevis told us that we need have no concern about delivering Four Seasons service anywhere in the world. We could carefully hire local people and give them the opportunity to master our standards, delivered in their own sincere way—just as John Stauss and his team had done in Nevis.

And that was what we would do from now on in establishing hotels in the world's most exotic but underdeveloped areas.

CHAPTER 24

Europe

For more than twenty years, we tried acquiring hotels in Europe. It was a long, formidable, expensive struggle, because our name was largely unknown; few Europeans equated our Inn on the Park in London with Four Seasons.

And Europe wasn't like North America, where empty city land on which to build could usually be found. In Europe every suitable site was taken. We searched in all the major cities—Madrid, Paris, Venice—finding just one site, in Rome.

In early 1972, I met a young real estate developer who drove me around in his sports car wearing black gloves although it was eighty degrees Fahrenheit. He showed me possible sites and what he had built, nothing too remarkable, though he proudly told me, "I've done all this, and I'm only forty years old." Then he asked me what I had done. I explained that the latest I had worked on was London's Inn on the Park and that I'd built the Four Seasons Sheraton in Toronto. And when he asked my age, I said I was thirty-nine. I remember this so well because the next day, October 8, I was forty.

Eventually we made a deal to build a four-hundred-room hotel on one of the seven hills of Rome. Our partner was a major Italian company, Condotte d'Acqua. Webb, Zerafa and Menkes drew up the plans. But it took seven confrontational years to get construction well under way, starting and stopping time after time to get approvals from politicians. We finally gave up, because it was shown that our building would block the view of the Vatican in a way that was objectionable to a few landowners. I sold our interest back to our partners and decided I now understood what they meant when they said, "Rome wasn't built in a day."

From time to time throughout the eighties, we followed up on leads and rumors of hotels for sale, talking to consultants, developers, and bankers, explaining the kind of projects we had in mind. Sometimes developers had come to us with ideas, but in almost every prospective case, their site or budget was inappropriate for a five-star Four Seasons. Another difficulty was that we were trying to sell Europeans a totally foreign proposition, a concept developed in North America: the idea of a management contract. Hotel owners in Europe wanted a lease and a guaranteed return that we couldn't ensure in advance.

In 1989, as eastern Europe was opening up, my youngest son, Anthony, who had an MBA from Yale, enlisted in our company's development department, which was headed by Roger Garland. Tony traveled to Europe with Roger and some of our other development people shortly after the Berlin Wall came down in late 1989. Most eastern European countries were converting to some form of capitalism, and East Berlin, though suffering from the sluggish German economy, was beginning a dramatic revitalization.

Roger discussed our situation with a British real estate consultancy group, Jones L. Wootten, which assigned one of its brightest young people, Thorsten Brudigan, a Moscow University grad, to work with Tony to find a suitable hotel site on Friedrichstrasse. The area was in the prewar business area of East Berlin, now undergoing a ferment of rebirth as developers from around the world jockeyed for position on this street near such attractions as the Opera House, the National Library, museums, cathedrals, historic monuments, and the city's finest shopping area.

One of the main blocks in the Friedrichstrasse district was earmarked for a major hotel development, so Tony and Thorsten, after assessing the area and recognizing its appeal, sought out the appropriate city planners. None of them spoke English, but Tony, who knew a little German, made a strong case based on the rising prestige of our brand name.

Competition was strong. Many firms, including Ritz-Carlton, wanted the site. But we prevailed, and the city planners gave us the right to develop a hotel on that block.

That wasn't the end of it, though. There were others who had owned that land before Hitler confiscated it. Many Jews who once lived there wanted to reclaim their property. Hypo Tirol Bank AG, an old and powerful Bavarian bank, owned a branch on a corner of that block, which would give it rights on what could be built there. Then Jones L. Wootten's British real estate consultancy group teamed up with Gerry Hines, an enterprising and influential American developer. Hines took over completely. He financed the land by bringing together a group of former landowners, satisfying both the Jews and the bank. Then he hired Professor Josef Paul Kleihues, the most prominent architect in Germany, to create for us a mixed-use development of offices, apartments, and a five-star hotel.

Four Seasons Berlin opened in September 1996 with 204 luxurious suites and guest rooms, the largest hotel in the city. It was a fine hotel, but our expectations for Berlin never materialized. It was widely assumed that the German government would move many major departments from Bonn back to Berlin, recreating it as the capital it was before the war. That never happened. Germany reunified but remained a kind of federation of cities, so that Berlin never regained the prewar dominance that would have made our hotel a worthwhile success, and seven years later, we sold it at a small loss.

Roger's next assignment for Tony was to help us get a hotel site in Prague. The Communist regime of Czechoslovakia had just been overthrown in a largely bloodless coup led by a famous writer and poet, Václav Havel, and Prague was in the early stages of trying to create an honest government of teachers, dentists, tradespeople, and other worthy citizens. But most had grown up with little knowledge of democracy and hadn't yet had time to gain enough political clout to easily contend with some less-ethical politicians who still held power.

Roger left, and Tony went on looking. He'd become friendly with a young lawyer, Yohn Tamza, who worked for a Canadian firm with a small office in Prague. Yohn introduced Tony to various government ministers, the mayor of Prague and his councilors, city planners, and property owners, a beginning that would later prove propitious.

One day, Yohn told Tony that the city had a site for sale on Golden Wenceslaus Square, a short, wide street rising up a hill in the very center of Prague. It was an outstanding location, and the city wanted a hotel built on it.

Tony hired Robin Clark to design an appropriate five-star hotel. He put that together with a financial offer for the land and a favorable description of our credentials, submitting it according to the city's rules of tender, but unfortunately, we lost.

Tony continued to meet with city politicians, officials, and consultants, and finally one of his consultants came up with a possible location. This was in downtown Prague, where the famous Charles Bridge spans the Vltava River. It was an interesting river site, incorporating three historical buildings, one each from the sixteenth, eighteenth, and nineteenth centuries, all of which had survived bombing in World War II. If we could get all three, we could build an exceptional hotel.

There were problems, of course, even more than usual.

One was that Ritz-Carlton also wanted this land. Another was buying the buildings, two owned by the city and the government and one by a family named Czechis. They had the biggest and most difficult to negotiate of the three sites, so Tony went after that first.

Here, as it turned out, he was both wise and fortunate. None of the Czechis family could speak English, but his friend Yohn Tamza negotiated for him. Mr. Czechis then hired a lawyer to represent the family, and the bargaining was so long and crucial for Mr. Czechis that he became ill. He had little money, and his lawyer was bargaining for a long-term lease that would give him several hundred thousand dollars or more a year, an extraordinary sum in his circumstances.

Eventually Tony got a deal, highly lucrative for the Czechis family and crucial for us, for Ritz-Carlton, which took the easier route, first approaching the city to buy the rights to its land, was now stymied. Tony told the city council that we now controlled the Czechis land, and if they dealt with Ritz-Carlton, they wouldn't have much of a hotel. It was obvious to our rival and the council that all three sites were required, so within a few months, the city sold us the balance of the land we needed, much larger than the Czechis site, at such a reasonable price that it offset what we had paid for the first section.

We drew up an architectural design for approval. But local architectural groups were concerned, some genuinely so, about what we might do with this important historic location, though others simply wanted to be paid for

Four Seasons Prague incorporates three historic buildings plus one modern structure.

their approval. A competition was held, but nothing was decided; they said they didn't like any of the designs. Tony believed some expected him to come to them and ask, "Whom and how much do I pay to put this through?" But because he wouldn't do this, nothing was decided. And it didn't help that President Václav Havel didn't like the idea of making these old historic buildings into a hotel. He opposed the project, speaking out against us and censuring us in the local newspaper.

The architects began to set up a second competition, so Tony brought in UNESCO, which designates heritage locations, to help get the architectural group to cooperate and perhaps set up a jury for the competition.

In the meantime, he met with city officials, explaining who we were and what we had done. Once he sent a group of city councilors and reporters to Milan to look at our hotel there, a dramatically remodeled fifteenth-century monastery on the exclusive Via Gesu, also an old and sensitive site, and that gave them illuminating impressions and us some favorable publicity.

We brought a similar delegation, including the mayor of Prague, to Toronto. I invited the mayor to our home to dine with us, and we had an engrossing and possibly useful discussion. In any case, since he'd never been to North America before, the trip for him was clearly an unforgettably pleasurable experience.

In the second architectural competition, Robin Clark hired a local architect to work with him, not only because he was needed (he had no experience with hotels), but also because he was a Czech. And because the city and the government were now mainly behind us, we finally got the necessary approvals. After a frustrating ten years, the hotel opened in February 2001.

It ended up as a somewhat small but unique hotel, which we had no problem selling as soon as it was built. Unfortunately, two years after it opened, the river overflowed its banks, as it did every hundred years or so, and we closed the hotel for eleven months. It eventually became a great success, a credit to the company, and very profitable. And that was due primarily to Tony's dogged determination to conclude a job that everyone said couldn't be done.

CHAPTER 25

More Bumps in the Road

B y late 1989, service was being depicted in the media as "the ultimate strategic imperative for the nineties" in our industry, and providing it had become our core competence. Year after year, in the annual surveys of the best hotels in North America, customers were putting us in first place. Our reputation had finally begun to pay off.

Our properties averaged 5 percent higher occupancies and up to 55 percent higher rates than our direct competitors. Our average employee turnover was less than two thirds that of comparable companies. And each year, we were getting first choice of some six hundred graduates from food service and hospitality schools, of whom we could hire only twenty.

I thought there was nothing to stand in the way of our growth, but I was wrong. On August 2, 1990, Saddam Hussein, president of Iraq, invaded his weaker neighbor, oil-rich Kuwait. The United States and the United Nations demanded that Iraq withdraw immediately. Saddam refused, and war began on January 16. Within thirty-eight days, it was over, leaving Hussein with a fractured Iraq and the Western world in a deep recession.

I think the best word to describe that period for us would be *turmoil.* And the best word for the period I saw ahead was *uncertainty.* The hotel business had never before faced a time so unpredictable.

Even before Kuwait was invaded, hoteliers had realized that eight years of growth had run its course. Costs had been rising faster than room rates, which were held down by oversupply, and we all knew that the expected recession was under way. But an imminent war was unusual. It made the last quarter of 1990 one of the worst in our industry's history.

The shooting war in the first two months of 1991 turned normality into aberration. The sudden threat of terrorism paralyzed transatlantic air traffic, and American businesses' travel bans cut attendance at intercompany meetings and conventions in the first quarter of 1991 by anywhere from one third to two thirds. TWA cut overseas service in half. Pan Am reduced seats by 45 percent.

Occupancy dropped sharply at most of our hotels. At Four Seasons Boston, for example, it fell 34.3 percent in the first quarter of 1991. Occupancy at our Inn on the Park in London dropped almost overnight, and for the first time ever, we had to temporarily cut staff.

These cuts left us shorthanded during brief flurries of activity. When our laid-off employees who had kept in touch with their fellow workers heard about this, they came in and volunteered their time. Dining-room servers stayed after their shift, voluntarily helping out at banquets. Neither group made it a big deal. No one said, "Look what we're doing for you." As I told the general manager, "They're just saying they appreciate how they've been treated over the years, so they're willing to accept and support what we have to do in bad times."

I'd assumed and declared that business would bounce back when the war ended and that this would mean great opportunity for us. I was wrong again. Australia, Britain, and Canada remained in recession for months. Credit for real estate dried up. Many companies were saddled with long-term debt. Our American business fell off, dropping our net profit from $17 million in 1990 to $2.8 million in 1991.

What happened that year had never happened before. We'd always had recessions, and we'd had terrorism threats, the previous one in 1986. But we'd never before had both at the same time, trapping the travel industry in the worst recession in memory.

Our business customers seemed to be saying, "Hey, we've been getting by with less travel; let's try to get by a little longer." Recovery was said to be under way, but it was definitely slower than usual, though I was now beginning to see our current situation as just another kind of recession— troublesome, but still a short-term problem in a long-term business. And recessions can have an upside as well as a downside. One of the problems in senior management during a long stretch of growth is that we seldom have reason to question how we operate—we're carried along by the buoyancy of the economic current, and we take it for granted that what we do is the best that can be done.

Tough times brought on by the Gulf War were testing such assumptions, forcing us to consider our response. We needed to come up with new ideas, do more with less, make short-term gains through greater efficiency, and prepare for long-term gains. That meant cutting every dollar possible in overhead and procedures while maintaining or boosting spending in three vital competitive areas.

Number one was product quality. World leadership demanded that we maintain world-class quality, and recession is generally a period when material and labor prices are lowest and room occupancies are down. So we renovated and refurbished at such normally busy properties as the Inn on the Park in London and The Pierre in New York at a time when revenue would be little affected and customers least inconvenienced. That meant we were spending when others were retrenching. We had followed that strategy in 1981–82, and the rebound from that recession had given us nine years of steady growth. I thought the odds were in our favor to score the same way again.

The second area was marketing. It's tempting during recession to cut back on consumer advertising. At the start of each of the last three recessions, the growth of spending on such advertising had slowed by an average of 27 percent. But consumer studies of those recessions had showed that companies that didn't cut their ads had, in the recovery, captured the most market share.

So we didn't cut our ad budget. In fact, we raised it modestly to gain brand recognition, which continued advertising sustains. As studies show, it's much easier to sustain momentum than restart it.

Third, we eased the workload and reduced costs by simplifying reporting methods. We set up a new system that allowed each hotel to recalculate its forecast, with minimal input, to year's end, then send it in electronically along with a brief monthly commentary. And anyone who needed it, including corporate staff in the field, had instant access through their personal computers. Recession was also a good time to prospect selectively for new developments. Land prices were down. Sellers outnumbered buyers. We now had an opportunity to look for premium locations that might soon be very costly or unattainable. Until now, we'd been more or less playing it safe, testing our capabilities. Now we knew that if we needed to, we could open five hotels in a year, so we would now be actively seeking the finest locations for global growth.

Best of all, recession had put behind us the excesses of overbuilding. Tax laws had changed. Lending requirements had tightened. Hotel construction was virtually at a standstill. Industry consultants were projecting that over the next five years, any net increase in hotel-room growth would be minimal, about 1.5 percent a year, far below the 3.5 percent growth of the eighties. And as the industry worked off its excess capacity, our occupancies, room rates, and revenues would rise, thanks to all the employees who were spearheading our growth through their continued commitment to making us number one.

The Gulf War made 1991, without question, a difficult year. But recession, as I saw it, was just a hiatus, setting the stage for a much stronger advance in the future. It had made us more cost-efficient and sharpened our focus on the customer. And looking beyond 1991, I expected that focus would be the key to continued leadership, steady growth, and profits.

CHAPTER 26

Regent

The Regent hotel chain opened its first hotel in 1970 in Oahu, Hawaii, a joint venture between Robert H. Burns and the Tokyo Corporation of Japan. Regent developed its five-star brand in Asia while Four Seasons operated the same product in North America and Europe.

Regent ran into business reversals with the collapse of the Japanese economy. By early 1991, Regent had already been up for sale for more than a year. We looked at it, but its problems, including debt load, precluded a bid. Then in late 1991, we heard that Wharf Holdings, the parent of Omni Hotels, offered to buy Regent for $100 million.

I got up early the following morning and, as always when contemplating a critical move, reconsidered, in the solitary stillness of predawn, the Regent situation as far as I then knew it. Most of that day, I discussed it with our head-office executives, following up with a great deal of necessary research.

We learned about EIE, which was put together by a onetime Japanese billionaire, Yoshinori Takahashi, who built a $5 billion portfolio comprising universities, airlines, oil, manufacturing companies, and hotels, ending up with 90 percent of Regent. But in mid-1991, Japanese interest rates had doubled, and Takahashi's bankers had taken over his company.

After much more discussion and reflection, I flew to Tokyo with Roger Garland, our executive vice president of finance, and approached Regent's bankers, led by the Long-Term Credit Bank of Japan.

We outlined a concept that at first must have seemed far-fetched. We said, in effect, "You have a billion and a half dollars invested in existing and uncompleted Regent hotels over which you have no control, and if

Four Seasons New York, 57 East Fifty-seventh Street.

Wharf Holdings buys Regent, they'll have control. But suppose you were to exercise your right of first refusal, then put up the hundred million yourself? You would then own one hundred percent of Regent. In other words, for one hundred million dollars, you will get complete control of your one and a half billion dollars in assets. And we will pay you that one hundred million if we can restructure the management contracts.

"Furthermore, because those properties are no longer worth what you paid for them, we will combine some of our real estate with yours and structure a deal that will save you from writing off those assets. And then, as Regent is linked to Four Seasons, each, as the foremost name in its sphere, will add strength to the other, and those assets will rise in value as part of a truly global hotel company that can dominate the deluxe market worldwide."

For months they investigated our record, checking all our references, including our relationship with Fujita and IBJ. They hired several top hotel consulting firms to advise them and solicited bids from other chains. It was not until all their information was in that they called us back and told us, "Yes, we are satisfied that what you said is true: You are probably the best company to handle this deal and make it a win-win proposition."

In August of 1992, they signed an agreement that gave us control of Regent—fifteen properties, most in choice Asian locations where we had no hotels and little hope of acquiring any suitable sites. Their acceptance made us the dominant high-end hotelier worldwide.

Tony Tsoi, an analyst for Toronto broker Nesbitt Thomson, seemed to see it that way too. "It was a once-in-a-lifetime deal," he told a writer for the *Financial Post*. "How often can you buy a major competitor at a reasonable price, and how often can you buy a company that will fit your long-term expansion strategy? I think the deal was made in heaven."

The Toronto stock market also approved. It pushed our shares up to $20. Analysts applauded, called it a stunning coup. They said our balance sheet was solid and our debt-to-equity ratio healthy, this despite the fact that recession the previous year dropped our earnings a shocking 84 percent. Dominion Bond Rating Service, however, concerned about the $102 million we were paying EIE, slapped a rating alert on our senior debt.

They were not the only ones who disparaged our deal. The *Far Eastern*

Economic Review said Regent was "being thrust into a potentially disadvantageous joint venture with Toronto-based Four Seasons Hotel. . . . Among the company's [Regent's] albatrosses are a soon-to-open New York hotel that is costing a whopping U.S. $1.2 million a room to build and a Milan property that is too small to turn a profit for at least four years. Closer to home, over-budgeted projects in Jakarta and Bali are behind schedule."

The *Review* had reasons for its opinion. Sixty percent of the customers of luxury hoteliers in Asia had been North American, European, and Japanese, mainly business executives drawn by Asia's economic growth. Low overhead and high returns for hotel companies brought numerous Asian magnates into the hotel business, some on their own, others in conjunction with the big American chains. So, as the *Review* noted, the number of top-end hotel rooms in Hong Kong soared, causing a collapse in historically high occupancy levels, setting off a room-rate war that was spreading to Bangkok, Kuala Lumpur, and Singapore, with Jakarta, Manila, and Taipei believed to be soon following suit. With the recession due to the Gulf War, the situation in North America and even in Europe was worse.

This disastrous drop in travel had clobbered us, too. Although we hadn't shown a loss in 1991, we earned only $2.8 million. It was by far the worst year we ever had.

But we had some advantages our rivals didn't share. Eighty percent of our customers were top-level business executives, many of whom traveled regardless of current conditions, so our occupancy rates were not excessively low. And our balance sheet was relatively good: only sixty cents of debt on every dollar of equity, because we hadn't overbought as others did.

The stock market seemed to reflect this. While in 1991 the Standard & Poor's index dropped 60 percent from its high of September 1989, our shares had remained stubbornly strong, even throughout 1990 and 1991. As Ross O'Reilly of Wood Gundy, Toronto, noted, "Investors appear to be focusing on an anticipated strong recovery in Four Seasons 1992 earnings."

I wasn't sure about that. But while our industry was deep in the doldrums, we still considered the Regent deal an exceptional opportunity to expand, for Asia would be the next big growth area. But it was a difficult market in which to find hotel sites. The only one we closed on was on the outskirts of Tokyo. Now we had eleven Asian hotels in Regent's name and one in ours, and I didn't buy the opinion of the *Far Eastern Economic Review* that this was a bad time to be getting into that market. Trouble, in my experience, could be opportunity in disguise. Sure, things were tough right now, but I couldn't see it lasting. Our research showed us that Asia was a demographic powerhouse, where governments were privatizing and deregulating, financing expressways, high-speed rail lines, seaports, telecommunications, electric power stations, and four multibillion-dollar airports, all financed internally by high savings rates, Japanese foreign aid, and large trade surpluses.

Surely all this testified that business in Asia would go on expanding, especially along the Pacific Rim, where wealth was being created faster than anywhere on the planet by venturesome multinationals and a very young and literate workforce: in all, a coming megamarket of 1.7 billion people whose household incomes would rise as farmers moved to the cities. Each worker's religious affiliation bolstered family stability and encouraged a principled work ethic.

Then coming up behind them was the rest of the Asian continent, a second mass market of 1.3 billion people, emerging more slowly but just as inevitably. Taken as a whole, Asia should have, in some twenty-five years, more potential customers than the rest of the world put together.

Nowhere on earth, we concluded, would it be more advantageous for us to establish an early high-end leadership position, because these first new Asian customers were following a pattern set by the Japanese, who stay in the best hotels, often spend more than Western travelers, and patronize the brand names recognized worldwide as the best. We hadn't reached that pinnacle yet, but we were well on the way, earning more awards every year than any other hotel group, even though we had only twenty-three hotels.

Now, in 1992, with Regent, we swelled to thirty-eight properties, counting five Regents still under construction. Two of these were among the top ten of *Condé Nast Traveler*'s Reader's Choice Awards. And *Institutional Investor*'s wide range of voters, ranking twelve Four Seasons and Regent properties among the top seventy-five in the world, once again chose Four Seasons as the world's best hotel company.

Taking over Regent was a tour de force, making us, almost overnight, a truly international company, something that otherwise would have taken another ten years. Now, to complete our coup, we had to convince our Asian hotel owners—none of whom knew us—that we could make their hotels profitable, especially the new hotels that were being renamed Four Seasons: Bali, Indonesia, Milan, and New York. And when a correspondent for *Trend Weekly* bluntly asked me, as others had done privately, "Why didn't you change the Regent name in Asia to Four Seasons?" I reminded him that the Regent name was as well known in Asia as Four Seasons was in North America, and that owners who'd never heard of us would probably balk at a name change.

We put Wolf Hengst in charge of the changeover. Wolf had risen in the company, becoming vice president for eastern North America, and we considered that his experience, judgment, and finesse made him an excellent choice as Regent's chairman in Hong Kong, as well as president of Four Seasons Asia.

We also set up an executive team to act as a management committee, supervising financing, giving preopening assistance, and controlling quality, design, and human resources, because when the deal went through at year's end, we were a much bigger organization almost overnight.

We now had 19,500 employees and thirteen sales offices, as well as central reservations and corporate facilities, which we would consolidate with Regent. This was no easy task. We'd have to ensure that both brand names were seen as top value, something we couldn't take for granted. As a senior Hong Kong hotel executive told a reporter, "If we [Four Seasons] tried to bring a North American mentality" to Asia, we were in for "a big shock." Even in America, many people were debating the wisdom of such a highly complicated move. "A bold experiment," a U.S. hotel owner, Lawrence Geller, called it. "You wonder if it is going to be synergistic or destructive."

First we had to meet and assess the people in charge of our new company, so Wolf and John Sharpe, who'd become Four Seasons president of hotel operations, visited all Regent hotels, getting to know their managers and finding, to their surprise, that some Regent GMs knew little of their company's business as a whole. Nor were they exchanging information, passing on ideas, or drawing on each other's experience as we did. Some, in fact, had never met, never held a meeting, and they were seldom supported by the corporate office; every manager was on his or her own.

Of immediate importance was getting a handle on Regent's costs. Its reputation for service had been won primarily in an environment where it was typical to hire three or four employees for every guest. With Asian labor costs rising, we couldn't let that go on and we gave fine service with one on one. We asked Wolf to first weed out and then retrain the staff in all Regent hotels, making them more efficient and bringing them individually up to Four Seasons' standards. This was crucial not only for top-end market dominance, but also to sell the real estate later at higher prices.

The Regent properties gave our company an equitable geographic balance, reducing our exposure to economic cycles in any one region. And I could see that once out of this slump, earnings before interest and taxes would be reasonably balanced: 40 percent from Asia, 40 percent from North America, and 20 percent from Europe.

That diversification proved to be key. Even in a disastrous year, Regent was paying off. In 1992, we lost $4.1 million in America, cut only by a little more than half by earnings in Europe. But with profits of $5.2 million from Regent, we were doing reasonably well in one of the worst years in memory.

We soon jettisoned Regent hotels in Melbourne, Auckland, and Fiji; all three were below the five-star standards required by Four Seasons quality guidelines. We renovated Sydney and reduced its number of rooms, though at 513 it still had too many. But in 2007, new owners were willing to spend money on it, so we're looking forward to a true Four Seasons in Australia's most exciting city.

We also kept Singapore and still run it.

In all, we now had forty-three hotels in seventeen countries, with five Regent hotels still under construction or renovation: New York, Milan, Bali, London, and the Beverly Wilshire in California. Each was exceptional, part of what I called the next generation of hotels. Among them all, New York, to me, was the prize: putting our brand on display in the most important city in America and at the time probably, for us, in the world. And it was not just another hotel but, as one reporter called it when it opened in June 1993, "the best . . . an architectural achievement," the creation of two eminent architects, I. M. Pei and Frank Williams. It was the tallest hotel in New York, splendidly situated between Park and Madison avenues, the most expensive hotel ever constructed in North America, and one that was destined to be a landmark.

The hotel drew a lot of early publicity, but with it came a problem. In 1961, when we opened our first Four Seasons hotel in Toronto, unbeknownst to us, a restaurant in New York had already opened with the same name. When this duplication was discovered, we came to an agreement with the restaurant owners, Classic Restaurants, that none of our hotel restaurants would carry the name Four Seasons and that any Four Seasons sign on any hotels close to New York would always include the word "Hotel" as part of the name. Also, we agreed that any future hotels in New York could not carry the name Four Seasons.

Of course, when this grand flagship hotel was built, there could be no other label. So again we negotiated with Classic Restaurants for the use of the name Four Seasons. Fortunately, both parties give it equal prestige.

I claimed, while building, that we would set a new standard in New York, but I hadn't picked an auspicious time to say that. Competition had become formidable. In addition to such historic notables as the Waldorf-Astoria and the Plaza, several new hotels had recently opened. And of course there was The Pierre, with whose board we eventually came to terms, allowing us a second hotel in New York, even one so close to theirs. This was my and Roger Garland's achievement with the help of a lawyer new to our company, a young lady with great potential who was rising quickly in the organization: Kathleen "Katie" Taylor, then our general counsel.

Industry analysts openly doubted that we could command the room rates required for such a hotel to succeed in the crowded New York market. Over the previous five years, occupancy rates in luxury hotels had dropped almost 10 percent. And in 1992, "The average New York hotel lost seventeen cents on the dollar," noted Randy Smith of Smith Travel Research. "It's going to be next to impossible for Four Seasons to make a profit."

Our company was "very over-invested," said Roger Cline, executive vice president of Hospitality Valuation Services. "With the top Manhattan daily rate at approximately $350 there would have to be an extremely high premium over the top rates to get this hotel within striking range of viability." Then, he added a postscript: "For those who are price insensitive, however, it's going to be the property of choice."

And it was. A great many people must have been price insensitive, for within six months of its opening in July 1993, it was not always possible to secure a Four Seasons reservation in New York, while today it brings in a premium of more than 20 percent above its nearest competitors.

New York was the main—but not the only—distinctive asset obtained from Regent. We also put our name on two other Regents under construction: Bali, an elegant resort on Jimbaran Bay, on an island long defined by travel magazines as the closest thing to a tropical paradise; and a fourteenth-century monastery in Italy's fashion capital, Milan, converted into what one correspondent called "fascinating . . . uniquely indigenous to its surroundings, radiating style, and at the same time drenched in history."

We could now offer business and leisure travelers a fine hotel experience in most of the world's major destinations. Offers flooded in for new projects; no other company could match what we brought to the negotiating table.

Our approach to the merger had been, as usual, financially conservative. We built in allowances for the downside and for every surprise we could think of. But we didn't expect the recession to be so long or recovery so slow. And we didn't foresee the widespread devastation of real estate markets. Despite this, neither the company nor our strategy was ever compromised. What happened was that our short-term problems diverted early market attention from the success of our long-term growth strategy. At the same time, we were integrating Four Seasons hotels in the western hemisphere and Regent hotels in the Far East into one world-spanning company—no small achievement in itself. We took over an oceanside resort in exclusive Palm Beach and prepared for further Four Seasons openings in Mexico, Singapore, and Thailand, as well as overseeing construction of additional hotels in Europe, Asia, and Hawaii and negotiating for others in key locations around the globe—a huge expansion of future business.

Our success in bringing so many hotel investors on board testified to the soundness of our position in a world now becoming, even sooner than we expected, one global economy, one vast commercial marketplace linked by international air routes and ever-expanding corporate relationships. More and more companies were doing more business abroad. International travel in 1993, despite the recession, rose 20 percent, setting a new world record. And the pacesetter was the Pacific/East Asian region.

What the World Bank was calling the East Asian economic miracle was already generating a fast-rising middle class: young achievers and consumers needing and wanting to travel to dynamic centers where we operated preeminent five-star hotels.

International business travel had no way to go but up. And of particular interest to us, a *Travel News* survey found that 51 percent of executives were "willing" or "very willing" to spend more to enhance productivity when the outcome of a business trip depended on how they felt emotionally and physically—a willingness on which we had built our reputation. Yes, they were shying away from ostentatious travel expenditures, but most of them were still traveling first class.

"To sum up," I told our shareholders at year's end, "earnings are rising. The industry is in growth. Four Seasons is now in an excellent position. Selling most major investments in hotels is reducing debt and real estate exposure. Our diversified locations give us protection from regional cycles. Our management expertise is in demand."

We had staked out a leadership position in the luxury segment of our industry. We held locations in top global destinations as well as in emerging major markets. We had an unmatched reserve of trustworthy employees and the two most powerful brand names in the top tier of the business, so profit couldn't fail to catch up with performance. Regent gave us growth we could never have gained any other way and helped get us through the worst decline in our industry's history.

Four Seasons Resort Bali, Jimbaran Bay.

At the resort opening.

CHAPTER 27

Prince Alwaleed

In the aftermath of the Regent transaction and all the deals we made on our own, which had doubled the size of our company in less than two years, I now had to consider my personal need for prudent estate planning, a need that sooner or later every owner of a company as closely controlled as ours must face.

Although my partners Eddie Creed and Murray Koffler had, for personal reasons, sold most of their stock, reducing their share of the company to about 8 percent, I had held all mine, turning it into multiple voting shares that gave me 29 percent of Four Seasons with 83 percent of the votes, ensuring that I would remain in control. But now, in my sixties, it was time to follow my partners while good health allowed me to manage the process properly.

In early fall of 1993, I began discussions with Goldman Sachs, a global banking and securities firm in New York. I told them my preference was to sell a portion of my Four Seasons holdings in a way that would allow all other shareholders to sell along with me. I said I'd consider selling the whole company, but I didn't really care to. I wanted to sell only 25 percent, and that only to an individual or a group who shared our views: our belief in personal service and the management that provides it. I wanted the buyer to be a person or persons willing and able to preserve and enhance the company's value for the benefit of our owners and employees as well as themselves. And I also said I expected to stay on for five years to ensure that any management changes would have all our people's best interests in mind.

In March 1994, I announced my intention to sell. Goldman Sachs had concluded its analysis of our firm and started contacting a hundred or so

Skiing at Four Seasons Jackson Hole in 2006 with HRH Prince Alwaleed and his daughter, Princess Reem.

prospective buyers. Setting up interviews with some fifty interested companies, they soon narrowed the field to six major corporations. We negotiated with all of these but reached no clear decision.

By August, I still hadn't found a buyer I wanted. I received a call from Chuck Henry, adviser to the Japanese bankers during our Regent deal. Chuck said he'd been working since April for an investment bank, representing a client, His Royal Highness Prince Alwaleed Bin Talal Bin Abdulaziz Alsaud of Saudi Arabia, who was considering the acquisition of a hotel chain. The prince was outbid by a huge UK firm for that hotel, but Chuck approached David Mongeau, vice president of mergers and acquisitions at Wood Gundy Inc., in Toronto (he had worked for us as general counsel from 1987 to 1992 and was extensively involved in the Regent deal). Chuck and David, who knew both of us well, discussed the possibility of Prince Alwaleed's buying Four Seasons.

The prince, Chuck disclosed, had three principal investment parameters. First, he preferred global industries: financial services, tourism, hotels. Second, he wanted companies with strong brand names but that were not too large. Third, he looked for capital-intensive businesses that offered the potential for enabling quicker growth.

Four Seasons seemed to meet his requirements, and Chuck quickly set up a meeting for me with the prince in late August.

I gathered what information was easily available on the prince, as I'm sure he did, perhaps even more thoroughly, on us. I learned that he was a grandson of King Abdulaziz Alsaud, the desert warrior and statesman who by 1932 had united the fiercely independent nomadic Bedouin tribes of Arabia, driven out the Turks, and founded a new semimodern Muslim state. The prince's father, Prince Talal (who plotted against the king and was exiled from Saudi Arabia), settled in Lebanon and divorced his Lebanese wife, who had raised the prince. At nineteen, the prince attended Menlo College, near San Francisco, a favorite school for Saudis. Then, with a small gift of money from his father, he went into real estate in Riyadh. He made several million dollars speculating in land, earned a business administration degree from Syracuse University, and then gave full attention to the stock market. His biggest early purchase was buying 10 percent of Citicorp, then close to bankruptcy, for $590 million. Before long, Citicorp turned around, which made him several billions, in what *Fortune* magazine proclaimed "a master-stroke."

A group from Four Seasons—including Roger Garland, my son Tony, two investment bankers from Goldman Sachs, and me—flew to Cannes to meet with the prince and Chuck on the prince's yacht. It was a beautiful day, and the size of the yacht was impressive. I was told it was 288 feet. The yacht reminded me of the status of the prince more than of his wealth, as well as of the incongruity of our ages and backgrounds: he in his late thirties, I in my early sixties, two people whose ancestral nations had fought a bitter war with ramifications that still engendered violence in the Middle East.

If these discordant thoughts occurred to the prince, he gave no sign of them. He made us welcome and quickly got down to business. He'd done his homework. He'd read up on the company and knew the stock was low as a result of war, recession, and a real estate slump.

We talked at length about a number of things, such as whether this was a personal investment for him or whether he was acting with other partners as part of a syndicate. I knew that, only the month before, he'd bought 50 percent of the Fairmont hotel chain, based in San Francisco. That bothered me, because owning different tiers of hotels might result in some brand confusion; to my mind, it might lessen the Four Seasons brand.

He assured me that wasn't his intention. "This is a long-term commitment for me," he said.

He asked me how I saw the deal.

"I see it as a partnership," I said.

"What would you say to the word 'alliance'?" he asked.

I was impressed. A partnership is a legal association to achieve some business purpose. But an alliance is a bonding of people to further their common interests, a much closer connection. This, I thought, is a man who does more than write checks. He understands that any lasting business relationship, which he assured me this was, must be solidly based on mutual respect and trust.

That first meeting told us a lot about each other but, as expected, we came to no immediate agreement. Flying to London that evening on one of the prince's planes, I asked our group what percentage of Four Seasons they thought he was interested in. They all believed he wanted the whole company. I disagreed, and I hoped I was right.

A few days later, Chuck Henry called and asked me to set a time for a meeting in Toronto to discuss a possible transaction. The prince, it turned out, wanted to buy 25 percent, as I had hoped. He also went against his advisers' proposals on how much he should pay. The prince, as I've since learned, listens to others but decides for himself. The only change he wanted was to add two people to our board: Chuck Henry and Mustafa Ibrahim Al Hejailan, director of the United Saudi Commercial Bank, both welcome additions. On September 2, 1994, His Royal Highness and I announced that we had signed a binding agreement. Prince Alwaleed would acquire 25 percent of our stock for $22 (Canadian) a share.

We met again when the prince visited Toronto in December 1994, and I remembered something he said: "I think we are both religious people."

I said, "I'm not sure what you mean, because I'm not what I consider religious in the observant sense."

"We have similar values, basic to all religions," he said. And for me, that was what our handshake symbolized.

We had rebounded from the recession but our stock was still in the $12 range, and various people in the industry said the prince overpaid for Four Seasons at $22, nearly twice our market value at the time. But as I told reporters, most of whom didn't believe anyone would buy without getting control, "If I had wanted to sell 100 percent of the company, the price would definitely have been higher."

"It's more than we would have paid," said Steve Bollenbach of Marriott, "but it's difficult to put a price on a unique luxury asset. It's like the Hope Diamond, impossible to say someone paid too much." Bollenbach publicly apologized for previous public criticisms, saying, "I was wrong. My notion was that when somebody buys a company, they want to control it too. I think it's a real vote of confidence for Issy Sharp."

I had "pulled a rabbit out of a hat," said one amazed money manager.

Completing the deal was an immense relief. It was a difficult and unpleasant year, beginning with a highly negative *New York Times* article and continuing with most of our senior executives believing that selling shares in the company with our stock at an all-time low was a sad mistake.

But now, with a visionary partner who had worldwide connections and influence, especially in the Middle East, where we were little known, we were riding high, exceptionally well positioned for future growth.

The first thing we asked of the prince was help in restarting Aviara, a Four Seasons resort that was part of a major residential development on a hill overlooking a thousand-acre southern California wildlife sanctuary. The site had been purchased by the Hillman family of Pittsburgh; the hotel was a joint venture of Hillman and Takeshi Sekiguchi, our original partner in Hawaii, each of whom owned 45 percent, while we owned 10. But the Japanese downturn had had a negative impact on TSA, our Japanese partner, delaying completion of Aviara for some four years.

The prince agreed, and we put the resort back on track. This enabled us to seize a new opportunity. In the early nineties, Marriott had developed a time-share project in Palm Desert, and while Rosalie and I were living at our winter home in Palm Springs, I investigated Marriott's venture and was impressed. They had sold 250 units and were building another 250. If they could do this in the desert, I thought, we could surely do better in Aviara, a much more attractive location. It was here that my son Tony began our time-share business.

He started by looking at what Marriott, Hilton, Disney, and others were doing, then hired an experienced manager, Jamie Cline, to help him get our time-share initiative off to a good start. The model used proposed building 240 villas, each 1,750 square feet, with two bedrooms and three bathrooms. Prices started at approximately $17,000 to $25,000 a week, but initially sales were slow, for their sales personnel had difficulty bringing in buyers at such high prices.

Then they took a more focused approach and began targeting Four Seasons' customers exclusively. The results were soon exceptional, facilitating a price increase of 25 percent, a significant premium over other time-share projects. Tenants could take a holiday with all the Four Seasons amenities in their own vacation home.

Once Aviara was up and running, we began two more: Scottsdale, Arizona, and Punta Mita, Mexico. By now we were selling longer intervals, four to six weeks. We changed the concept to that of our current fractional residence club, and before too long, we had residence clubs in Costa Rica, Jackson Hole, Wyoming, and Whistler, British Columbia.

In a sense, our residential business had begun long before, starting in 1981 with The Pierre and the service we provided to our co-op owners there. This was followed in 1982 by residences in Four Seasons Boston. But it wasn't until the late nineties that this business evolved to what it is now, when 65 percent of our new projects include some form of residential.

Aviara was one of several projects that our deal with the prince advanced. After Aviara, he became a half partner in Four Seasons Cairo, overlooking the Great Pyramids, and Four Seasons Resort Sharm el Sheikh, as well as a 30 percent partner in Amman, Jordan. Later, he developed hotels in Riyadh, Beirut, and Damascus and also invested in Mauritius and Marrakech. He's also owner of the Four Seasons in Toronto. But his most important contribution came with the George V in Paris.

The George V was a special hotel for the prince. As a child, after his father was expelled from the kingdom, he spent most of his summers at the George V and was clearly still attached to it. I remember his asking me, "If I bought the George V, could you make it the best hotel in the world?"

"If you followed through in doing everything required," I said, "we could. And it would give us a major strategic position in Europe."

So that was what he did, and that was what we did. He bought the hotel and closed it for a year while we restored it from bottom to top, spending at least a million dollars a room. We also brought to the hotel the Four Seasons brand and standard of service. The result is so spectacular that recent awards have indeed recognized the Four Seasons George V as the best hotel in the world.

The hotel's excellence eventually helped us win our bid to manage two hotels in Lanai owned and controlled by David H. Murdock. Near the end of the negotiations, I went out to meet with Murdock in his office in Westlake Village, California.

He greeted me graciously and asked me to sit down to hear a story. He then described his recent experience at our Four Seasons Hotel George V in Paris. He was in Paris on business and was staying at his usual place, the Bristol Hotel. He was not pleased about the way he was received and treated, and he remembered that we had a hotel in Paris and decided he would try us out.

Making a cold call, Murdock was told that the hotel was sold out, but the reservation clerk, Michèle André, suggested that she would check if she could find a way to accommodate him. She called him back and said that she found a room, but he told her he wanted a suite in the interior courtyard. She then followed up and was able to accommodate his request.

He arrived at the hotel without any formal recognition of who he was. He spent two days there and enjoyed two or three meals in the dining room. He told me that he was so impressed with the way he was treated as just a regular customer. It was at that point he decided that he would make the deal with Four Seasons.

This experience, typical of all of our hotels, has brought us together with many of our partners. It emphasizes the importance of *all* our people in the company.

CHAPTER 28

A Few Bad Apples

In 1994 an industrialist from India, Captain Krishnan Nair, approached us. He headed a publicly traded company, Leela Group, which owned and operated two hotels, the Leela in Mumbai and a resort in Goa on India's Malabar coast. He wanted us to manage a group of five-star hotels that he intended to build in India.

The Indian government was then in the midst of a long-overdue attempt to join the global economy and had for the past three years been approving new investments by companies like DuPont, General Motors, IBM, and other big American firms. India's managerial and technical workforce was extensive and well trained. It included the largest middle class in the world, 300 million people, now growing faster than any other sector of Indian society.

We went to India and visited Nair's hotels. His resort in Goa needed an expensive renovation, but his Leela Hotel was clearly successful. I mentioned that to him and asked, "Why do you need Four Seasons? Why bring us in?"

"My family and I," he said, "can manage these two hotels. But I have a dream, a vision of what the Leela Group could be." He outlined a plan for five five-star hotels in such major cities as Bangalore, Delhi, and Madras. "We couldn't manage all these alone," he explained.

Captain Nair's plan sounded reasonable, perhaps a propitious opportunity. He was also a delight to be with, for he told entertaining stories about his experiences. And as we talked, I could see why he thought more than two hotels would be too many. Hotels were not his original business. He was a manufacturer of fabrics.

He explained how he made a killing from one type of fabric. The story began when he supported the young Liz Claiborne, then just a budding designer, in a buy-now, pay-later scheme. This led to more buyers, notably Brooks Brothers, a leading U.S. clothier. One of their New York representatives sifted through his line of fabrics and chose a bright madras plaid in red, yellow, and green.

"No, no," Captain Nair said. "That fabric is not at all suitable. We make it only for the African market, where it is used for just one night, the wedding night bedsheet. The parents then check the sheet to confirm that the bride was a virgin."

"But I like it," this buyer said. "I think it's great. Let me buy it."

"No, no," Captain Nair repeated. "You can't use that fabric. It's not colorfast."

But the buyer persisted until Captain Nair finally agreed to sell it. Brooks Brothers turned it into colorful shorts and sports jackets. But when they were washed, the dye ran, making Captain Nair very worried.

Brooks Brothers continued to sell the jackets, calling the fabric bleeding madras, because every time the jackets were laundered, the colors merged. Bleeding madras became enormously popular and was soon Captain Nair's main business, making him very rich.

The captain and I negotiated, eventually agreeing on a business arrangement. It started with Bangalore, where we developed the concept and design for what would become a spectacular hotel. But Captain Nair insisted that we first renovate and redesign his Goa resort, turning it into a five-star property. I told him what we would have to do: literally gut it and rebuild. "Are you sure you want to do that?" I asked him. "It's doing a reasonable business, and this will cost you a lot of money."

"Yes, I want to do it," he said. "I want it to be a true Four Seasons."

We brought in our designers and consultants and made many changes, minor and major, taking off the lobby roof, raising it to make a grand entrance, creating for him an outstanding five-star resort.

We completed Goa in mid-1998, furnished it, brought in an experienced Four Seasons GM, Dieter Janssen, along with a team to train our Indian employees. We were just about to open when Captain Nair aborted, refusing to move forward with our agreements and taking over the hotel.

I was shocked by this sudden, unexpected turn of events—though we had seen signs that Leela Group was then overextended. We might have pursued legal remedies, but instead we focused on transferring our managers and staff, helping them resettle in other Four Seasons. Some wonderful employees who joined us there are still with the company.

Soon enough, our presence in India brought us a more promising deal. The Suri family, who controlled a pharmaceutical company, the Morepen Group, had decided to branch out and asked us to build them several hotels. This was a reputable firm; we drew up agreed-upon plans and a letter of intent was signed. When the company's founder, a young man of thirty-eight, suddenly died of a heart attack, with him also perished all plans for any Morepen hotels.

We were then approached by a senior member of another family, the Oberois, a famous hotel name in India. Its chairman was Biki Oberoi, whose father had founded the company, which now owned and operated some of India's most magnificent hotels, boutiques, and castles. What brought them to us was our global brand name.

Biki Oberoi and I began to talk of an affiliation, a kind of marriage, in which we would manage their five-star hotels in India. Biki was a fine gentleman, a pleasure to deal with. I thought our operating philosophies were similar and felt very comfortable with him personally.

But the Oberoi group, like us, was a management company, and there were many things to decide about how we could work together. Our discussions about this went on for approximately two years. They would start and stop, start and stop, once for almost six months. Finally, Biki told me, "I don't think this is really going to work." We parted, then he rethought and called again.

One of our problems was the name of our hotels. Each of us felt strongly that his own brand should be on top. How to manage the hotels was also a topic of many long discussions; we were, after all, two separate management companies.

In the end, we concluded there wasn't a basis for partnership, even though getting into India might take another ten years. I apologized to Biki, told him I would have enjoyed working with him but I didn't think it was good for our company in the long term. Biki was his usual gentlemanly self about it, and we parted, I believe, still friends.

Then, just as we were about to give up hope on India, a Mr. Jatia approached us. He and his family owned a very successful Hyatt in Delhi and had talked with Hyatt about another in Mumbai. But they thought in all the circumstances a Four Seasons might be a better match for them. We explained the difference between our hotels and the ones they'd been considering, and although many changes were required, and it would be more costly to build, Mr. Jatia decided to make it a Four Seasons.

On October 24, 2003, with Canadian prime minister Jean Chrétien standing by, I signed an agreement with Mr. Jatia to manage Mumbai's finest new hotel: a sleek, glass-clad, thirty-three-story tower in the emerging Worli district. Already such companies as Goldman Sachs and Deloitte & Touche had opened offices nearby, and our hotel would no doubt draw more.

Four Seasons Mumbai opened on May 12, 2008, with 202 guest rooms and suites, many with a view of the Arabian Sea. A planned second phase will include serviced apartments and a major ballroom.

Now, with a foothold in India, we have four new projects under way as of this writing: Gurgaon, Hyderabad, Bangalore, and Kerala, plus a second hotel in Goa with the Jatia family. With its economy growing so quickly, India can support a half dozen more Four Seasons, and eventually that is surely what we will have.

Sometimes, thinking back about how and why we first came to India, I can't make up my mind about Captain Nair's actions. Had he intended to take advantage of us from the beginning? Or was he prompted by a problem in financing his new hotels? No doubt I should have seen trouble sooner, but I had little experience with him at that time.

INDIA was not the last place where we made an unfortunate choice of partner. The second was in Venezuela in the mid-1990s. Carlos Barrera, a developer in Caracas, the capital, asked if we'd manage a Four Seasons hotel there. We had a hotel in Mexico but nothing in South America, so we were interested and flew down to see him.

He had a magnificent site in the center of the city and wanted to build a hotel of two hundred rooms or more with an equal number of adjoining condominiums. It seemed promising; we accepted his offer.

We had no difficulties negotiating our business deal and agreed that we would also invest some money ourselves. Barrera began construction, taking complete charge, letting us guide him on what should be built but doing personally much of what we would normally do. I guess his reluctance, indeed refusal, to relinquish any control should have signaled a warning. But Barrera kept saying, "Look, what I'm doing is good for us both. I'm not going to disappoint you." And though he wasn't cooperating with us as partners typically do, he was indeed building very well, and we ended up with an excellent hotel.

We brought in an experienced Four Seasons GM and the many other managers needed to recruit and train a large staff of young Venezuelans. But Barrera hadn't yet put a Four Seasons sign on the building. That, of course, concerned us. We questioned it. He told us the sign was on order, coming soon. We complained again when the sign hadn't arrived for the hotel's opening. But he kept on reassuring us, saying, "It's coming, it's coming, don't worry."

The hotel opened in January 2001, and slowly Barrera began taking out money to pay various bills, which our contract allowed him to do. Then it reached the point where we couldn't access enough cash to run the business. Barrera then began taking all the money in the hotel bank accounts, and no matter what we said or did, we could not retain it to pay the operating expenses.

We tried our best to keep the hotel in operation, but we'd never had a problem like this before. Some of Barrera's employees hacked into our computer systems, which is against the law in the United States.

This put a great many young Venezuelans out of work. I recall that shortly after we opened, I was visiting the hotel during a general staff meeting. A young man stood up. "Mr. Sharp," he said, speaking in Spanish through an interpreter, "do you realize there are many of us here who have a very good education? This room is filled with what I would classify as intellectual capital much greater than the job we're doing. But we joined Four Seasons because we see it as an opportunity for a better life."

I remembered this when we closed the hotel. We asked our hotel managers everywhere if they could use these people, and jobs were found for many. Quite a number of them are still working for us.

This was the only time we had a problem so significant. We invested well over $10 million in that hotel. We've gone through many court actions in the United States and have so far prevailed in every significant case, but the owner challenged the enforcement of the arbitration tribunal's ruling, and since that was three years ago, it seems evident that under the current Venezuelan system we may never be reimbursed.

The Barrera family also lost a great deal of money, which is incomprehensible, for by simply opening the hotel as a Four Seasons they could have made up what we had both lost and eventually made much more.

Barrera and Captain Nair are the only two of many partners with whom we had a bad relationship. Most of our partners became good friends, coming back to us time after time, always supportive, sometimes invaluable. And when I consider all the friendships our business has brought me, these two experiences merely make me value those other friendships more.

OUR EXPANSION around the world continues to bring new challenges. For example, in 1998, business at the Four Seasons Jakarta was terrible. The government was being overthrown, the country was in turmoil, and our hotel became a rare safe haven for the Chinese and Indonesians. People slept in the ballroom on cots as if it were a refugee camp—with tanks surrounding the building.

Jim FitzGibbon, our president of worldwide hotel operations, remembers that on leaving the hotel around that time, the driver said to him, "Do you want to take the long way that is really, really safe, or do you want to take the short way that is not so safe but it's OK?"

"What will happen if we take the short way?"

"We'll come to a riot," the driver said. FitzGibbon looked alarmed. "Don't worry about the riot. You have a hundred dollars?"

"Yes, I do."

"Fine. Just keep it handy."

They set out away from the hotel and came to a spot where, as the driver predicted, there were people waving flags and looking menacing.

"OK," the driver said. "Now is the time to give the hundred dollars to that guy over there."

FitzGibbon held the hundred dollars out the window to a guy who appeared to be in charge, the mob gently parted, and the car drove off.

Four Seasons Mumbai.

PART VI

IN A LEAGUE OF OUR OWN

The great law of culture is: Let each become all that
he was created capable of being.
—THOMAS CARLYLE

Four Seasons is the sum of its people—many, many good people.

CHAPTER 29

A Great Place to Work

I n 1997, *Fortune* magazine announced the beginning of a yearly ranking of "The Hundred Best Companies to Work for in America."

Hearing about it, our marketing team persuaded *Fortune*'s editors to consider Four Seasons, because half our hotels were located in the United States. They agreed to include us, then asked that we complete a comprehensive twenty-nine-page questionnaire on employee benefits. A key part of this effort was a survey to be filled out by 225 employees selected at random, giving them the chance to rate their work experience with Four Seasons. In 1998, we were voted by these employees to be part of *Fortune*'s inaugural ranking, an inclusion we have maintained ever since, one of only fourteen companies to keep this honor and the only one headquartered in Canada.

In its accompanying cover story, "Why Employees Love These Companies," the magazine declared that most of the raves workers give their employers were based on three corporate traits. First, "a powerful visionary leader," one who "demands but also inspires them to give their best." Second, "they offer a physical environment that makes work enjoyable." Third, "they frame their work as part of a deep rewarding purpose that employees find fulfilling." It also stated that "high morale and outstanding performance emphatically go together."

This article followed another 1997 *Fortune* poll of ten companies acclaimed by the magazine as "America's Most Admired." All agreed that "the single best predictor of overall excellence was a company's ability to attract, motivate and retain qualified people" and that "corporate culture was their most important lever in enhancing this key capability," which could "set the context for everything a company does."

Our culture always provided a big edge in acquiring good people, but the competition that year would be stronger, for we no longer had an exclusive claim on top customer service. Every upscale chain in our business was now advertising their superiority in service, depicted by the media as "the ultimate strategic imperative for the decade." Not that this was new. Books and magazines had, for a half dozen years or more, been billing customer service as the number-one business priority and the business mantra for the nineties. What was new was that more business travelers had begun to appreciate service and were switching to companies that provided it. This prompted more hotel brands to focus on service.

I didn't see this increased competition as worrisome. In one sense, it was actually a benefit: to stay ahead, we'd have to continually do better what we were already doing well. And unlike our rivals, we didn't need to change procedure or attitude. We had only to ask a little more from employees and continue to strengthen the culture.

Skills come with experience, and our low turnover rate gave us an unusually high proportion of long-term people. These employees were focused on more than their jobs; they were concerned about guest comfort and their ability to enhance it. And our ability to attract, develop, motivate, and retain such people made our creation of culture a rare advantage.

My conclusion was by no means unique. I seldom read business books. Whenever I need specific information, I turn to people more skilled than I am in acquiring it. But in preparing for our management conference in 1995, I wanted some information on companies that had retained their competitive advantage over a very long term, fifty years or more. John Richards, our executive vice president of marketing, suggested I read *Built to Last*, the top-selling business book of the midnineties, a six-year study by two Stanford professors on what makes a company preeminent.

The authors compared the performance of eighteen outstanding companies, averaging nearly one hundred years of age, with a control group of well-known similar companies. The top companies' stocks grew fifteen times faster than those of the general market, the control group's only about twice as fast.

This study was called the first scholarly attempt to isolate the elements common to companies that decade after decade, despite setbacks from time to time, turn in a surpassing performance. And it found that these companies had eight things in common, including promotion from within, willingness to be innovative, and setting audacious goals. But the key factor was culture. And though no one culture was right for all, it was the depth of belief in the culture, its permeation of the organization from top to bottom, that gave it its dynamism. In strong cultures, the study showed, employees share such a clear corporate vision that they know almost instinctively the right thing to do and how to do it.

We were quick to create such a culture but slow to realize its power. If someone had mentioned *culture* to me when I first spelled out our credo, I'm not sure I'd have known what it meant. Now it was being touted as a company's most valuable competitive asset, and we had spent a quarter century or more developing what we considered the strongest culture in our industry—first by hiring more for attitude than experience, later by establishing career paths and promotion from within. And whenever we had to give up a hotel, we made every effort to ensure that our employees didn't lose out. A typical example was when a soft Texas market had forced us to sell one of our two hotels in Dallas. Two Four Seasons executives, John Young and Jim Brown, spent their entire Christmas holiday working with every hotel in our chain to locate vacant positions. By the completion of the sale, every employee able to move had been placed. And within hours, the company grapevine was telling people in all our hotels about the efforts management had made to help employees get a new start.

We also showed respect for our staff by soliciting their opinions through regular surveys. We passed on any compliments on their work, usually individually, but sometimes companywide, as we did when *Fortune* magazine sent a reporter to check on service in New York's luxury hotels.

"At Four Seasons," the reporter wrote, "the only problem was to find a problem."

And one day in Italy, where rotating strikes go on all the time—newspapers even list them in advance—the Milan paper reported: "Workers at all hotels will be on strike today." Italian unions are powerful, and Milan is highly unionized, but Four Seasons workers ignored the order and showed up for work—an unprecedented demonstration of commitment to the company, which we felt would be of interest to all our people.

We reinforced togetherness by eliminating things that divide. Managers and staff dine together in our cafeterias. And unless something private is being discussed, executive doors are always open to employees with a problem or complaint.

Employees quoted by *Fortune* had exuberantly given their opinions: "I'm treated like a five-diamond hotel guest . . ." "Free meals in the company cafeteria . . ." "Tailored uniforms cleaned and pressed daily . . ." "Great pay, great benefits, a great 401k plan . . ." "Free stays at any Four Seasons hotel in the world."

CHAPTER 30

Meeting Expectations

F our primary elements make the difference between other hotels or resorts and a Four Seasons Hotels and Resorts property: service, quality, culture, and brand. All four defining characteristics are on display and in practice daily in the ritual of the morning meeting.

Egos are not allowed in that meeting. We're there for one reason, and that's the guest. From Toronto to Tokyo, from Los Angeles to the island nation of Nevis, the morning meeting is conducted the same way.

In most cities, the meeting begins with our guest relations manager, who recaps who is staying at the hotel. On our organizational chart, this person's job is the equivalent of a department head. He or she goes over the hotel's new arrivals, extended stay guests, VIPs, and special attention guests. Because of the caliber of our guests, the rates they pay, the expectations they have, and how much we drill down to get it right for them, we couldn't live without this position.

At the Four Seasons New York, Johannes Waltz is the senior guest relations manager. Johannes has an amazing rapport with our returning guests (and there are a lot of them). Whenever they arrive, he makes them feel welcome. He gives them a sense of home when they come here, that they don't have to worry. He is also very proper. You could lock him in a room with a *Daily News* reporter, and he wouldn't give up a word of good gossip. Partly this is due to his inherent sense of decency, but he also knows when not to share something that could harm the hotel or its guests.

The guest relations manager runs through the VIPs who are coming in that day as well as a recap of return customers. "How do we get the house ready?" he or she will ask. "Are the rooms prepared? Who needs a hypoallergenic pillow?"

Then we go through the special attention guests. They might be people who need gluten-free food or are allergic to peanuts or want us to empty out the minibar and put only bottled water in it. We really don't stop short of anything here. A different mattress, more pillows or hypoallergenic pillows, extra hangers, a special shampoo if they're allergic to what we routinely stock—it doesn't matter: we go out and get it.

Next up is a review of the previous day's mistakes in something we call the Glitch Report. Every department in the hotel is represented at the morning meeting, and each has a printout detailing what's gone wrong and what steps may have already been taken to correct course. The Glitch Report ensures that every hotel department knows what happened and which guest it affected.

We might have missed a guest with something as simple as turndown service, and everybody listens to the department head responsible as he or she articulates what went wrong. That person will go to the root cause of the problem and tell everyone what will be done to fix it in that guest's eyes. Whatever the issue, making it right starts with a sincere apology. It can also mean trying to do something else for them later on in their visit. It can mean an amenity such as flowers or fresh fruit skewers or a bottle of wine. It can mean an appropriate adjustment or consideration on their bill. For each guest, we strive to find the right approach in the apology.

We give our staff the tools they need to do the job, and we let them know what the expectations and standards are. "This is what we want to happen at check-in." Then, we measure. "What happened? Why did Mr. Andrews not do the standard upon check-out?"

And things do go wrong. This is how one report read:

> Ms. Jones [a pseudonym] in room 212 notified telecom operator 21 that her room "smells like smut." Guest reaction: Guest was upset.
>
> The operator informed the hotel's assistant manager on duty. He called the guest in her room and apologized. He then offered to freshen up the room. The guest accepted, and an air purifier was sent to the room by the

housekeeping leader, followed by an amenity and a personal card from the manager on duty. Guest will be met at check-out. A team leader went to the room and apologized. The guest was fine. Room exchange was offered. Guest declined.

Here's another example:

> Mr. Brown's [a pseudonym] reservation due date was incorrect. He checked in with the hotel manager, who informed Mr. Brown that his reservation was for yesterday. Mr. Brown was adamant that the reservation was incorrect and he was to check in today. We apologized and offered him a room in another hotel. This one is unresolved and requires follow-up.

If we make a mistake, we're sorry and we're sincere about it, we apologize, and we fix it right away. And when the guest comes to check out, we say, "I'm sorry about your room."

The second stage is ensuring that the guest doesn't have something else go wrong during the rest of the visit. That is another great value of having these department leaders together in the morning meeting. We share the glitches, and someone will inevitably look at her notes and say, "You know what? That guest has dinner reservations with us tonight. We'll make sure a manager goes by the table to recognize and connect with them."

The hotel manager (who works directly under the general manager) usually runs the morning meeting and may offer further guidance.

"Let's also make sure the timing and everything else with their meal is right, but we don't need to bring up the problem that happened yesterday, they probably want to leave that behind."

The whole question of glitches is central to how we provide service. It comes full circle to employee job security and confidence. If they feel secure in their job, they won't mind telling us the things that didn't go right.

From the Glitch Report, we'll move on to discuss how the hotel performed the previous day. This takes a minute or two in which numbers, finances, occupancy, and average room rate are reviewed.

Topic three looks forward to the day ahead. What groups are coming in?

What are the types of movements? What's the timing on them? Who's an extended-stay guest? Mr. and Mrs. Smith? Tell me about them. What do they like to do?

Sometimes we can have perfect staffing, but customers don't all arrive and depart as we please. Even we can't afford to overstaff the entire hotel and have fifty-five bellmen. We try to read the business all the time and have the right number of staff on hand.

A hotel that handles a great deal of group business will spend more time on this topic. "Callaway is here today. Toyota is here, as is Diageo. They are all looking at us and comparing us against the competitors. How will we create an experience here for them so that they will say, 'I have to bring my business back to Four Seasons?'"

We ask who did some standards testing the day before. And then there's a bit of sharing that goes around the room, in which each colleague gets a chance to present something new that's going on in their area or something we need to focus on. "How are we doing on accidents on the property? How many days have we gone without a lost-time day?"

We deliberately make the morning meeting tough on ourselves. But we think, "If we don't get better, somebody else is going to do this better than we do. We don't want to hear 'Four Seasons *used* to be a great company.'"

The GM or hotel manager usually finishes with a solid message of the day that we want the department leaders to take away, one that we would like our people to be focused on, and then we all go on our way.

We keep the morning meeting as condensed as possible; forty-five minutes is a long one. The purpose is to rev everybody up, tie up loose ends from the previous day's business, and get in the right frame of mind for the day ahead.

CHAPTER 31

The Front Lines

We pride ourselves on our great diversity of people. Years ago, if you lined up a group of business executives, they all would have had the same look to them—clean-cut, same type of suit, same type of dress. It was true of many companies of the era. There was—and still is—an expected appearance. Not at Four Seasons. We look at people in terms of their personality, their attitude. If you lined up Four Seasons people, there wouldn't be anything physically that ties them together at all—more the reverse, actually, because the whole essence of what we talk about, day in and day out, at every level of the business, is tolerance.

When we talk about what the Golden Rule stands for, it really is just that. All people are equal in our eyes, whether guests or employees. We see them that way from the start of the hiring process. There is absolutely no discrimination. I made a statement, and I have continued to do so, that we could go anywhere in the world and bring together a core of people from the community who could rise to this level of excellence in service delivery and attitude.

I speak to our people about Four Seasons culture and the Golden Rule and how we preserve it. "Look," I tell them, "this isn't of my making. This is not something I invented and you have now bought into. This is the way you were brought up and this is the way I believe you bring your children up, with certain principles, work ethics, and values. That is what brings us together. We are different in our personalities, beliefs, and backgrounds, and we take pride in those differences. The tie that binds is our value system, the principles that we believe in, and that is what makes the company homogeneous. Not that we are all the same, but our beliefs are similar."

Several years ago, I asked Rosalie to find out where the Golden Rule came from. When did it start? Who were the scribes who originated these wonderful sayings?

She came up with a list of ten religions that honor the Golden Rule, the first law of human rights.

I was in a Muslim country, and I said, "Let me read to you what it says in your Koran about Islam," and I read the statement. The whole audience stood up and clapped and cheered, because what we're saying about the Golden Rule represented their beliefs and my beliefs. Even though we're from different parts of the world, the rules are exactly the same. "Are we different because we're Muslim or Christian or Jewish? No," I said. "Whether it's Christianity, Judaism, or Islam, the words are different, but the meanings are the same. That's why our culture is embedded in a way that it will never be lost."

We've brought people together from so many different backgrounds. Even more important, when people ask about the success I have and what's most important to me, my real satisfaction of success has been just that, that there are so many people whose lives have been enriched.

Hans Willimann, a thirty-year veteran, would be a perfect example of this. He says openly that his children have a better life because of his having come to Four Seasons, that the company's philosophy changed him as a person and inspired him to raise his own children with a hands-off approach. To me, that's what success is: it's not what you do on your own; it's how many people have come along with you to reach higher than their expectations ever were.

And our employees continually do amazing things, going beyond what anyone would normally expect from customer service. I'm reminded of an event at Four Seasons Chicago, about six months after it opened in 1989. The event was a small black-tie fund-raiser for sixty people hosted by President and Nancy Reagan to support Children's Memorial Hospital.

Every gentleman in the room wore black tie—except one.

Hans overheard a man off to one side speaking with his wife as donors lined up to get their pictures taken with the former president and first lady.

"You could have told me that it was black tie!" he complained to her. "If you had, I wouldn't feel like an idiot."

Hans moved close enough to hear this, and he approached in classic Four Seasons fashion.

"I'm sorry," he said, "but I couldn't help but overhear your conversation. I work here. I understand your dilemma, and I think I can help."

Hans invited the man to follow him to the uniform office.

"Khaled, this gentleman doesn't have a tuxedo. Can you help him?"

Khaled invited the gentleman to have a seat in his office, excused himself, changed out of the tuxedo he was wearing, put on his civilian clothes, and rushed to the laundry to press his very own tuxedo for the guest to wear. The pants were a little bit too big, so the staff seamstress came up and fixed them, and the gentleman rejoined the party.

The next day Hans received a lengthy and effusive letter of praise from Mr. Steingraber expressing his gratitude. The letterhead indicated that he was the chairman and CEO of a major global strategic consulting firm, A.T. Kearney. And he felt that if his consultants had the kind of attitude that Hans and his banquet manager had demonstrated, the company could be twice their size.

This company has since spent millions at the Four Seasons on food and beverages for many years. From that time forward, all of A.T. Kearney's functions were held at our hotel. And, at every one that once-tuxedoless gentleman would rise and retell his Four Seasons story so that his colleagues would never forget what the standard was for exceeding expectations in providing a service.

On another occasion, one Mother's Day during the Clinton administration, the restaurant at Four Seasons Washington received a call from the Secret Service. President Clinton and his wife, Hillary, were just leaving church and wanted to come for Mother's Day brunch.

The restaurant manager didn't know what to do, because the restaurant was already packed with reservations. He handed the call off to GM Chris Norton, who only asked, "Where do they want to be? . . . Not a problem, don't worry about it."

Sunday brunch is all over the area as you walk into the hotel, and then it continues downstairs to the fine dining area. The Secret Service indicated that the Clintons wanted to be downstairs, so Chris led a team who wedged in one more table with two seats and told people around it, "We're really sorry, but we have a special guest coming."

Chris went to the front door to welcome the Clintons. He thanked them for once again choosing to dine with us and led them through the lobby toward the table downstairs.

"You know what, Chris?" President Clinton said. "I think we really want to be upstairs, not downstairs."

"Of course, Mr. President, of course. Not a problem at all," Chris said.

And as he walked leisurely, pretending to be relaxed, the Secret Service turned left to go downstairs, but Chris turned *right* with the president and First Lady. He walked toward a young assistant manager who was manning the podium as maître d', and the manager's eyes popped open wide as he saw Chris leading the president and First Lady toward the restaurant.

Chris held up his hand with two fingers, and said, "Heinz, a table for two, please."

He slowed down his steps, and the staffers ran like mad. Meanwhile, the Secret Service went wild, because the president had wandered off from them. Heinz skillfully added a table in the middle of the dining area, and Chris personally apologized to a second group of guests: "We're really sorry, but we have to move you over a little bit, because we had a guest arrive at the last minute."

A French couple was among the affected diners, and they were not too happy about being relocated a few centimeters . . . until they saw who sat down. It turned out they had stood on line for hours the day before for a White House tour, and now suddenly the president of the United States was sitting right next to them. They got an autograph and beamed with delight. The restaurant became oddly quiet, and President Clinton graciously stood up and walked through the restaurant doing Chris's job, greeting everybody, saying hello, and making sure everybody was enjoying the Mother's Day brunch.

It was just another ten-minute episode from the life of a Four Seasons hotel manager. But sometimes our employees go even further above and beyond. A doorman at Four Seasons Chicago literally saved the life of a four-year-old child in 2008. Upon seeing a young child wander out of a car and into the street in front of our hotel, he ran out and grabbed the child before a speeding vehicle could hit him.

He's a hero, absolutely a hero.

CHAPTER 32

Marketing Our Brand

O
ur company didn't actually manage a hotel under the Four Seasons brand name in the United States until 1979—the Four Seasons in Washington, D.C. We did, however, have a presence there under names like the Clift in San Francisco, the Olympic in Seattle, the Ritz-Carlton in Chicago, and after 1979, The Pierre in New York. The company was building a presence but not necessarily a name.

Between Washington in 1979 and the opening of the Four Seasons Chicago in 1989, we opened hotels in Houston, Austin, and Dallas, under the Four Seasons brand name. We also opened Four Seasons hotels in Philadelphia, Newport Beach, and Los Angeles.

The market was changing. The same forces that allowed Four Seasons to open so many new hotels in the United States also permitted the market to expand and other companies to open new hotels. I came to believe that brand marketing would become important to the future success of the company.

One reason was the rapid worldwide advance of telecommunications and the recent emergence of electronic commerce on the Internet. Now the suddenly increasing reach of international marketers and the wide variation in product and legal standards between one jurisdiction and another made familiar brands the most trustworthy choice.

Another reason, I believed, was a changing consumer lifestyle. Many consumers in the early 1990s began using no-name products, wondering if, in paying a brand name premium, they were merely underwriting the cost of a company's advertising. Now, with prices falling and products multiplying, brand names were more valuable and more powerful than ever before.

But name recognition, while crucial, was no longer enough. Today's customers were more discerning. No amount of advertising, by itself, would keep them buying. They wanted not only a safe buy but also a smart buy. A known brand-name product now had to live up to its claims. The prevailing popularity of a leading global brand name lay in its power to turn a single transaction into a lifetime habit.

Until the 1990s, we had evolved by developing one hotel after another, the reputation of each contributing to the eventual success of the next. Our brand name had been growing, but slowly, for it usually takes a long time to build top-of-the-mind brand awareness. In the mid-1980s, Four Seasons was relatively unknown, and when travel agents were polled and asked to name North American chains, only one in ten mentioned our company. Synergy was low; some of our hotels were not yet carrying our name. Yet within five years, all the annual surveys of the leading travel publications ranked us the foremost name in North American luxury lodging.

The hotels we were now designing had status to spare. All were showpieces of outstanding quality, set in select locations virtually impossible to duplicate: global financial centers, industrial hubs, and glamorous resorts.

Our properties were matched by our management contracts. These were contracts that ensured us control of standards, and if the hotel was sold, they couldn't be canceled. They averaged more than fifty years, some as long as eighty, whereas the average duration of hotel contracts in this decade was six years.

I was sometimes asked if we could sustain the competitive advantage our brand conferred. Indeed, I had sometimes asked myself the same question. But the history of great brands said yes. Most of the top brands that began sixty-five or seventy years ago—Wrigley, Eveready, Kellogg's, Gillette—still dominated their market sectors. Brand momentum, once gained, goes on and on, lasting as long as a company maintains its customers' trust in what built the brand: in our case, our culture, which grows stronger every year.

When the time was right, we made an investment in the best marketing, advertising, and public relations people and brought significant resources to bear. People talked much more about marketing than about brand in those days, but the idea was that we would succeed in the future as much because of the power of a brand as the quality of our service, and that became a belief that I enthusiastically shared with the organization and with the partners who owned hotels with us in the Four Seasons system.

Barbara Talbott and Susan Helstab joined Four Seasons to lead our marketing effort. One of Barbara and Susan's first responsibilities was to write a definitive marketing strategy to build brand value.

We knew that Four Seasons' service was a unique competitive advantage, one that could be protected and extended because there was something behind it that's deep and durable: we listen to our customers, and we listen to each other.

Service is the heart of everything, and guests experience that truth through the comfort we provide during their stay. One component of that comfort is the art and science of giving guests the best possible night's sleep, a concern that goes all the way back to the company's origins. As far back as 1961, I thought about the soundproofing in rooms when they were constructed, quiet plumbing, blackout curtains in the windows, and custom-made beds, which we've had for over thirty years. The essence of what you get from staying at Four Seasons is a better night's sleep.

So the marketing department developed an ad in which the headline "Cancel the warm milk; I don't think I'll need it" appears over an image of a guest blissfully asleep in one of our rooms. The copy read:

> The advantages of a Four Seasons Hotel are obvious even in the dark. There's the sensation of slipping between fine cotton sheets, thoughtfully French folded for dream-like comfort, the luxury of curling up under our duvets, the back-soothing firmness of our mattresses, each custom-made to Four Seasons specifications. Awakening hours later, you'll feel as if you haven't slept so soundly in years, so we do apologize in advance for the promptness of our wake-up call. The demands of business demand nothing less.

As time went on, we discovered that the idea of sleep was so important, we returned to the theme time and time again. We photographed a house-keeper in a beautiful black uniform with a white cap and apron, and the headline said, "If we didn't give you a bed this comfortable, how would we sleep at night?"

Another one of my favorite campaigns was one that we called "Por-traits." It consists of beautiful black-and-white portraits of actual Four Seasons employees, such as Liloo, the concierge at the Four Seasons To-ronto. The headline: "Liloo is warm, knowledgeable, gracious, absolutely ruthless in the fulfillment of your every wish." The copy below continues,

> Not only can our incandescent concierge find you a secretary fluent in Japanese but also deftly corner the last first-class seat on the evening flight. Moreover, she possesses the worldliness that opens doors to the newest bis-tros and makes sold-out tickets appear before your eyes. For Liloo, like all our employees, believes accommodating you must not merely be a liveli-hood but a life passion.

That campaign debuted in 1990, and it ran for several years. Eventually the market evolved once more, and what followed it was something that has both a problem and a solution. The slogan we developed was "The Demands of Your Business Demand Nothing Less Than Four Seasons."

A new downturn in the world economy led to worries in our industry that no one would stay at luxury hotels. But what we heard from our guests was quite different. They told us that service was even more impor-tant than ever. "I have a lot on my shoulders," they said. "I'm traveling for a purpose."

We turned that around and advertised, "This isn't about frills; this is about the services that you need to do business effectively. You've left your home and office support system at home, and that's what we're here to pro-vide." This campaign brought that alive. It notes the sleeping experience, because what can we do if we're not rested? The twenty-four-hour room service became crucial, because people were working longer hours. One of the ads in the campaign had a guest calling the front desk and saying, "I'd love some sushi, but it's late. Is there any place that's open, and how far do

I have to go?" And the clerk replies, "We'll get you sushi right here. It'll be up to you in a few minutes." Anyone can claim to have twenty-four-hour room service, but no one else was bringing sushi to guest rooms around the clock at that time.

Let me tell you a story. A fellow in one of the focus groups in New York was a frequent guest at one of our hotels, and he couldn't get in on a particular trip. Our hotel was sold out, so his office booked him a room at a different hotel. He told us, "I got to the airport, picked up my rental car, but I couldn't make myself go to the other hotel. Instead, I went to the Four Seasons. I know every one of the valet parkers, I know the doorman. I threw myself on their mercy: 'Can you find me a room?' And they did."

That led to an ad called "Is It Possible to Be Homesick for a Hotel?"

It sounds deceptively simple—"We listen to our guests, and we listen to each other"—but in effect, that's what we do. People are conscious of how important Four Seasons service is and that others are talking about service. It was a real eye-opener when some of the people who operated boutique hotels started talking about service. We heard that and thought, "OK, what does that mean at your property?"

We responded with a white paper called "The Power of Personal Service." Service is hard to sound-bite, so initially we only wanted something to use internally, but then ultimately it was published by Cornell. It talked about what service is, why it matters, and why it's so hard to do.

That, in turn, led to "When Life Feels Perfect." If other people were going to talk about service and if our aspiration was leadership, then we had to go a step beyond, right? And what we heard was that that was how we made guests feel—perfect. The other thing we were hearing from people was how bombarded they felt in their lives, the round-the-clock e-mail, cell phones, information—all these things coming at them nonstop. There are no words beyond the headline; we created a generosity of space and a feeling of serenity and beauty that would telegraph to people that we understood that what they loved about being with us was that it felt so calm and peaceful—whatever it was that they wanted it to be. It wasn't always about being calm and peaceful. Sometimes it was about lots of fun, family fun or couples being together.

What you will never see from us is marketing that ignores the intelligence of the reader. We see our guest as someone who not only understands service but also appreciates value and refuses to be taken in by gimmicks. We understand, most of all, that when offering the best possible experience, we must still remind people that what they are purchasing is worth every penny.

CHAPTER 33

Continuing Growth

We had planned to make 1998 a distinctive year of growth. In fact, we exceeded our expectations. Industry analysts called it outstanding, sensational, even fantastic, and although this was somewhat exuberant, it was nonetheless gratifying.

I hadn't forgotten, of course, that growth could bring risk along with success. In becoming too big too fast, you can fall into a numbers trap: a preoccupation with figures, judging everything by numbers and size, quantity rather than quality. It could gobble up capital, starve cash flow, and create a liquidity crisis.

But we believed growth for us would have precisely the opposite effect, since we had become mainly a management company. Now the head-office cost of a new hotel was so much less than the revenue it added that growth expanded rather than shrank cash flow and liquidity.

The only risk that growth could now pose would be a drop in our service standards. But this didn't concern me. Growth gave employees greater job security, more prospects for promotion, and the lure of transfers abroad. This was raising retention rates, creating a pool of long-term employees who could train and act as role models for new hires. We were now more than ever our industry's employer of choice, able to attract and retain the best graduates of the best hotel schools, allowing us to keep service standards high as we grew.

So our growth, already strong, was now accelerating: fourteen hotels due to open in the next twelve to eighteen months, plus another fifteen under construction—and I felt we could do this without compromising in any way the cachet of our brand. And I believed that we could do it anywhere in the world, even in areas where hotel experience was nonexistent.

Everyone in our company knew that our core competence had evolved from the core values of our credo, which underlay everything we do. I doubted there was even one person in the organization who didn't understand what our brand name represented: distinctive quality, exceptional service.

We were now revamping our Web site to better inform all customers about everything we were offering. Our site was already delivering some 5 percent of individual bookings, well above the industry average of 1.7 percent. In the not too distant future, we could see it cutting marketing costs and raising occupancies by giving customers detailed visual presentations of all our hotels abroad. We had a state-of-the-art reservations system linked to our customer database so our marketers could speed up service, check performance, focus on pockets of higher growth, and identify groups and opportunities that would shift market share our way. As a recent Internet study by Goldman Sachs had noted, Four Seasons' customers are "more tech savvy than most, which should allow the company to be a leader on the Internet."

This study had also noted what it called "the dark side of the Web." All too soon, it would put every week's best hotel deal at every traveler's fingertips, raising the specter of unusually lethal periodic price wars, and every hotel chain would face an unwelcome choice: whether to lower profit margins or lose market share.

Every hotel chain except us: We weren't into discounting. We didn't compete on price. Our product was not a commodity; it was a unique prestige-value buy. Bridging the old and the new economy, we were the one hotel company that could take full advantage of the new without any problems.

But most important by far to our earnings was our brand, now evolving into a special class of its own. More and more, it was showing up in popular novels and films as a backdrop to convey an impression of elegance or glamour or the social standing of a character, giving our reputation a broader significance. I remembered an interviewer saying to General

Schwarzkopf during the Gulf War, "Here you are in the middle of the desert. What are the accommodations like?"

"Well," General Schwarzkopf said, "it's not the Four Seasons."

Like the Ritz at the turn of the century, our brand was entering the realm of folklore as a generic term for the ultimate in quality.

Four Seasons was not a purely luxury product but a service. Recessions had much less effect on us than on vendors of products. We charged only twenty, fifty, or a hundred dollars more a night to ensure the comfort, facilities, and frustration-free, time-saving service that our customers would sooner pay somewhat more for than forgo. So we were a luxury item, yes, but our functional value outweighed cost. We were becoming a necessity, not a discretionary expenditure.

Considering this, I realized we were also in a period when successful firms in the past had felt they had it made and no longer had to strive so urgently. And although I had no reason to think this could happen to us, I decided to help ensure continued leadership. So at our shareholders' meeting in 1999, I said we were setting a new Four Seasons goal: to be recognized and accepted as a company that Wall Street calls a blue chip, one of the stellar mainstays of the market. "That may seem presumptuous," I said, "since we're relatively small. But Four Seasons' situation is unique. I believe we can earn blue-chip status, not by size but by what a blue chip truly represents: a global brand name, a dominant market position, and a sustainable competitive advantage, something most companies only dream of."

Our growth continued into early 2001, when I began my comments to our shareholders with an unequivocal affirmation: "Year 2000 was the best year in the history of our company."

We had increased our 1999 after-tax earnings by 20 percent. RBC Dominion Securities was now ranking us a strong buy, as were four or five other firms, but what really interested me in RBC's comments was a statement that Marriott had announced a joint venture with Bulgari that "will appeal to guests who seek high value from an individualized contemporary Italian style," while Ritz-Carlton, our closest competitor, which Marriott owns, "provides guests with refined elegance, combined with easy luxury. It would appear," said RBC, "that Marriott is virtually conceding that Ritz is having difficulty competing with Four Seasons and that a different product offering is required."

Credit Suisse First Boston, who also recommended our stock, noted that we had put in place "a unique oversight structure to coordinate day-to-day hotel activities," explaining that "every hotel general manager, whose average length of service is thirteen to eighteen years . . . reports directly to either a regional vice-president or an area vice-president" in all "seven regional teams. . . , a management structure not only effective but durable, a strong foundation of stability over time."

Also helping financially, the worst in Asia was now behind us. In 1999 our situation in Asia had begun to show a little improvement, and in the fourth quarter, our Asian hotels had posted a 4.7 percent RevPAR (revenue per available room) increase, rising slightly in year 2000.

In 2000 we had successfully opened five new properties, while readying five more for opening the following year, three of them in operation as I spoke in 2001 and the other two on schedule. And when I said "successfully opened," I didn't just mean that they all came on stream according to plan, for during the year we had hired and trained some two thousand employees. And from day one, this frontline staff was able to meet customers' high service expectations, contributing to profitability well ahead of forecasts.

And each new hotel incorporated the latest and best in design, function, and comfort; we were assembling a new generation of twenty-first-century five-star hotels that were head and shoulders above any other hotels then in existence.

We had already achieved blue-chip status, and to maintain momentum I announced that we should again raise the bar and set a new objective: to be seen, over the next three to five years, as a member of a select group of blue chips, what I would call a special category—leaders of their sectors, the best of the best: companies like the Walt Disney Company, the Coca-Cola Company, LVMH Moët Hennessy–LouisVuitton, Sony Corporation, the General Electric Company, and Wal-Mart Stores, Inc.

Again, it was not that we'd be comparable in size, but rather in sharing those special qualities that set such companies apart: their ability to retain sector dominance and to maintain, as they have, an average growth rate of

20 percent. And most important, we'd continue to enhance, like them, the worldwide drawing power of our brand name, which now, because of the Internet's clutter, was the most valuable asset in business history, causing such companies to merit, regardless of market conditions, price-earnings multiples well beyond those of competitors.

All these companies had remained sector leaders year after year on their ability to sustain their competitive advantages. For General Electric, it was superior product. For Sony, miniaturization. For Wal-Mart, logistics. And for us, of course, impeccable personalized service.

Ever since our decision to concentrate solely on five-star management, we had focused on customers' needs and desires. Our core competence thus derived from more than a quarter century of continuous cumulative learning—a long head start on competitors who had failed for many years to recognize service as our sector's ultimate competitive advantage.

In the past, success was believed to depend primarily on product and location, and both, of course, were still imperative. We continually upgraded convenience and comfort to ensure we never fell behind. And each property we developed was also aesthetically individual, reflecting the culture and traditions of its locale.

But while product was essential to sector success, product, unlike service, could be bought. Product alone was not the sustainable competitive advantage required to join the ranks of dominant sector leaders.

Another requirement was location. Location was basic. This was why we'd acquired hotels in select locations: the capitals of sixteen nations, global financial centers, some of the world's most exotic resorts. And the annual *Zagat Survey of Top International Hotels, Resorts and Spas,* based on ratings by more than twelve thousand frequent travelers, had named Four Seasons the World's Top Hotel Chain.

We would certainly not have scored twenty-nine out of thirty points if these hotels had not been in premier locations. But that was not the reason we scored so highly with these travelers. According to the *Zagat Survey,* it was our "consistently superb experiences . . . thanks to an incomparable mix of style and service."

The preeminence of service figured large in our growing revenue from branding and managing residential projects as a component of our hotels and resorts. It's interesting that as residential sales went up, so did prices, and our partners in these ventures attributed this to a growing realization that the accompanying availability of a full range of Four Seasons' services was becoming, for well-off, time-conscious vacationers and retirees, the epitome of luxury.

For all these reasons, I believed that our core competence—delivering error-free service—which kept on getting better and better, more and more consistent as more and more employees steeped in our values stayed with the company, was a truly sustainable competitive advantage. And the numbers seemed to bear me out. Our profit margins, still expanding, were among the highest in the industry. Our average revenue per room had topped that of our closest competitor by 39 percent. And we were trading at a market premium comparable to an outstanding sector leader like Wal-Mart.

These competitive advantages were summed up in our brand name, fast gaining worldwide awareness on multiple levels. It was a symbol of status and quality, but it wasn't a discretionary item. For those to whom time was money, it implicitly guaranteed value. And every day, we gave thousands of guests a favorable experience, often emotional and therefore memorable, that lodged our name in the forefront of their minds. As the president of Protravel International in New York had said the previous year, "The branding is so strong that travelers will say 'Four Seasons' when what they mean is 'book the best hotel in the city.'"

"So our new goal," I told our shareholders in May of 2001, "is to be seen as one of a special category of sector leaders, which may not be as brash as at first it might seem. As I said two years ago, it may sound audacious, but experience shows that it's not at all unrealistic."

PART VII

STAYING
AHEAD

When you've got something to prove,
there's nothing greater than a challenge.
—TERRY BRADSHAW,
Pro Football Hall of Famer

CHAPTER 34

Creative Crisis Management

September 11, 2001, was a day unlike any other. Less than five months after announcing our best year ever, we were caught in the aftermath of an unforeseen calamity unique in the history of business. Nineteen al-Qaeda terrorists had hijacked four passenger airliners, flown two of them into the twin towers of the World Trade Center in New York, flown another into the Pentagon, and crashed a fourth in Pennsylvania, killing all aboard when the passengers tried to regain control of the plane.

As soon as I heard of the attack, I immediately called a meeting of our senior people to decide what we should do, for this was more catastrophic than anything we'd ever dealt with, and it called for some immediate critical decisions.

We agreed that our competitors would most likely do what they'd done in the Gulf War: cut costs by every means possible, including employee layoffs. What would happen, we asked ourselves, if we followed suit? What would it do to employee morale? To the service our reputation was based on? To our customers' perception of us? How would customers feel, in this period of increased tension and decreased confidence, if the service they would now be more than ever dependent on was no longer reliable?

I heard everyone out, then said, in effect, "We've agreed the downturn will be severe but temporary. So we're not going to change the product. We'll deal with it as we dealt with the Gulf War. We won't let people go. We'll continue giving our customers what they expect when they stay with us. And we'll do it in the most cost-effective way: by being creative. Control without compromise will again be our direction to all our hotel managers. And we'll tell them not only in writing but personally."

That same day, Wolf Hengst, now our president, was due to be in Washington, with a small group of business leaders invited to meet with President Bush. I asked Wolf to cancel his White House meeting, because he and Kathleen Taylor, president of worldwide business operations, along with me and perhaps several other top executives, would be traveling around the world to personally inform the management at every Four Seasons hotel of our position on this crisis.

Within a few days, it was obvious that our conclusions were correct. A great many people had ceased to fly. The airlines were devastated. Travel and tourism suffered a deep slump. The economy began drifting into recession. For hard-hit hoteliers, the outlook was bleak. And other hotel companies were responding as we had thought: focusing on squeezing costs, cutting staff, cutting product standards, cutting everything.

Three days later, concerned that our employees were worried about our future and their jobs and perhaps about the possibility of terrorist attacks against their hotel, I wrote a full-page letter that went to every employee in the company. I said, "Though we face a period of great difficulty and uncertainty, we do so as a company with the best locations, best facilities, best partners, best brand, and above all the best people in the world. Our people come from all races and religions, and we trust you will continue to deal with one another in the true Four Seasons spirit of the Golden Rule.

"Our long-term future," I assured them in ending it, "is secure . . . and we will emerge from this crisis, with your help, stronger than ever, able to resume the growth plans for which we are fully prepared."

On October 10, I wrote a second letter, extending "sympathy for those who lost colleagues, friends, and family members in the tragic events in New York and Washington." Then I pointed out that we were "in the strongest position in our history, with eighteen projects under construction and ten more about to begin. . . . Through these difficult times I urge each of you to join me in looking to the future with hope and optimism."

We had reason for optimism at this time. Although the New York credit agency Standard & Poor's had put seventeen lodging companies on Credit Watch eleven days after the terrorist attack, Four Seasons was exempted because of what was called "a stable outlook owing to its solid liquidity position and modest debt level." In fact, one year's cash flow would have reduced our debt to zero.

But the travel outlook continually worsened, depressing the number of business trips and hotel stock prices. We reconsidered our strategy. Almost alone among hoteliers, we still adamantly refused to cut either room rates or staff, and as fourth-quarter 2001 revenue dropped, we were taking flak for this stand from consultants and analysts, even from some of our long-standing hotel owner-partners. They knew our competitors were cutting back and feared our approach was costing us market share, resulting in their hotels losing money.

A few of them put a lot of pressure on us. "You guys have got your head in the sand," we were told. "Business isn't the same anymore."

We empathized with their feelings. But believing our approach would give us the best results in the long term, I told them, "We're staying with our plan. It's the right strategy for all of us. We will come out of this as we always have, and when we do, we certainly don't want to find that we jeopardized our future by compromising our product."

In fact, all our hotels were handling this unprecedented situation remarkably well, as we had expected. Every hotel's general manager had immediately called a meeting of all employees and explained the company's dilemma: forced to cut costs but unwilling to lay people off. Then separate staff meetings were held by all department heads to hear what their people had to say.

In most of our hotels, employee opinion had been almost unanimous. Even people who knew their jobs were not at risk had voted to work four days a week instead of five, so that we wouldn't have to let anyone go. The only exceptions were a few unionized hotels, where inflexible union rules would not allow us to negotiate work-hour reductions. But employees in these hotels understood that this left us no choice but to temporarily lay some of them off.

Everywhere else, flexibility had ruled. Our hotels cut costs in whatever way matched their situations. They created work pools: an employee might one day be waiting on tables and the next day be tending the grounds, or a maid might be assigned to help out in the laundry. Some employees voluntarily took unpaid leaves of absence. Others, when we assured them that their benefits would be preserved, chose to use up accrued vacation time.

A prescheduled employee survey at Four Seasons Maui in Hawaii, which we couldn't cancel, was taken two weeks after September 11. It gave us an enlightening glimpse of how our people really felt about the course that we had chosen. Our employees knew that the response of many of our competitors was simply to lay off staff; that was not our approach. Horror stories from other island hotels were their major topic of conversation. And for employees who had been coming to work dreading what might happen, the contrast between how we and how the others responded to the situation was striking.

Basically, what our employees told us was, "You could have acted like everyone else and fired us. You didn't. You stuck to what you've always said about people coming first. And your credibility in our eyes couldn't be higher."

Credibility—belief in the company—was the unseen but central factor behind the results that Wolf and Katie reported after their trips to our hotels. "It was astonishing," Katie said, "completely voluntary. We didn't have to mandate anything." I agreed, for I too had made a special effort shortly after September 11 to visit over thirty-five hotels, explaining to employees what our company was doing worldwide and giving them, I hoped, a little more comfort and security.

It had been an exceptional demonstration of initiative, cooperation, and compatibility in a workforce of many different cultures and nationalities. As a result, we maintained or enhanced our market share in most regions, contrary to the predictions of various industry experts. And we did it while holding room rates at the level reached in 2000, an all-time high.

We had also successfully opened new hotels in Dublin, Prague, Caracas, Shanghai, and San Francisco and assumed management of two properties in Buenos Aires, Argentina, and Carmelo, Uruguay, hotels now rebranded Four Seasons. Yet despite the unprecedented disruption, we closed this extraordinary year with the strongest balance sheet in our history, thereby reducing our long-term debt by 70 percent and giving us unprecedented cash reserves to fund future growth.

"We are well positioned," I told our shareholders in May 2002, "for the economic recovery expected later this year."

CHAPTER 35

Our True Competitive Advantage

Though our employees had done a splendid job in getting us through the first four months of the worst business period in memory, we had a small decline in revenue in the fourth quarter that year. It deepened in 2002, shrinking the top line by 6 percent and our profits by 75 percent. The trend continued through late 2002 and into 2003 as the terrorist bombing in Bali and then the outbreak of SARS further reduced travel demand. For the first time in Four Seasons history, we had two successive years of RevPAR declines.

The greatest impact was from SARS (severe acute respiratory syndrome), a highly contagious illness that had started in China and spread around the world, creating far-reaching impacts on travel. SARS hit our industry hard, and though we were still meeting our objective in funding new developments, I told the *National Post* that we couldn't give them a 2003 earnings forecast even though trends were improving. "This period is so severely affected by the war in Iraq, by terrorist alerts and SARS," I said, "that it's too difficult to estimate what occupancy levels will be."

It didn't help that we still owned some hotels that were losing money. The Pierre, previously a good contributor to earnings, had lost $708,000 in 2001 and $4.9 million in 2002. And Four Seasons Berlin, with declining bookings and an expensive lease arrangement, had been down $1.5 million in 2001 and $3.9 million in 2002, and we didn't expect any improvement in the near future. Gabor Forgacs, assistant director of Ryerson University's School of Hospitality and Tourist Management, said that we had done a lot of things right, but our "ambitious expansion may have spread management a little thin . . . it could dilute the product." He continued, saying that our managers should

> keep their eyes out for a possible attitude shift among American corporate clientele. As the price gap between rate-cutting competitors and Four Seasons widens, [businesses may be] concerned about a spendthrift image. This is the first time that U.S. business travelers haven't minded going after value. They haven't traditionally been penny-pinchers, but now they're not afraid to bargain and don't feel embarrassed to say cheap is chic and value is king. It is definitely a culture change.

Wayne Lilley of the *National Post* took the same view. "These days," he wrote, "businesses are loath to be perceived by their shareholders as taking the luxury route. As well, rising insurance, energy and labor costs make it tricky to cut expenses without lowering service levels."

But RBC Dominion Securities analyst Irene Nattel disagreed. "The customers who would be drawn by lower rates," she wrote, "likely aren't typical Four Seasons guests and wouldn't become a sustainable market in better times." It would "risk dampening the impact of a future upturn. . . . You need to support your brand. Then, when the world becomes a better place again—and it will—you've done nothing to compromise the integrity of your market position."

I couldn't have said it better myself. And despite still facing conditions of unprecedented severity—all the worst imaginable happenings occurring at once in the economic equivalent of a perfect storm—by the spring of 2003, I had no hesitation whatsoever in telling our people, our partners, our board, and our shareholders that we had never been so well positioned as we were now.

Some of my listeners thought that an odd pronouncement in those times, but I said it with assurance, because it was based on solid fact. In all areas, our strategy following September 11 had worked as planned, increasing our competitive edge. And most analysts agreed that our 2002 balance sheet was the strongest among all lodging companies.

By every measure of competitiveness, our leadership had been confirmed, prompting Britain's *Sunday Telegraph* to call us, at year-end 2002, "the reigning sovereigns of high-class hospitality," a comment certified by the effectiveness of our brand name, which *Forbes Global* had called "the most lucrative in the world."

Underlying and justifying my view of the future was what Warren Buffett, the world's most successful investor, in his latest year-end discourse, had called "the only competitive advantage that matters: a barrier to entry." This was what I believed our competitive advantage now provided.

Our barrier to entry, as I saw it, was twofold. One was our portfolio of hotels, especially those built over the past decade. It was the largest group of authentically first-class hotels in the world, a physical product no other company had to the same degree, to which we'd be adding fourteen properties by the end of the following year. These were exceptional assets almost impossible to duplicate, all in the very best business and leisure locations around the world.

Not too long ago, the three essentials for a hotel's success were said to be location, location, location. And location was still an imperative, especially for business travel. But location was no longer foremost in getting and keeping customers. Now it was people, people, people. This was now the decisive factor in our twofold barrier to entry.

We had by far our sector's lowest employee turnover rate, 23 percent per year compared to an industry average double that rate, in some cases as high as 100 percent. And the pride and satisfaction our employees took in their work could be seen in our annual awards.

For fifteen years, Jim Collins, a distinguished management consultant and bestselling author, had been studying how merely good companies become great. Now, in a *National Post Business* column, he had summed up his conclusions: "Great companies first build a culture of discipline . . . and create a business model that fits squarely in the intersection of three circles: what they can be best in the world at, a deep understanding of their economic engine, and the core values they hold with deep passion."

I concluded that Collins was describing, in exact detail, our business model. We had built an economic engine—service—by understanding our customers' needs, and we'd made it the best in the world. And we had maintained and perfected it through the discipline of a culture based squarely on deeply felt core values. We see the effect every day in every hotel. Employees develop a camaraderie that deepens year by year, creating a sense of community that makes cooperation the norm.

This was strikingly illustrated during the tsunami that struck Southeast Asia, including our resort in the Maldives, on December 27, 2005. As the huge wave descended, all two hundred employees acted intuitively to help save the lives of our guests and one another. Some searched our swimming pool for guests washed into it. Others dove into the raging waves to rescue people swept out to sea. In the aftermath, they did everything possible to offer comfort, sleeping on the beach that night so guests could be sheltered in the staff quarters, which were still standing. Within twenty-four hours, the team had evacuated the island, working with our owners to charter a plane that flew guests out to safety. Miraculously, no one was seriously injured.

One of the guests whose life had been saved later wrote: "Let me stress that your group's strength . . . rests on rock . . . made up of the local employees who, having been selected for doing their job well, have shown in a time of utmost crisis a level of dedication that no training and no amount of money can ever generate."

IN THE CHALLENGING FIRST YEARS of the new century, our market position became important for a different reason. America's largest energy company, Enron, had been experiencing spectacular growth, rising from sales of $19 billion in 1996 to $101 billion in 2000. Then in 2001, Enron suddenly became "the largest corporate bankruptcy in history," as the Public Citizen Foundation called it, "a tangled web of deceit." Enron's chairman and founder, Kenneth Lay, and his second in command, Jeffrey Skilling, were found guilty of conspiracy and fraud.

This was followed in 2002 by the bankruptcy of WorldCom, wiping out stock worth $115 billion at its peak and resulting in a twenty-five-year jail sentence for its chairman and CEO, Bernard Ebbers. Charges of conspiracy, grand larceny, and fraud were made and proved against half a dozen other company leaders, making ethics for this period prominent not only in the news but also in the minds and conversations of investors, citizens, and business executives. Ethical values had become visibly crucial to corporate success.

Only a few years before, most business executives had considered ethics primarily a matter of personal conscience. Now, when companies were paying dearly for loss of investor trust, an ethical reputation was rising rapidly in value. Ethical standards were no longer something nice to have as long as they didn't conflict with short-term profits. They were the unseen factor that everything else depended on.

Thirty-odd years before, as we had started to spread out, I had made our implicit credo, the Golden Rule, explicit. It wasn't a strategy or tactic, nor was it novel. Many companies professed the same thing. But unlike most others, we upheld and enforced it until it was now our ruling discipline and guide, our ethical cornerstone.

Trust was the emotional capital of Four Seasons, our ethical imperative for long-lasting success, a code and a compass enshrined in the corporate culture. It underwrote the conversion of one-shot deals into long-term relationships. It was the precondition for workplace cooperation—without it, we weren't believable. Through trust, I had given dissent free rein, which benefited us because it took dissent and disagreement to bring out all aspects of a problem. Only with trust could we give those working with us at all levels the freedom to act independently and the flexibility needed for fast decisions, for seizing opportunities as they arose.

Trust, we agreed, had been the primary reason for our success, crucial to the reputation that precedes us in every deal, in every hotel opening, and in all our operations. It's a precondition for employee commitment because it gives management credibility, making communication believable and impelling employees to open up, cooperate, and share information. Like the invisible hand that regulates the free market, the invisible hand of trust had been our guide and our dynamic. And every year, as trust rose, our reputation rose with it.

This idea held true more broadly as well. We had always perceived our host community's problems as ours, and community service gave many of our GMs their deepest satisfaction. In fact, all our corporate relationships—with communities, investors, and employees—thrived on mutual self-interest. And all were converging to move ethics from the periphery of our corporate consciousness to the center.

It wouldn't, of course, happen overnight. Business schools were still teaching that the primary purpose of business was to maximize shareholder wealth. That's an important purpose, of course, but not the only one, in my view. If our responsibility was not also to customers, employees, and the public, any admission of error that called for costly restitution could make management and directors legally accountable to owners. Worse, because maximization was more common, it put those who might otherwise follow their conscience in a gray area of decision making.

There's a complex distinction here between personal and corporate ethics, and I didn't have any easy criterion to separate them. But we'd seen a start on reforming the law in both the United States and Canada, and reports showed that ethical awareness was on the rise. According to *U.S. News & World Report*, twenty-five to thirty business schools had set up a chair of ethics on grants by business philanthropists. And a University of California business scholar, Bill Ouchi, had found that "among the fastest-growing, most profitable major American firms . . . profits are regarded not as an end in itself . . . but a reward for providing true value to its customers, helping employees grow, and behaving ethically as a corporate citizen."

It now seemed to me that the greatest challenge for business leaders this coming century would be to align corporate values with human values—not just by giving the corporation a human face, but by giving it a human spirit and cohesion as a community. The corporation can be an ethical organism, evolving as people grow, appreciating tangible and intangible value continually through training, teaching, and learning.

OUR GROWTH, despite our industry's daunting problems, was now on track to deliver five to seven new hotels a year, about half with residential components. We had not only weathered the most precipitous meltdown in modern travel history; we'd come out of it, as in the last two recessions, stronger than we had ever been before.

This was growth based solidly on the foundation of a culture that continued to extend the global power of Four Seasons' brand while raising the barriers to entry that made our market position unassailable. And since research by the World Travel & Tourism Council indicated that travel over the next ten years could double, I thought we had every reason to look forward to our next decade as the most fruitful we had ever enjoyed.

CHAPTER 36

The Best of the Best

I n May 2004, while considering my annual report to shareholders, I
recalled that three years earlier, I had set a company goal that I'd
termed "audacious." We would become, I had claimed, a market
mainstay known as a blue chip.

In the following year, our best ever, I'd considered our goal achieved
and set a new one: to be recognized as a sector leader like Louis Vuitton,
General Electric, or Sony: the best of the best. We would not be comparable in size, but in the power of a worldwide brand name, the power that
gives sector leaders, regardless of market conditions, better than average
growth rates, with price-earnings multiples to match.

Now, assessing our performance these past three years, I believed we
could tell our shareholders, with confidence, that this goal, too, had been
attained. In 2000 we had our and the industry's all-time-highest room
rates. Since then, all our competitors had continued to lower their room
rates. We had not only maintained ours but in various instances raised
them. And yet we had retained and in some cases increased our market
share. This indicated that our customers thought what we gave them was
worth the price we asked.

Our 2003 figures were conclusive. Four Seasons shares were now trading at an all-time high. Despite our many hotel investments, terrorism,
SARS, and Iraq, our balance sheet was in good shape. As analyst Steve
Kent of Goldman Sachs had noted, "It appears that everything is coming
together for Four Seasons . . . occupancies are coming back, leisure travel
remains strong and business travel is showing signs of life . . . the outlook
is bright."

Our brand was now preeminent, an intangible factor of unparalleled power in our sector. It would be very difficult for competitors to duplicate, because it hadn't evolved, like most brands, primarily through advertising. It grew through promises kept, to our guests and staff. It grew through vision and conviction underpinned by ethical values.

Like all great brands, it aligned internal and external commitment by continually giving travelers what they most wanted and needed. And over the years, the resultant relationship had solidified, creating committed customers who passed on their opinions to friends, the most believable and therefore the most effective form of advertising. And this customer intimacy had shielded us from a major pitfall of great brands: loss of relevance. Repeat customers were constantly telling us what they liked and wanted, which helped keep us in touch with changing tastes and trends. And as the last three years' experience had confirmed, the Four Seasons brand also signified value.

Value was also evident in the number of developers who came to us first when they wanted to build hotels. In these worst of times, we had been offered and had accepted twenty-eight new projects, thirteen of which were already under construction. All these were what I've referred to previously as "the next generation of five-star hotels." They incorporated plasma TVs, as we had once introduced armoires. We hired specialty restaurant designers to create exciting new dining concepts, and we introduced unique spas in our destination resorts and city hotels.

This latest growth phase was taking us into eleven new countries. In Europe, where construction sites were nearly impossible to procure, we had acquired historic properties in cities such as Florence, where we converted a formerly private Florentine palazzo into an intimate 118-room hotel, and in Moscow, where the former Hotel Moskva on Red Square was being rebuilt as a Four Seasons.

Under way in Pacific Asia were six new city-center hotels and three resorts. In China, we were opening a second hotel in the Pudong district of Shanghai, as well as a hotel in Beijing and one in Macau, the new gambling capital of Asia. We were also opening new resorts in such destinations as Bora Bora in the South Pacific and Mauritius in the Indian Ocean, along with a second property in the Maldives. Then in the United States, we were building ten new hotels and resorts, while in Canada, our new hotel in Toronto included private residences.

In addition to these projects, now under way or confirmed, we had over forty new developments under discussion, some in emerging markets in Eastern Europe, South America, China, and India. And every new project was governed by long-term management contracts averaging more than sixty years.

Our brand was now, in effect, a global franchise, preselling each new hotel and raising its revenues well ahead of customary expectations. And with each new hotel in a new country, our brand power was extended through word of mouth and visibility.

Could we sustain the competitive advantage our brand momentum conferred? we asked ourselves. The history of great brands told us we could. Though the average company lifespan was only twenty-five years, most worldwide companies with leading brands were more than sixty years old. A top brand securely based upon a compelling idea and supported by resolute purpose and ethical values is a growth machine that never wears out, as long as it is maintained and as long as a company retains its customers' trust in what built the brand.

It had taken us more than forty-five years to get to where we were now, mainly through two decisions: to operate by the Golden Rule and to distinguish ourselves through exceptional service. And the contrast between our performance and that of our competitors these past three years had proven beyond dispute that service was a product that travelers, in growing numbers, demanded. By consistently meeting and sometimes exceeding their expectations, we had created something akin to a patent on service delivery, thus becoming a sector leader, the best of the best.

CHAPTER 37

The New Leaders

As the company spread out, we brought in numerous new executives, though not as many as our competitors. I had decided that promotion would always come from within, except when we needed talent we didn't yet have.

This had nothing to do with tenure. This was a meritocracy. It was all about who had acquired a built-in knowledge of our business. We wanted people who had learned what to do and how and when to do it, people who had proven themselves and earned the right to move up. And this had given me an understanding about our growth, the how and why of its continuity in the five-star class. It had been something akin to the perfect passing of the baton in a championship relay race.

I believe the failure of many entrepreneurs is due to their inability to delegate responsibility and authority. The complete trust and faith I had in all our very senior executives gave them the self-confidence and desire to train and develop the top people now reporting to them, and this respect and trust went right down the line, giving us the opportunity to attract and retain the brightest and the best—because they believe their opportunities lie in their own hands.

We'd had many changes of senior leadership over forty-eight years, all of them promotions from within. Following Ian Munro and Michael Lambert came John Sharpe and Roger Garland, both playing a vital role in the growth of the company, extending our portfolio throughout North America, then taking us into Europe, Asia, the Middle East, and South America.

John retired in 1999, Roger a year later, both having contributed tremendously to our success and having shared in the results. As a public company, we had an extensive stock option plan for all our senior people, including GMs of all our hotels and every corporate person at management level.

Wolf Hengst, after a series of achievements in many parts of the globe while president of Regent International, took over from John Sharpe as president of worldwide hotel operations, and Kathleen Taylor took on Roger's responsibilities as president of worldwide business operations. Katie and Wolf served as copresidents until Wolf retired in 2006. By then, within the company around the world, we had experts in every discipline, about 150 top-level officers.Many of them were on headhunters' lists, for they're all adaptive, decisive, assured, confident, self-motivated, and trustworthy. I call them our bench strength, ready to take over when their turn to lead comes.

Of these, eight are currently members of our management committee, headed by Kathleen Taylor. Katie is my good right hand, a perfect endorsement of promotion from within. She joined us as a young lawyer in 1989, and I soon noted that she had good business sense and an expansive way of thinking well beyond legal aspects. I began involving her in business dealings, finding her so effective that when Roger Garland retired, she was clearly the one to take over the tasks of managing acquisitions, directing the company's worldwide hotel and residential developments, and supervising our corporate planning, human resources, and administration.

Katie is both a generalist and a specialist, an individualist but a team player, bright and with great sensitivity for others, tough when necessary but always compassionate—the complete executive. So in 2007, I created a new position, chief operating officer, assigning it to Katie. Clearly she had earned it, along with the respect of everyone she has ever worked with.

Jim FitzGibbon was promoted to president of worldwide hotel operations when Katie became COO on Wolf Hengst's retirement. Jim is one of the longest-serving employees in the company. Born in Youghal, Ireland, where he still maintains a home, Jim is an expert horseman and a pretty fair golfer. He began with us in 1976, an assistant manager on the desk at the Inn on the Park Toronto. He eventually became a GM in Philadelphia and Dallas, moved up to regional vice president in 1989, then followed Wolf Hengst in taking over our Asia Pacific operations before assuming his current post.

Jim's office is now in our Toronto headquarters, but he's seldom there. About half his time is spent traveling around the world. He frequently spends time with our senior operations teams in all the major regions, ensuring that we retain and nurture the people we need and that our guests' experience continues to be the best, ever evolving as it should. He also visits our hotels, now in more than thirty countries, getting opinions on product and service from employees and customers, certifying that new hotels are meeting our guests' expectations, and checking with key managers and owners on market conditions, competition, profit, and politics in their part of the world.

Supporting Katie and Jim are other management committee members, each highly proficient, often exceptional in some areas. They're not in any particular order as far as importance or rank is concerned. I'll begin with Antoine Corinthios because we recently celebrated his thirtieth year with the company.

Antoine is president for Europe, the Middle East, and Africa, responsible for overseeing our growth in those areas. Born in Cairo, Egypt, he's a naturalized U.S. citizen with an economics degree from York University in Toronto. He came up through the ranks as general manager of our hotels in Montreal and Chicago, becoming area vice president for the Midwest, West Coast, and Asia. With his command of five languages, he helped us expand abroad, building strong, lasting relationships with foreign partners.

Another veteran is Nick Mutton, now twenty-eight years with Four Seasons, a general manager who advanced to an area vice president. Then when we needed someone who understood how to train and deal with thirty-eight thousand employees of many different cultures and languages, Nick made an unusual and, for us, opportune switch: from senior vice president of operations to executive vice president of human resources. And when John Young retired at the end of 2003, Nick not only developed new service people, he reorganized our pension plan and helped design a designated contribution program. His interests, as might be expected from someone who successfully makes such an offbeat move, are extraordinarily wide. He loves fast cars, wing shooting, and fly-fishing; he's a director of the Canadian Opera Company and a member of the International Advisory

Board of L'École hôtelière de Lausanne and of the Governing Committee of the International Business Leaders Forum.

Then there's Barbara Talbott, our former executive vice president of marketing. Her outstanding depth of knowledge was always useful on the Management Committee, and her role in building our brand was invaluable. She serves on the board of Cornell's Center for Hospitality Research and has been given a lifetime achievement award by the International Hospitality and Marketing Association. Other recipients of this award in recent years have included Michael Eisner, Sir Richard Branson, and Barry Sternlicht.

Barbara retired in December 2008, after twenty years with Four Seasons, when Susan Helstab took over as executive vice president of marketing. When Susan joined Four Seasons, in 1987, each of our hotels was creating its own sales and marketing literature, each different from all the others. She developed a uniform marketing and advertising platform for our hotels, built around our exceptional service.

If Susan presented something to me for input and approval, I had a blunt way of providing feedback about a piece that missed the mark. I'd say, "This doesn't *feel* like Four Seasons." Capturing the essence of Four Seasons in everything we do has always been critical. Over the years, as her familiarity with our operation grew, she heard it less and less often.

We have Randy Weisz, who came to us in 1998 after fourteen years with Goodmans, a major Toronto law firm, where he had been our legal counsel for ten years, negotiating, structuring, and completing corporate transactions and the agreements for many Four Seasons properties. Goodmans' founder, Eddie Goodman, once told that us that Randy was a lawyer's lawyer, which I took to mean he'd be the right guy for a tough legal problem. I considered that an exceptional compliment, and getting Randy was a stroke of luck. He has the ability to understand and stay tirelessly focused on the most complex of issues in managing our worldwide legal and business affairs. In July 2002, he was a crucial addition to our management committee and is now executive vice president of business administration and general counsel, reflecting his role in helping to manage the business affairs of the company.

Scott Woroch, executive vice president of worldwide development, is a recent team member who joined us in 2000. I recall sitting in a meeting with him some years ago when he was in charge of acquisitions and development for Strategic Hotel Capital, having previously overseen all Asian and European development for Westin Hotels. He had impressed me greatly then, so when Katie Taylor was looking for someone to head our Asian development department and Scott accepted our offer, I was delighted. As a lawyer with extensive real estate experience, he has been an outstanding deal maker for us.

John Davison, executive vice president and chief financial officer, listens, then works heroically to ensure that Four Seasons has the best balance sheet for the long term, rather than the short haul.

And then there is John Davison. John is exceptional. He was president and chief financial officer of Imax until he came to us in 2002 as senior vice president of project financing. In 2005 he took over from Doug Ludwig as our executive vice president and chief financial officer, handling our intricate financial problems in becoming a private company as well as heading our Residence Clubs business. John continues to be responsible for our residential developments, but his primary role is managing our financial department worldwide, bringing to it an expertise and work ethic that is setting a new and higher standard.

These are the people who confirm our management strength and reinforce our culture.

Kathleen Taylor, president and chief operating officer. Katie is a true leader, because people follow her out of respect. She is selfless and empowering and could take over from me anytime.

James FitzGibbon, president of worldwide hotel operations, hails from the unpronounceable city of Youghal. He juggles owners and managers alike with his great head for numbers and an Irish smile.

Antoine Corinthios, president for Europe, the Middle East, and Africa, speaks Four Seasons Golden Rule lingo in five languages. He's a great maven of human nature and has the diplomacy of a statesman.

Nicholas Mutton, executive vice president of human resources, brings heart and soul to his job of making sure staff members find the job closest to their dreams. He speaks very softly but makes his point.

Barbara Talbott, former executive vice president of marketing, always came up with new plans for which she found words that no one else had thought of. She was a master at defining us.

Susan Helstab, executive vice president of marketing, has an innate understanding of the power of the brand, and how best to present Four Seasons to consumers and travel professionals alike.

Randy Weisz, executive vice president of business administration and general counsel, brings immaculate integrity and sound judgment to his job. Everyone benefits from his wise counsel and business advice.

Scott Woroch, executive vice president of worldwide development, has brought a staggering number of new opportunities to the company. He is very effective at creating relationships and deal making for the company.

CHAPTER 38

Three Partners,
Four Seasons

I n late November 2005, an institutional investment adviser familiar
with Four Seasons came to us with an interesting proposition. He
was an adviser to several financial institutions, and one in particular, he thought, could be very interested in buying into Four Seasons, in partnership with me and a small number of long-term strategic
investors, to take the company private.

I considered this proposal for several months. The more I thought about
it, the more compelling it became. Until then, it had never occurred to me
that you could sell the majority of a company and still maintain control. As
far as I knew, it had never been done before. But thinking about it, I saw
how it could facilitate the orderly transition of ownership of the company
in a manner consistent with the interests of all our stakeholders.

On March 1, 2006, I flew to Paris to discuss the proposal with Prince
Alwaleed, Kingdom Holdings being our largest shareholder then. He
thought the idea was worth pursuing and indicated he would support ex-
ploring the possibility. In that meeting, we also discussed the idea of such
a transaction being pursued on a basis that would involve consideration of
approximately $100 (Canadian) per share.

Back in Toronto, I refined the concepts the prince and I had discussed
and outlined them for our board. Then in April, our president, Kathleen
Taylor, went to Riyadh to discuss our conceptual framework with the
prince.

Kingdom had recently bought, with a partner, the entire Fairmont
hotel chain. Alwaleed thought Bill Gates, chairman of Microsoft, might be

interested in the proposal. Gates, through one of his companies, Cascade Investment, already owned shares in Four Seasons.

Over the next two months, representatives of Kingdom and Four Seasons met with a small number of potential investors, including Cascade. During this same period, representatives of Kingdom and Four Seasons continued to discuss and refine potential deal terms.

Finally we agreed on terms. On November 3, 2006, I received a proposal from Kingdom and Cascade confirming the terms on which we would pursue the privatization of the company at a price of $82 (U.S.) per share. On November 5, the board reviewed that proposal, and on November 6, it was announced to the press that I, through my company Triples Holdings, Bill Gates, through Cascade Investment, and Prince Alwaleed, through Kingdom Hotels, had made a proposal to buy Four Seasons for $3.83 billion (U.S.). Gates and the prince would each own 47.5 percent of the company's outstanding shares, leaving me with 5 percent. But I would still remain, by contract, in control of operations and strategy as chairman and chief executive officer.

This was a unique deal—Kingdom and Cascade brought an expertise to the company that could ensure the Four Seasons legacy for the foreseeable future. It would be a new alliance (a word that the prince commonly uses to describe our partnership) that could set the stage for our next decade of growth.

On the same day the company announced its receipt of the sale proposal, I wrote a letter to all Four Seasons employees, advising them of "an important proposed step in the evolution of Four Seasons." I explained the proposal to take the company private and gave some background on how and why it had come about. I told them it would ensure that we would continue to distinguish ourselves as the leading operator of luxury hotels throughout the world, and I thanked them for their continued dedication and commitment.

The next decade would be the most interesting and exciting period in our history, and I was looking forward to it. By the end of 2008, we had eighty-two hotels in thirty-four countries, and over the next ten years, we expect to double that number. I don't see this as either risky or unusually difficult. We'll be growing on the same strategy that took us where we are now: by giving our customers, worldwide, the experience they expect. In many cities and areas, we are considered the best, though we began, more than forty years ago, merely with hope and self-belief. Now our property owners are building new hotels that are dramatically better, more impressive than ever before—magnificent new buildings, the best of the best. And these will comprise, in a decade, some 85 percent of our offerings.

Even our older hotels will be luxurious, with no scratches on the doors or furniture, no worn carpets; they've been constantly maintained with loving care, repaired, redecorated, and upgraded. Recently, for example, I visited Four Seasons Washington, built back in 1979. It had just been redone; everything now the latest. It looked splendid.

In the past, I said that our objective was to have the best hotel in every location. At the time, Four Seasons could only aspire to such a goal. Today, more of our hotels have been proclaimed the world's best than those of any of our rivals, and I am confident we can lengthen that lead.

We not only have capital and technical expertise; we also have, in every hotel, an assemblage of committed employees who will be, as before, the single primary element allowing us to prevail.

That was what I meant in saying we had an impenetrable barrier to entry: the ability of our people to deliver a quality of service that hasn't yet been duplicated on a worldwide scale by any other hotel company is our paramount prerequisite for leadership.

I brought up this matter of leadership in May 2006 at a two-day conference of all our senior people. And at the closing dinner, I put forward our next strategic objective: to become the undisputed leader of luxury hospitality—the global gold standard.

Then I explained why this was a sound business decision. Our chief financial officer, John Davison, had shown in his presentation that although we were generally able to charge higher rates than our closest competitors, our occupancies were just about the same overall, some 70 percent. "If we could improve our occupancies by just one or two percent," John pointed out, "the difference to the company's bottom line would be dramatic."

We should surely be able to do just that, I had thought, for in London in the early seventies, up against the finest hotels in the world at the time we performed well. If we could do it there, then why not everywhere now?

And I'd considered the quality of our people at this conference. Most, still in their forties, had been with us fifteen to twenty years; some had never worked for another company. All were efficient and enthusiastic, the brightest and best, as their records confirmed. People in other hotel companies were doubtless just as good in their end of the industry, but in the five-star class, none could match this group. Indeed, good was not the right word—they excelled.

Now I told them what Rosalie said the morning after the opening party at our house: "I looked around at our people, most of whom I have seen in action in their hotels, and I was struck by the wealth of talent, goodwill, and cerebral capital marshaled in one room."

"That really says it all," I added. And in my closing remarks, I went on to say, "As you know, we've grown on four pillars: quality, service, culture, brand. And now our next strategy, our fifth pillar, is to become our industry's undisputed leader, known globally as number one—again setting an audacious goal for ourselves.

"I'm not sure how long it will take," I said. "Three, five, ten years, it doesn't matter, because in aspiring to do it, we will continue to become better."

Unlike forty years before, when I'd declared much the same goal, I now had no doubts that this goal was attainable.

That was largely why we became what we are today, why my new partners and I can look ahead with absolute confidence to continued financial success and global growth—to more than 150 hotels in more than forty countries, all still with one philosophy.

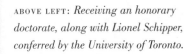

ABOVE LEFT: *Receiving an honorary doctorate, along with Lionel Schipper, conferred by the University of Toronto.*

CENTER LEFT: *With George H. W. Bush.*

BELOW LEFT: *With Bill Clinton.*

BELOW RIGHT: *Made "Officer of the Order of Canada" by Governor General Ramon John Hnatyshyn.*

AFTERWORD

We now come to the end of the book but not to the end of Issy Sharp's career. Having created a luxury hotel company that now encircles the globe, transcending every rival, he continues to expand Four Seasons with an entrepreneurial insight unique in the history of the industry.

His accomplishments are legendary, for Issy has not only built more top luxury hotels than anyone past or present, he also continues to raise all five-star hotel standards worldwide.

Isadore Sharp, as *Luxe* magazine put it, "is arguably the most innovative hotelier of the century."

Issy gave nobility to the word *service*. When the business pages of newspapers and magazines disclosed that Four Seasons' success was primarily due to superior service, the service factor became a prominent agent in making business better throughout North America.

Issy is well known for his philanthropy, for which he has received countless awards, including Officer of the Order of Canada.

But of all his contributions, the one he finds most gratifying, I believe, is setting up and directing the Terry Fox Run, raising millions of dollars a year for cancer patients around the world. At least that's what he once told me. It seems appropriate for a man whose legacy is built around superior service, to customers as well as for the greater good.

ALAN PHILLIPS
September 12, 2008

Here's our talented team of leaders. What a great group of stars! Some aimed to be poets or painters, physicians, finance experts, or astronauts. But luckily they chose us.

ACKNOWLEDGMENTS

Alan Phillips has done a heroic job of knitting together my life and my work. Now in his nineties, Alan is still at the top of his form. He was my ideal choice because he and I have worked together on speeches for twenty-five years and we're well attuned to each other. Mai Phillips transcribed all my recollections from a tiny Dictaphone that produces an indecipherable page-long word with no spaces.

Nan Wilkins, my friend and helpmate, was the go-between who coordinated the steady flow of material to Alan and his wife, Mai.

Rosalie, as always, has my best interests at heart, and she edited the book many times as well as writing some anecdotes and the captions for the photos. Thanks to Greg Sharp for his insights and for suggesting more anecdotes.

Thanks to Katie Taylor, Barbara Talbott, Susan Helstab, and Elizabeth Pizzinato for reading the first draft and making useful recommendations.

My gratitude to Portfolio publisher Adrian Zackheim for his expertise and guidance, as well as Will Weisser, Allison McLean, Courtney Young, Joe Perez, Francesca Belanger, Tricia Conley, Bruce Giffords, and Fabiana Van Arsdell at Penguin Group (USA) and David Davidar, Andrea Magyar, Yvonne Hunter, and Alina Goldstein at Penguin Group (Canada); and Beth Tondreau of BTDNYC.

I'm grateful to Michael Levine for his wise counsel and support through the maze of publishing possibilities.

Thanks to Randy Weisz, Sarah Cohen, Anita McKernan, Joe Conforti and Jonathan Lampe for their legal guidance.

Bob Andelman added some good stories from his interviews with Four Seasons staff.

There were many others who helped along the way during the two years of compiling and remembering: Jordan Sharp, Anthony Sharp, Jim FitzGibbon, John Davison, Nick Mutton, Scott Woroch, Roger Garland, John Sharpe, Wolf Hengst, Christopher Hart, Robert Cima, Christopher Norton, John Stauss, Dimitrios Zarikos, Armando Kraenzlin, Hans Willimann, Dirk Burghartz, Kurt Englund, Delores Hayes, Nicola Blazier, Mary Gatti, Matthew Gridgeman.

I acknowledge the former board of directors (when the company was public) for its diligence, guidance, and personal interest: William D. Anderson, Brent S. Belzberg, Nan-b de Gaspé Beaubien, H. Roger Garland, Charles Henry, Heather Munro-Blum, Ronald W. Osborne, J. Robert Prichard, Lionel H. Schipper, Anthony D. Sharp, and Simon M. Turner.

OUR GOALS, OUR BELIEFS, OUR PRINCIPLES

WHO WE ARE

We have chosen to specialize within the hospitality industry by offering only experiences of exceptional quality. Our objective is to be recognized as the company that manages the finest hotels, resorts, and residence clubs wherever they are located. We create properties of enduring value using superior design and finishes, and we support them with a deeply instilled ethic of personal service. Doing so allows Four Seasons to satisfy the needs and tastes of our discriminating customers and to maintain our position as the world's premier hospitality company.

HOW WE BEHAVE

We demonstrate our beliefs most meaningfully in the way we treat each other and by the example we set for one another. In all our interactions with our guests, customers, business associates, and colleagues, we seek to deal with others as we would have them deal with us.

WHAT WE BELIEVE

Our greatest asset, and the key to our success, is our people. We believe that each of us needs a sense of dignity, pride, and satisfaction in what we do. Because satisfying our guests depends on the united efforts of many, we are most effective when we work together cooperatively, respecting each other's contributions and importance.

HOW WE SUCCEED

We succeed when every decision is based on a clear understanding of and belief in what we do and when we couple this conviction with sound financial planning. We expect to achieve a fair and reasonable profit to ensure the prosperity of the company and to offer long-term benefits to our customers, our employees, our hotel owners, and our shareholders.

Senior Staff Tenure by Position

(Effective October 2008)

		YEARS OF SERVICE
TOTAL: AVERAGE YEARS OF SERVICE		**15**
MANAGEMENT COMMITTEE: AVERAGE YEARS OF SERVICE		**22**
Isadore Sharp	Chairman, CEO, and founder	48
Jim FitzGibbon	President, worldwide hotel operations	33
Antoine Corinthios	President, Europe, Middle East, and Africa	31
Nick Mutton	EVP, human resources and administration	29
Susan Helstab	EVP, marketing	21
Katie Taylor	President and chief operating officer	19
Barbara Talbott	EVP, marketing (retired 2008)	19
Randy Weisz	EVP, business administration, and general counsel	11
Scott Woroch	EVP, worldwide development	8
John Davison	EVP and CFO	6
SENIOR VICE PRESIDENTS: AVERAGE YEARS OF SERVICE		**21**
Alfons Konrad	SVP (retired 2007)	33
Ivan Goh	SVP (retired 2008)	29
Chris Garland	SVP, finance	29
Chris Hunsberger	SVP, operations, Americas	27
Chris Hart	SVP, operations, Asia Pacific	25
Mike Duwaji	SVP, finance operations	25
Craig Reid	SVP, operations	19
Barbara Henderson	SVP, corporate finances	18

Sarah Cohen	SVP, corporate counsel, and assistant secretary	11
John MacKinnon	SVP, design and construction	10
Michele Sweeting	SVP, capital planning and procurement	8

VICE PRESIDENTS: AVERAGE YEARS OF SERVICE		**12**
Debbie Brown	VP, human resources, Americas	31
David Crowl	VP, sales and marketing, Europe, Middle East, Africa	26
Karen Welch	VP, global compensation and benefits	24
Scott Taber	VP, rooms, Americas	23
Jeff Blakeman	VP, operations finance, Asia Pacific	23
Jonathan Sicroff	VP, sales and marketing, Americas	22
Paul Iacovino	VP, sales and marketing, Asia Pacific	21
Susan Devins	VP, sales and marketing, Asia Pacific	19
Guy Rigby	VP, food and beverage	19
Ellen duBellay	VP, learning and development	18
Robert Dunigan	VP, operational analysis	17
Doug Leung	VP, financial reporting and analysis	16
Tom Hubler	VP, sales, North America	15
Heather Jacobs	VP, human resources, Europe, Middle East, Africa	14
Yu Jin	VP, information systems	12
Dana Kalczak	VP, design and construction	10
Sam Zarlenga	VP, design and construction	10
Steven Garber	VP, design and construction	10
Dean Hyry	VP, residential operations	10
Elizabeth Pizzinato	VP, public relations	9
Paul White	VP, residence clubs	9
Laurel Vanderjagt	VP, senior associate, corporate counsel	7
Robert Skyvington	VP, procurement	6
Christopher Wong	VP, development, Asia Pacific	6
Sandip Rana	VP, corporate finance	6
Janet Deline	VP, planning and procurement services	5
Joel Monson	VP, senior associate, corporate counsel	5
Michael Minchin	VP, marketing planning and residential	4
Rosemary Christopher	VP, taxation	2
Mary Sullivan	VP, corporate human resources	1
Wilke See-Tho	VP, development	1

REGIONAL VICE PRESIDENTS AND GENERAL MANAGERS: AVERAGE YEARS OF SERVICE **15**

William Mackay	RVP and GM, Hong Kong	26
John Stauss	RVP and GM, London	26
Robert Cima	RVP and GM, Aviara	25
Thomas Gurtner	RVP and GM, Westlake	20
Peter Weber	RVP and GM, Shanghai	20
Christopher Norton	RVP and GM, George V	19
Ignacio Gomez	RVP and GM, Singapore	16
Christoph Schmidinger	RVP and GM, New York	16
Radha Arora	RVP and GM, Beverly Wilshire	14
Marcos Bekhit	RVP and GM, Bosphorus	14
Patrick Ghielmetti	RVP and GM, Chicago	14
Thomas Steinhauer	RVP and GM, Maui	13
Bahram Sepahi	RVP and GM, Dubai	13
Dimitrios Zarikos	RVP and GM, Toronto	12
Andrew Humphries	RVP and GM, Nevis	11
Olivier Masson	RVP and GM, Cairo at Nile Plaza	10
Armando Kraenzlin	RVP and GM, Maldives	9
Christian Clerc	RVP and GM, Washington	8
Rainer Stampfer	RVP and GM, Bangkok	7

GENERAL MANAGERS: AVERAGE YEARS OF SERVICE **14**

Hans Willimann	GM, Vail	30
Kathleen Horrigan	GM, Palm Beach	29
Royal Rowe	GM, Maldives at Landaa Giraavaru	29
Doug Housley	GM, San Francisco	29
Rene Beauchamp	GM, Terre Blanche	29
Stephen Lewis	GM, Sydney	27
Tom Kelly	GM, Scottsdale	25
Martin Sinclair	GM, Regent Singapore	24
Yves Giacometti	GM, Buenos Aires	23
Simon Pettigrew	GM, Vancouver	22
Thierry Kennel	GM, St. Louis	21
Harry Gorstayn	GM, Philadelphia	21
Mehdi Eftekari	GM, Los Angeles	21
Randy Shimabuku	GM, Cairo (at First Residence)	21
Mark Herron	GM, Whistler	20
Denise Flanders	GM, Chicago	20

Tom Segesta	GM, Austin	19
Tracy Mercer	GM, Silicon Valley	19
Simon Casson	GM, Doha	19
Michele Grosso	GM, Ritz-Carlton Chicago	18
Antoine Chahwan	GM, Macao	18
Colin Clark	GM, Hampshire	18
Greg Pirkle	GM, Langkawi	18
Bill Taylor	GM, Boston	16
Vincenzo Finizzola	GM, Milan	16
Patrizio Cipollini	GM, Florence, Italy	16
Mark Hellrung	GM, Las Vegas	16
Vikram Reddy	GM, Jakarta	15
Karen Earp	GM, Santa Barbara	15
José Silva	GM, Geneva	15
Michael Newcombe	GM, Dallas	14
John O'Sullivan	GM, Bali at Jimbaran Bay and Sayan	14
Ben Trodd	GM, Seattle	14
Todd Cilano	GM, Chiang Mai	13
Gerhard Stutz	GM, Amman	13
Rebeca Selley	GM, Mexico City	13
Andrew Harrison	GM, Mauritius	13
José Soriano	GM, Dublin	13
Dan Normandin	GM, Atlanta	11
Stefan Simkovics	GM, Beijing	11
Ricardo Acevedo	GM, Miami	11
Michael Branham	GM, Tokyo at Marunouchi	11
Robert Whitfield	GM, Hualalai	11
Julien Carralero	GM, Budapest	10
Tarek Mourad	GM, Istanbul	10
Vince Parrotta	GM, Jackson Hole	10
Alastair McAlpine	GM, Maldives at Kuda Huraa	9
Luis Argote	GM, Costa Rica	9
Markus Iseli	GM, Seychelles	8
Guilherme Costa	GM, Lisbon	8
Stephan Killinger	GM, Alexandria	8
Martin Rhomberg	GM, Damascus	8
Tom Roelens	GM, Koele	8
Jean-Claude Wietzel	GM, Sharm el Sheikh	6
James Kostecky	GM, Exuma at Emerald Bay	6
Dirk Burghartz	GM, Houston	5

Sebastien Carre	GM, Bora Bora	5
Michael Purtill	GM, Canary Wharf	5
Masahito Mochinaga	GM, Tokyo Chinzan-so	5
Vincent Hoogewijs	GM, Mexico	5
Alper Oztok	GM, Punta Mita	4
Rami Sayess	GM, Riyadh	3
Davide Barnes	GM, Prague	2
Brent Martin	GM, Koh Samui	1

ABBREVIATIONS

CFO	Chief financial officer
EVP	Executive vice president
FSH	Four Seasons Hotel
FSR	Four Seasons Resort
FSRC	Four Seasons Residence Club
GM	General manager
RVP	Regional vice president
SVP	Senior vice president
VP	Vice president

PHOTOGRAPH CREDITS

Page x *center right:* West Preparatory Junior Public School

x *all others,* 2, 5, 28, 52, 74, 108, 153, 161 *above, center,* and *below right:* Sharp Family Collection

xiv: Toronto Star Archives

12 *above:* Courtesy of Forest Hill Junior and Senior Public School

12 *below left, center,* and *right:* Copyright Ryerson University

16, 19, 137, 279 *center left* and *below left:* Isadore Sharp Personal Collection

22, 27: Photo by Gerald Campbell

30, 32 *above,* 47, 51, 66, 82 *above right* and *center,* 90, 148, 151 *left,* 154 *above, left* and *right,* 155 *above left,* 155 *below, left* and *right,* 161 *below left:* Four Seasons Archives Collection

32 *below:* Cecil R. Forsyth, *The Bulletin,* March 1945, The Great-West Life Corporate Archives

39: Canadian Post Card Co., Ltd., Four Seasons Archives Collection

42: Herb Nott & Co. Ltd., Four Seasons Archives Collection

55, 57, 62: Courtesy of Sir Robert McAlpine Ltd.

80: Ty Warner

82 *above left:* Photo by Ron Bull/*Toronto Star*

82 *below:* Nicola Blazier

84: Robin Clarke Architect

85: City of Toronto Archives, Fonds 1244, Item 1946

87: Granite Club

95: Peter Peirce/Peter R. Peirce, Inc.

96: © John Reilly

107: Richard Feldman

116, 120: Four Seasons Hotel Washington

126, 274 *above right:* Michael Rafelson

151 *right:* Beatrice Eisen

152 *left:* Edmund Creed

152 *right:* Murray Koffler

154 *below, left* and *right,* 155 *above right:* Paul J. Lawrence, www.paullawrencephotography.com

156: Photo by Hudson Taylor

166: Media Systems, Inc.

171: Gensho Haga

178: Catherine Tillmann

191, 226 *above* and *below right:* Peter Vitale

INDEX

Page numbers in *italics* refer to illustrations.